ROMANÉE-CONTI

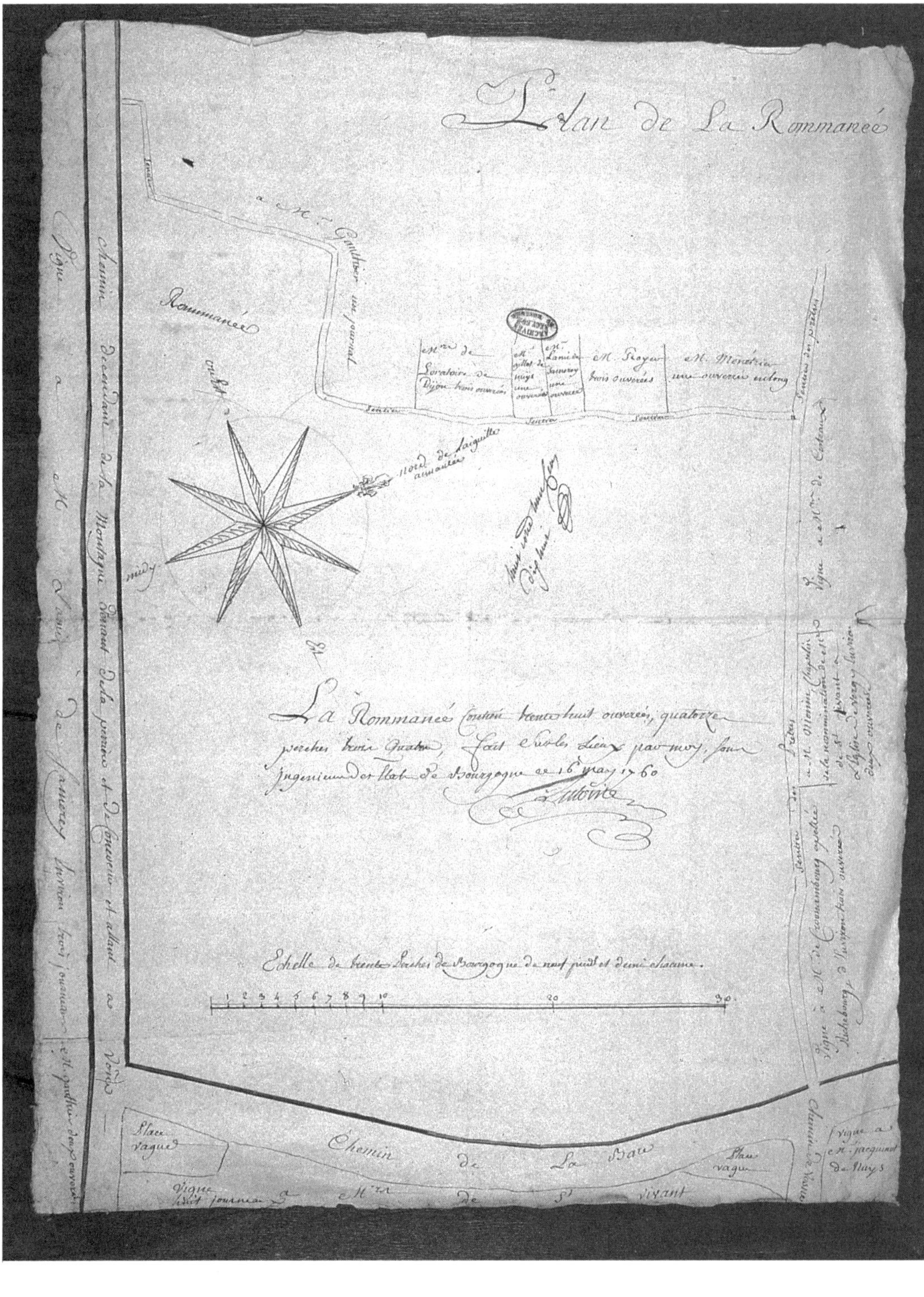
Plan de La Rommanée
Rommanée
Sentier
M. Royer trois ouvrées
Nord de l'aiguille aimantée
midy
La Rommanée contien trente huit ouvrées, quatorze perches trois quatre, fait sur les lieux par moy, sous Ingenieur des Etats de Bourgogne ce 16 may 1760
Echelle de trente Perches de Bourgogne de neuf pieds et demi chacune.
1 2 3 4 5 6 7 8 9 10 20 30
Chemin de La Bau
Place vague
Place vague

Romanée-Conti

The World's Most Fabled Wine

Richard Olney

Rizzoli

A Note to the Reader

When citing eighteenth-century sources or earlier documents, I have respected the orthography of the original (Conty instead of Conti, Vône or Vonne instead of Vosne, for instance). Quotes from modern editions of eighteenth-century works, in which spellings have been modernized, as in the Pléiade editions of Saint-Simon and Rousseau, stand as modified by the editors.

Richard Olney

First published in the United States of America in 1995 by
Rizzoli International Publications, Inc.
300 Park Avenue South, New York, New York 10010

Library of Congress Cataloging-in-Publication Data
Olney, Richard.
Romanée-Conti : the world's most fabled wine / by Richard Olney.
p. cm.
Includes bibliographical references and index.
ISBN 0-8478-1927-2
1. Domaine de la Romanée-Conti (Firm) 2. Wine and wine making--France—Burgundy. I. Title.
TP553.045 1995
641.2'2'09444—dc20 95-30200
CIP

Design by Big Fish Books

Woodcuts by Neil Shigley

To my nephew John Olney

Table of Contents

A LEGENDARY WINE

I

A FABULOUS THING—mysterious, sensuous, transcendental, the greatest wine in the dukedom of Burgundy, once reserved for the table of princes, its origins blurred in the mists of time—cannot help but spawn fabulists. For two centuries, no wine—no vineyard—has so deeply and so consistently motivated man's mythologizing instinct as La Romanée-Conti.

The most ethereal wines of Burgundy issue from a slender ribbon of vineyards about 30 miles (50 km) long called the Côte d'Or, a contraction of Côte d'Orient, or "east-facing hillside." The name dates from 1790, when France was broken into departments, named after typical geographical features, for the most part rivers. (The Côte d'Or narrowly escaped being named "La Haute Seine" or "Seine et Saône," thanks to the inspiration of a local deputy and lawyer, André-Rémy Arnoult.) In Burgundy this chain of vineyard hillsides has always been called simply the Côte. It is composed of two sections, the Côte de Beaune and the Côte de Nuits. The Côte de Beaune is renowned for its delicate red wines and for the most sumptuous of white Burgundies. Within the Côte de Nuits, the shorter and narrower northern section of the ribbon, the most prestigious red growths of Burgundy are strung, chainlike, just beneath mid-hillside, for a stretch of about 6 miles (9.7 km).

In the Côte de Nuits, equidistant from Dijon and from Beaune, lies the village of Vosne, to which by government decree, 11 April 1866, the name of its most celebrated growth, Romanée, was attached (a number of other villages in the Côte d'Or later adopted this commercially astute measure, which has led to a deplorable, albeit intentional, confusion in the mind of the general public). Above Vosne-Romanée lies Romanée-Conti, the paradigm of great Burgundy—4.46 acres (1.805 ha) of vines, the most celebrated and the most coveted *terroir* in the world, from which is eked an average of six thousand bottles, or about twenty *pièces,* of wine per year (less than one-fiftieth the production of Château Lafite, for instance. Even Pétrus, which by Bordeaux standards is diminutive, covers more than six times the area of Romanée-Conti and produces nearly ten times the quantity of wine).[1]

Except for the stark majesty of the Château de Vougeot, rising from a sea of vines, there is nothing visually spectacular about the Côte de Nuits. "Upon leaving Dijon," wrote Stendahl (*Mémoires d'un touriste,* 1838), "I am all eyes for the famous Côte d'Or . . . Were it not for its admirable wines, I would find nothing in the world to be so ugly." It may be that a consuming passion for its wines helps one to understand the unusual beauty of the Côte de Nuits, the inevitability of its landscape. The vines are mercilessly confined, from east to west, between the plain and the steep upper slope of the Côte; to the north and south, as far as the eye can reach, they have been cut like a jigsaw puzzle, into eccentric shapes by ancient footpaths and narrow dirt roads, punctuated by the bell-towers of the village churches. It is a timeless picture of infinite order, comforting and reassuring. The villages are secretive and silent, the streets uninhabited. In Vosne-Romanée, whose population is less than six hundred, one must feel one's way to discover the side street in which stand the gates to the courtyard of the Domaine de la Romanée-Conti. A few of the buildings in Vosne-Romanée, like the eighteenth-century houses in the prior's courtyard adjoining the vines of Romanée Saint-Vivant, have the charm of their antiquity, and the house called La Goillotte, built by the prince de Conti, breathes a genuine air of mystery. For the most part, however, the houses are outwardly undistinguished and inexpressive. Yet, behind the closed shutters of these mute facades and within the Domaine's gates, in the cellars and in the vines, *la Bourgogne profonde* is alive and well.

In the Côte d'Or words do not always mean quite the same thing as they do elsewhere. For instance, a *climat,* in the specifically Burgundian sense of the word, is the ensemble of physical characteristics of a particular *terroir*—composition, texture, and depth of the soil; exposition; altitude; degree of incline and other microclimatic factors—which defines a growth, or *cru*, differentiating its wine from all others. In short, a climat is a set of circumstances; a cru is the product of those circumstances, the wine itself.[2] The boundaries of a climat are legally consecrated, but not necessarily God-given, for though some, like Romanée-Conti, have remained unaltered for centuries, others have expanded, by court decision, in this century.

In Bordeaux the words, *domaine, château,* and *cru* mean roughly the same thing. A Bordeaux cru is a judicious assemblage of wines from a château, or domaine, which is an often vast estate composed of a variety of microclimates, terroirs, and grape varieties. By contrast, in the Côte d'Or a domaine is an estate composed of a number of different climats; often mere fragments because of the extreme parceling and multiple proprietorship within each climat. Each Côte d'Or cru represents the production of a single grape variety from a specific climat.

The Domaine de la Romanée-Conti today is a company-owned estate, shared in equal parts by the de Villaine and Leroy families.[3] It is composed principally of seven climats, each of whose wines is classified Grand Cru:[4] Romanée-Conti, La Tâche, Richebourg, Romanée Saint-Vivant, Grands Echézeaux, Echézeaux, and Montrachet. Romanée-Conti and La Tâche are *monopoles,* belonging in their entirety to the Domaine.

The Domaine de la Romanée-Conti, high altar of the Côte d'Or, symbolizes tradition and supremacy. For eighteen years, Aubert de Villaine and Lalou Bize-Leroy shared the responsibility of maintaining that ideal; today, Aubert de Villaine shares that responsibility with Mme Bize-Leroy's nephew Henry-Frédéric Roch. A total dedication to the Domaine permits of no flaw in the care of the vines and of the wines. The directors believe deeply that all aspects of viticulture and vinification should permit each wine to express, as completely as is possible within the framework of its vintage, the climat, or terroir of its origin. It is this absolute respect which defines the Domaine's signature; the wines, in fact, have such a distinctive style that foolish rumors have for long circulated to the effect that the Domaine possesses a well-guarded secret formula of vinification. In attempting to define the uniqueness of the Domaine's wines, writers often cite "oriental spices," an association which evokes notions of luxury, opulence, and exoticism.

Upon tasting the six red growths of the Domaine, side by side, in examples all of the same vintage, from neighboring climats with similar soils and similar expositions, extracted from mature pinot noir vines of the same strains and origin, and all vinified by the same person, one is over and over again transported in wonderment at the striking differences of personality from one cru to another, despite some family resemblance. These characteristic differences are repeated from vintage to vintage, however precious and unique the contributions of a particular growing season may be. I asked Lalou, Aubert, and Aubert's father Henri de Villaine to help me in defining the personalities of these wines. They worked hard to do so (the following passages in quotes are theirs), although initially they responded in unison, "Words are not the language of wine!" Of course, they are right. Attempts to describe wine usually rely on codified associations of scent and taste and abstract considerations of balance, texture, and structure. Many tasting notes could apply as well to an Hermitage as to Romanée-Conti; the notes are not necessarily at fault—words are simply inadequate.

Echézeaux, of all the Domaine's wines, is the most forward, the least complex. It opens out before the others with a ravishing clarity of expression, uncomplicated and cleanly etched; a caressing softness cloaks a steely skeleton which permits it to evolve with elegance. "It is the younger brother of Grands Echézeaux, the glorious eldest whose fortune Echézeaux aspires to equal. It sometimes comes very close, as in 1986, where it speaks the muscular language of the conquistadors. It is a wine which one can approach simply without the complications or the detours of other, more feminine growths . . . Each year, Echézeaux clears the paths which will be taken, each in its turn, by the Domaine's other growths in their evolution, first in barrel, then in bottle." Echézeaux is a reflection of Grands Echézeaux with, perhaps, a certain loss of detail; they share the same qualities but, in Grands Echézeaux, one senses greater variety, depth, and mystery. "It is 'GRAND' before being Echézeaux. Many fail to realize its place amongst the greatest growths. Grands-Echézeaux is a country gentleman, aristocrat and dreamer, who idles willingly with the unhurried step of his horse in a forest filled with the scents of sundry mushrooms, of mosses, of dead and decaying leaves, of furtive small game, which spill forth in a multitude of shifting alliances. All of that is expressed delicately, in a refined, musical tongue, concise and pure like the message of a Mozart quartet."

Romanée Saint-Vivant is flirtatious. "Each year, Romanée Saint-Vivant casts a spell of awe before the miracle of its delicacy and its femininity, its irresistible determination to seduce, before which one is helpless. Its perfumes are bewitching; one cannot help loving it and, only then, does one realize that behind this grace resides a strength in such perfect balance that, at first, it was imperceptible."

Richebourg, although perhaps less diversified, with greater power and less nuance, is closer in spirit to Romanée-Conti than the other growths; they are separated only by a footpath, the sentier des Raignots, once known as the sentier des Prêtres, because it led from the Clos de Saint-Vivant to the priory of Saint-Vivant (a *sentier* measures one step and a half, or 58 inches [1.46m]). In fact Romanée-Conti has one foot planted on the Richebourg side of the path. In the last century, Dr. Morelot noted that the two growths would be of the same quality were it not that part of "les Richebourgs" reached up steeper slopes. When tasted young, Richebourg is explosive, its fruit (in particular that which is associated with wild cherries, or *griottes*) the most violent and intense of all the growths.

> In contradiction to an opinion common amongst connoisseurs, Richebourg's personality is not wholly contained in its name. It is true that, by nature, it is the most opulent of the Domaine's growths, but, although it is "rich," it is not "bourgeois"; it may sport a velvet waistcoat but it certainly hasn't the "bread-basket" or "bran-belly" which an old dictum attributes to plush Burgundian city-dwellers. This immediate neighbor of La Romanée-Conti remains—willingly—in the antechamber of the salons where the latter reigns supreme. He escorts Her Majesty with good-natured ribaldry. He is a king's musketeer who likes company, likes to laugh and to sing, to feel that the somewhat brutal strength of his athlete's body is admired. He loves fêtes, loves to love and to be loved. Exuberant youth of Richebourg! More than any other, Richebourg demands the passage of time to discover the serene balance which it sumptuously displays, for example, today in a vintage like 1959.

La Tâche and Romanée-Conti vie for complexity, but they are different complexities. That of La Tâche is contained within a svelte, lean, sinewy, and aloof body. Romanée-Conti is fuller, more spherical; it has the feel of volume, it is more voluptuous. La Tâche is ultimate elegance; to its fruit, it typically joins scents which are more vegetal, memories of the gentler labiate herbs, fresh-mown hay, wild salads, the smoke of burning fruitwoods, decaying leaves. "La Tâche is elegance and rigor. Nothing evokes La Tâche so much as the wonderful portrait of Richelieu by Philippe de Champaigne, which expresses the Cardinal's fiery and angular authority, a nervous hand posed on the hilt of his sword, while the sword itself is drowned in a luxurious cascade of ermine and velvet. Likewise, in La Tâche, beneath the frequent hardness of its tannins, passion is aflame, restrained by an implacable, courtly elegance."

Romanée-Conti has been collecting adjectives, analogies, and hyperboles for two centuries. Ever since M. de Cussy (the same who, according to Dr. Lavalle, "never said simply Montrachet, but, with eyes cast heavenward, 'divine Montrachet'") described a bottle of Romanée, offered by the prince de Conti to the archbishop of Paris in 1782, as "bottled velvet and satin," velvet and satin have become part of the repertoire. As the vocabulary of wine tasting has become more sophisticated, these textures have been joined by the scents of violets, wild cherries, raspberries, strawberries, plums, spices, licorice, truffles, game, undergrowth, and other essences. There is always a sense of drama as one approaches Romanée-Conti after having tasted all of the other growths in the cellar—and one is never disappointed. It is as if all the stops had been pulled on a great cathedral organ, not in the sense that the wine is overpowering, for it is all delicacy and nuance; it is the infinite complexity which makes one catch one's breath.

> La Romanée-Conti is above all a complex wine. Its name, which savors of history and legend, fits like a glove: the wine of princes, it is velvet, seduction and mystery. Its personality is not defined by a singularity of character, but in terms of a complex ensemble whose unity each year is dictated by the laws of a subtle orchestration. These laws, immutable, but with changing forms of expression, constitute the real genius of the terroir. More than in any other growth, in Romanée-Conti lie somnolent treasures of delicacy and harmony which, it must be emphasized, years of silent repose, alone, can, little by little and progressively, bring forth. Romanée-Conti is the most Proustian of all the great wines: concealed in the secret perfume of fading rose petals in a Romanée-Conti 1954, is it not the intense and pure sensation of the past recaptured which arrests us and enchants us? As if, in this square of earth, the gods had bequeathed us a memory, the fascinating vestige of a timeless perfection, whose expression is like that of music, gentle and enveloping; its authority is that which emanates from majesty.

Although "Son Altesse Serénissime Monseigneur Louis-François de Bourbon Prince de Conti Prince du Sang," the most fastuous prince of the eighteenth century, was keenly aware of the grandeur of his title,[5] it was neither he nor his son, the last prince de Conti, who attached the name Conti to their proud possession La

Romanée. The two words were joined together, at the time that La Romanée was confiscated by officials of the Revolution, who, despite their goal of effacing all memory of the ancien régime, were loathe to surrender the prestige of the name Conti. This prestige, at a time when the name of a climat and the precision of its boundaries were defined by tradition but were not legally protected as inviolable property rights, had already excited covetous instincts among La Romanée's neighbors: the first transgressor was the priory of Saint-Vivant, whose vines, the Clos de Saint-Vivant, assumed the name La Romanée de Saint-Vivant five years after the prince de Conti's purchase of La Romanée in 1760.[6] After La Romanée de Saint-Vivant was seized by the revolutionary government and sold at auction in 1791 to Nicolas-Joseph Marey, he renamed a small parcel of lesser quality Le Clos Saint-Vivant (today called La Croix Rameau), and the remainder he called La Romanée. The name didn't stick; Marey's "Romanée" is now Romanée Saint-Vivant. In 1827 the vines which lay above Romanée-Conti, formerly "Aux Echanges," were baptized La Romanée; it is these vines which today bear the name. Other "Romanées" appeared and disappeared in the century to follow; the last to disappear was La Tâche-Romanée in the early 1930s.

Well before the prince de Conti removed La Romanée from the marketplace, reserving its entire production for his private table, it had attained the title of the first wine of Burgundy, its price was five to six times that of the most distinguished neighboring growths and it was rationed to clients, as it is today. For two centuries, since the birth of wine writing, Romanée-Conti has been consistently blessed with the epithet "Best Wine of Burgundy" and, often, "Greatest Wine in the World." The French minister of agriculture recently pronounced it to be "like a cathedral." The quality of awe that the very name Romanée-Conti inspires in us was perhaps better expressed in the more modest observation of Comte Alexandre de Lur Saluces, proprietor of Château d'Yquem, who writes "Romanée-Conti, this dream wine whose name, in my family, was mentioned only in hushed tones."

The history of Romanée-Conti, from its beginnings until the Revolution, can be pieced together from the Bourbon-Conti file in the Archives Nationales in Paris, the Archives de la Côte d'Or in Dijon, and in particular, the records of the priory of Saint-Vivant de Vergy. That these documents have survived centuries of wars, plagues, famines, and uprisings—above all, the conflagrations of the Revolution—is awesome. Since the Revolution, while these treasures lay dormant in the archives, a fabric of legends—a mythical history—has been woven around Romanée-Conti, embroidered upon as it passed from author to author, some altering dates, others inventing or falsifying documents to emphasize or extend the reputation of La Romanée's antique renown. Some of the legends sound plausible—the myth of Romanée-Conti's Roman origins, for instance; the frivolous legend of La Romanée and Louis XIV's miraculously cured fistula appears to have evolved out of a silent conspiracy among writers of the past to play a joke on succeeding generations. The sometimes incoherent mythical history of Romanée-Conti is the product of a sort of game, played over a period of two centuries, in homage to a great wine. Because it is the only "history" generally known, it constitutes a serious stumbling block to the presentation of a factual history, contradicting and accusing at each step. It became evident, finally, that the history of Romanée-Conti could not be written until each legend had been traced to its source and demythologized; it was a fascinating pursuit, with many detours, which produced a number of surprises.

The seeds of the fictive history can for the most part be traced to the eighteenth-century historian Abbé Courtépée. The first of seven volumes entitled *Déscription générale et particulière du duché de Bourgogne,* by Courtépée and Béguillet, appeared in 1775. The two authors rapidly parted ways; Courtépée, alone, is responsible for the work. The abbé was a tireless traveler within the boundaries of his beloved Burgundy and an impassioned taker of notes concerning anything Burgundian, be it statistics, natural history, geography, commerce, architecture, legend, folklore, history of village parishes, or critical judgments of wine; he was also an agile leaper to conclusions. It is often difficult to sort out the data from rumor, hypotheses, and wishful thinking.

The Fable of La Romanée and the Roman Occupation

Following a passage in praise of the Roman emperor Probus (for having repealed, in A.D. 282 Emperor Domitian's edict of A.D. 92, that half the vines of the empire be torn up and none replanted), Courtépée wrote, "One would be led to believe that, in gratitude to the Romans, Vosne will have given to its best *climat* the name of Romanée (à Romanis)" [L'on seroit porté à croire que, par reconnoissance pour les Romains, Vône aura donné à son meilleur climat le nom de Romanée (à Romanis)].

Dr. Lavalle, the greatly respected author of *Histoire et statistique de la vigne et des grands vins de la Côte d'Or,* published in 1855, suggested that La Romanée may have belonged to the Roman emperors or may have been the site of a Roman military camp; he concluded, "The only point that is almost certain is that the name of Romanée was given in souvenir of some event relative to the Roman domination." Forty years later, Danguy and Aubertin, authorities following in Dr. Lavalle's footsteps, attempted, with an evident lack of conviction, to justify Courtépée's suggestion. Among more recent writers, the suggestion has crystallized into an assertion of fact; reservations have vanished and peremptory statements permit of no doubt that La Romanée dates from the Roman conquest. Maurice des Ombiaux, jumbling legends, misinformation, and historical periods, wrote, "La Romanée was the wine of the grand siècle. The vineyard dates, as its name indicates, from the Roman conquest; part of it was ceded to the house of Conti, who were very proud of it. Following a long illness, Louis XIV's doctor, Fagon, prescribed for the entire period of his convalescence the wine of Romanée-Conti."

In fact, the name Romanée appeared for the first time in the middle of the seventeenth century; Louis XIV died in 1715, the prince de Conti purchased La Romanée in its entirety in 1760 and La Romanée was not known as Romanée-Conti until 1794. Moreover, the vineyard, one of the four Clos de Saint-Vivant which would later become La Romanée, was acquired by the priory of Saint-Vivant during the thirteenth century; it had certainly not been planted to vines before the end of the twelfth century at the very earliest.

Imaginary Gifts and Sales

Courtépée did not know that La Romanée, under another name, had once been part of the Clos de Saint-Vivant. He declared, "La Romanée de Saint-Vivant, in Vosne, was given [to the priory of Saint-Vivant] by Alix de Vergy in 1232." This is the most attractive of all the myths, if only for the beautiful and mysterious name of Alix de Vergy, duchess of Burgundy for the first half of the thirteenth century and one of the most beloved figures in the history of Burgundy. The declaration has been interpreted to mean "the vineyards which are now known as La Romanée de Saint-Vivant . . . " and the assertion has never been questioned. However, there exists no record of an acquisition of vines by the priory of Saint-Vivant in 1232. Moreover, the legend is too perfect to be true. Canon Jean Marilier, medieval ecclesiastical scholar and principal authority on the priory of Saint-Vivant produced an astonishing document, which he translated into modern French: Courtépée's act exists and the date, 1232, is right;[7] it concerns a lifetime gift—or loan—of vines by the prior of Saint-Vivant to "Aimon d'Aiserey, provost of Saint-Jean". Alix de Vergy's role was to bear witness to the transaction and to impose her seal. These vines were in Les Maizières, a climat unrelated either to La Romanée or to the vines known today as Romanée Saint-Vivant. The document is precious in that it furnishes certain proof that the priory of Saint-Vivant possessed vines under cultivation as early as the beginning of the thirteenth century. Courtépée was separated from Alix de Vergy by five and a half centuries; it is hard to comprehend how rumor and a misinterpretation concerning an act of no importance, the contents of which were unknown, could have endured for so long. However that may be, it is certain that Alix de Vergy made no gift of vines to the priory of Saint-Vivant.

Following the phrase concerning Alix de Vergy, Courtépée wrote, "Ponce de Blaisy sold his vineyard in Vosne to the prior in 1246." There was no sale of vines to Saint-Vivant in 1246. However, a sale was recorded in the Saint-Vivant ledgers thirty years later: "October 1276, Sale to Saint-Vivant by Jean de Vosne, chevalier, of all the lands belonging to him in the finages of Vosne and Poncey, with the exception of those having belonged to Thomas de Poncey and his brother." In a declaration of property holdings made by Jean de Vosne four years earlier in 1272, the property which had belonged to Thomas de Poncey and his brother, as well as "the fief which I hold from Poincet de Blaisy," are mentioned.[8] Reading between the lines, one must assume that Jean de Vosne was Ponce de Blaisy's son-in-law and that he had received Ponce de Blaisy's vines in his wife's dowry. Ponce de Blaisy did not sell his vines to anyone, but eventually Jean de

Vosne sold to the priory of Saint-Vivant the vines which had once belonged to Ponce de Blaisy. That a folk memory and half-truth can have persisted for over five centuries to be gathered into Courtépée's anecdotal history is as mysterious as the legend of Alix de Vergy's gift of vines. Though they contradict the actual history, both anecdotes would be harmless, were it not that they are generally accepted as fact.

Louis XIV and La Romanée

The tale of Louis XIV's miraculous recovery from an anal fistula thanks to his doctor's prescription of La Romanée, is familiar to everyone who has read the anecdotal histories of Burgundy wine.

The historical facts are banal. In November 1693, Guy-Crescent Fagon, who had been doctor to the royal children, was elevated to the position of king's doctor, after which he prescribed "old Burgundy," in place of champagne, to relieve Louis XIV's periodic attacks of gout.[9] Courtépée wrote, "The initial celebrity of the wines from the côte [de Nuits] goes back only to Louis XIV, for whom, after a dangerous illness in 1686, Dr. Fagon prescribed the most decongestive wine and indicated that of Nuits as being the most suitable for reestablishing his diminished vitality."

The historian is deliberately inventing history: 1686, seven years before Fagon became the king's doctor, was the year in which the king's surgeon, Monsieur Félix, operated on Louis XIV for an anal fistula; in court circles, it was known as *La Grande Opération*. Linking the years of *La Grande Opération* to Fagon's equally famous prescription of seven years later cannot be attributed to a natural tendency to muddle dates and events. Courtépée proclaimed the superiority of the wines of "Nuits," by which he meant Côte de Nuits, over those of Beaune, and the superiority of those of Vosne over the other "Nuits." This undoubtedly explains his sly transformation of Fagon's generic "old Burgundy" into "Nuits."

Sixteen years after Courtépée's text appeared, La Romanée was seized from the prince de Conti to be sold at auction. The revolutionary government's appointed experts, in their evaluation of La Romanée, incorporated Courtépée's anecdote into their report, defining the "dangerous illness" and concluding with a sardonic observation, completely out of context, about the sans-culottes (the most bloodthirsty of the revolutionists, from the Parisian working classes, so named because the men wore pants instead of the culottes, or breeches, of the upper classes): "Louis Capet, 14th of that name, having been treated for a fistula, had sunk into a deplorable and alarming state of weakness. The doctors assembled to find a way of reviving his strength. They were of the opinion that the most efficient remedy would be to choose the most excellent old wines from the Côte de Nuits and Vosne. Purchase was made of them, the invalid put them to use, and his health was promptly restored. That of La Romanée would undeniably work ('opéreroit, sans contredit') the greatest of marvels on our defenders, the sans-culottes."

In 1855, Dr. Lavalle published an abridged version of the 1794 expertise, noting that the Archives de la Côte d'Or housed the original but failing to indicate that he had eliminated entire sections, trimmed or rewritten sentences, and altered a number of details to suit his taste. The most remarkable bit of trimming consisted in lopping off the last six words of the above quotation so that the final sentence reads, "That of La Romanée would undeniably work the greatest of marvels."

Later authors reproduced Dr. Lavalle's version, while altering the last line to read, "That of La Romanée undeniably worked the greatest of marvels." [Celui de la Romanée *opérait,* sans contredit, les plus grandes merveilles (emphasis added).]

So it is that, at present, the accepted version of this fable is the altered version of Lavalle's altered version of the experts' altered version of Courtépée's altered version of a moment in history which concerned neither the king's fistula nor La Romanée. Thanks to Courtépée's misrepresentation of Dr. Fagon's prescription, the principal thoroughfare in Nuits-Saint-Georges today bears Fagon's name.

Two Centuries of Falsified Documents

Courtépée fiddled with dates and failed to verify his claims; Dr. Lavalle had his little joke by eliminating a few words from a text to completely alter its message; but the nineteenth-century writer Charles Theuriet invented documents that never existed. He wrote that Alix de Vergy ceded a "field" to the priory of Saint-Vivant: "The deed which mentions this event says that she harvested a few *émines* [1 émine = 16 bushels] of oats from her field; it is known that this field, in the hands of the monks, became the incomparable vineyard of La Romanée." Theuriet also invented a Romanée fountain: "At the marriage of duke Philippe-le-Bon, in the fifteenth century [two centuries before the name Romanée actually first appeared], there was a fountain from which flowed the wine of La Romanée." A five-page anecdote—which Theuriet claims to be taken from Dr. Fagon's memoires, and into which he introduces the prior of Saint-Vivant, a wily monk, Erasmus, and Dr. Salins—finishes with Fagon addressing the king in these words: "The wine of the monks of Saint-Vivant in Burgundy is suited to a robust temperament like yours, it is more stimulating, more astringent, more generous [than the wine of Guyenne]. It more easily supports the addition of water; in small quantities it produces marvelous effects. That is why, sire, I prescribe it in preference to Your Majesty."

In this century, Pierre Andrieu altered Theuriet's prescription, transforming the water into holy water, and presented it as Fagon's authentic prescription, without crediting the source; Pierre Forgeot lifted Andrieu's text without crediting the source, simply presenting it as Fagon's "well-known prescription."

Andrieu and Forgeot have employed other tricks to extend the antique celebrity of "the Romanées." However, for these to make any sense, it must be emphasized that Beaune's celebrity is much more ancient than that of La Romanée, and a slight digression is necessary to throw things into focus: partly as a result of Dr. Fagon's recommendation that Louis XIV drink old Burgundy in preference to the wines of Champagne (which were predominantly non-sparkling and reddish at that time), a foolish public quarrel flared up between Champenois and Burgundians. In response to an attack on the wines of Burgundy by the Faculty of Medicine in Reims, Dr. Salins, doyen of the Doctors of Beaune, was elected to defend the honor of Burgundy. In 1704 he published *Défense du vin de Bourgogne contre le vin de Champagne*, in which he spoke of "the Beaune, served in Venice by the doge Morosini at the banquet offered to the senators after the conquest of Morea [1684]." Andrieu then wrote, "*Romanée Saint-Vivant* was served at a banquet offered to the senators by the doge of Venice after the conquest of Morea [emphasis added]."

Inspired by Andrieu's daring, Forgeot employed the same technique, substituting "Romanée" for "Beaune" in an uncredited text by Courtépée, who wrote of Philippe-le-Hardi, "He made rich gifts to the pope, Benoit XIII, residing in Avignon, gave to the cardinals of Albane and of Viviers twenty *queues* of Beaune." Forgeot's version: "Thus in 1395 the cardinals, Albane and Vivier [sic], at the papal court of Avignon, received twenty *queues* of Romanée."

The Other Romanées

Andrieu wrote, with an absolute insouciance, "In 1240, the archbishops of Lyons were proprietors in Pommard, thanks to the generosity of the duchess Alix de Vergy who, twelve years later, gave a part of La Romanée to the priory of Saint-Vivant.

Ever since, this climat has been called Romanée Saint-Vivant, so as not to confuse it with Romanée-Conti and La Romanée." This very confusing passage is reproduced simply because it has often been read and, if not clearly understood, believed in essence. As far as "the Romanées" are concerned, it contains no fragment of truth. Alix de Vergy who, in her lifetime, made no gift of vines to the priory of Saint-Vivant, died in 1251, a year before the author credits her with this gift. Until 1584 the vineyard that was to become La Romanée in 1651 and Romanée-Conti in 1794 was part of the Clos de Saint-Vivant; the other vines in the Clos de Saint-Vivant were for the first time referred to as "La Romanée de Saint-Vivant" in 1765, more than five centuries after Alix de Vergy's reign. The third Romanée dates from 1827.

Affixed opposite the label on bottles of La Romanée is a fantasy/legend which reads: "Originally there was only one Romanée. . . . La Romanée was broken up in the 15th Century as a result of some sale or inheritance or other: the eastern section, bought in 1760 by the prince de Conti, still bears his name. The western section, or simply Romanée, as you see it today, has been since 1815 the monopoly of the Counts LIGER-BELAIR, Châtelains of Vosne-Romanée."

The parcel of vines lying above Romanée-Conti, which today takes the name of La Romanée, is a creation of the last century, the brainchild of Lieutenant-Général Louis Liger-Belair. It was originally composed of six small properties, varying in size from one *ouvrée* to one *journal*, in the climat, or lieudit, of Aux Echanges (or Aux Changes, Es Echanges, or Esange) and described in the Saint-Vivant property declaration of 1512 as "belonging to Monsieur de Fangey because of his wife, to Jehan Breton and to several others"; the surveyor's map of La Romanée (see frontispiece), prepared for the prince de Conti in 1760, indicates the six neighboring properties, their proprietors' names, and their surface measures.[10]

In October 1791, in the first attempt by the new regime to classify vines for purposes of taxation, the community of Vosne was broken down into fourteen lettered sections. Section J was composed of Romanée-Conti, Les Richebourgs, and Les Verroilles (today part of Richebourg). The six properties in the climat of Aux Echanges were included in Les Richebourgs. One of these properties belonged to a widow, Madame Lamy de Samerey. On 17 October 1791, she had declared in Section J, "one *ouvrée* of vines lieudit Aux Echanges." Her children had emigrated, and at her death in 1797 the property was confiscated by the government. It was sold at auction, 6 Frimaire, Year VI (26 November 1797), to Claude-François Viénot-

Rameau and Jean Bruet-Cretenet, *négociants* in Dijon; three years later, it was acquired by Nicolas-Guillaume Basire, the future father-in-law of Louis Liger-Belair, who received it at the time of his marriage to Claire-Cécile Basire, in 1815. In the course of the twelve years to come, he acquired, one by one, the five remaining parcels in the lieudit Aux Echanges. On the first day of July 1827, on the cadastre in the town hall of Vosne, Louis Liger-Belair registered these six properties, assembled into one, as "La Romanée."

In sum, Romanée-Conti is the only Romanée which possesses the historical right to the name La Romanée.

Eleven Centuries of History

II

THE VINES THAT were to become La Romanée originally belonged to a monastery, the priory of Saint-Vivant de Vergy, protected by a seventh-century fortress, the Château de Vergy.[11] The château rose from the summit of the Mount of Vergy in the back hills of the Côte de Nuits, while the monastery's foundations were carved out of the mountain's steep southern slope. Repeatedly restored, enlarged, demolished, and rebuilt over the centuries, Saint-Vivant's last alterations date from just before the Revolution.

As one wanders today in the lonely beauty and silence of the ruins of Saint-Vivant, the high wall of the terrace still impervious to decay, the remainder long ago destroyed, except for the crumbling walls of the chapel and two lower levels of vaulted cellars, mostly intact but condemned to collapse, with bramble and undergrowth choking the approach; time recedes.

Although the present ruins are eighteenth century, one is swept in revery to a moment eleven centuries ago, to a Burgundy dominated by warlords and roving bands of outlaws, menaced by the terrible invading Normans and scattered sparsely with monasteries, rare havens of hope and security, which also bore the promise of salvation to the warlords who supported them. The near-impenetrable Château de Vergy (destroyed in 1609 by order of Henry IV, to rid France of "nests of thieves and leagues" [nids de voleurs et de ligues]), built in the form of a ship, 1,920 feet (585 m) long and 35 feet (10.7 m) deep, and incorporating fourteen towers, was the stronghold of one of the most powerful of these warlords.

The Priory of Saint-Vivant

Manassès I, seigneur de Vergy, founded the monastery of Saint-Vivant around the year 900.[12] Manassès was count of Chalon, of Beaune, and of Oscheret (later part of the county of Beaune) and lieutenant to Richard le Justicier, first duke of Burgundy. A. DuChesne, in his *Histoire de la Maison de Vergy*, 1625, describes Manassès as the "very intimate and familiar friend of Richard and the most powerful and the richest seigneur of his court"; he bore the unique title of "*Preux,* which signifies magnanimous and valiant." [très intime et familier amy de Richard et le plus puissant et le plus riche Seigneur de sa cour . . . Preux, qui signifie magnanime & vaillant.]

Unlike his friend le Justicier (who legend claims refused on his deathbed to repent for all the lives he had taken, because he felt that for each scoundrel slaughtered he had saved many innocent lives), Manassès was persuaded by his wife, Ermengeard, daughter of Boson, defunct king of Burgundy and brother of Richard le Justicier, and his brother, Gales, bishop of Autun, to expiate his sins by providing a sanctuary for the relics of Vivant, the fourth-century saint, and the twenty-eight monks who, fleeing the invading Normans with the saint's body, liturgical essentials, and household utensils, had first abandoned, in 868, their monastery in Poitou and, later, a monastery in the Jura, burned by the Normans.

The new priory of Saint-Vivant was said to have been lavishly endowed by its founders and benefactors, Manassès and Ermengeard. Manassès died in 918; Ermengeard lived much longer.

The priory of Saint-Vivant was first reformed around the year 1000, under the orders of Saint-Bénigne, in Dijon; in November 1095, at the Council of Clermont, Pope Urban II pronounced Saint-Vivant's affiliation with Cluny, which in succeeding centuries furnished a number of priors to Saint-Vivant. Throughout its history, the wealth of Saint-Vivant depended largely on the wealth of its priors.

By a deed dated 13 November 1131, Hugues II, duke of Burgundy, ceded to the priory of Saint-Vivant "all the uncultivated lands, woods and fields [that he owned] in Flagey and in Vosne."[13]

This deed may be only a reiteration or a confirmation of part of the original endowment, conferred two centuries earlier by Manassès and Ermengeard; such was the assumption of Dr. Lavalle, who wrote, "These fallows were, at that time, so worthless that the great priory of Saint-Vivant, which to all appearances had received this land as part of its endowment, the ownership of which had been newly consecrated by the duke, Hugues II, had abandoned it, reserving only the right of the tithe."

Until the Revolution and the abolition of monasteries and feudal rights, the priory of Saint-Vivant collected dues and tithes on much of the territory in Vosne, Flagey, and Nuits, and on the Clos de Vougeot, the vineyard that was pieced together by the Cistercian monks during the twelfth, thirteenth, and fourteenth centuries.[14] All of these lands were either part of Manassès and Ermengeard's original endowment or of Hugues's gift, and most of them were relinquished early on through emphyteutic, perpetual leases, which assured the monastery of a continuing income without the necessity of occupying itself with the cultivation of the lands.

Emphyteusis, a legacy of the ancient Greeks, was originally a perpetual lease of land by a collective, abstract being destined to live eternally (the priory of Saint-Vivant, for example). An emphyteutic lease imposed annual dues or rental fees, a tithe (literally a tenth, but broadly interpreted to mean a small percentage of the harvest or its worth in coin), and the obligation to improve the property. It carried rights of succession but the original leaser retained seigneurial rights, which included *lods* (an undefined sum of money due to the prior of Saint-Vivant at the time of signing the lease and, subsequently, each time that the property changed hands), *retenue* (the right of the seigneur-prior to reclaim or "buy back" the property), and *remuage* (the right of transfer; a property could change hands only with the consent of the seigneur). There is no perfect equivalent in the modern world to the medieval concept of perpetual lease. It is best understood if one considers the priory of Saint-Vivant as an abstract being or government, the lease a rights contract, and the dues and tithes as taxes owed to the government.

The monks of Saint-Vivant were never numerous and they were not worker monks; their business was prayer. The few lands which had not been disposed of by emphyteutic leases were let on short-term leases (usually six or nine years) to vignerons who created new vineyards or cultivated already existing vines. These leases, or tenant contracts, were on a *moitié-fruits,* or half-harvest, basis, a system akin to sharecropping; the vineyards were tenanted but remained the property of the monks, who received 50 percent of the wine harvest, or its equivalent in coin, for rent, as opposed to the 10 or 12 percent that they received from vines surrendered to perpetual lease. The priory of Saint-Vivant did not, in Dr. Lavalle's words, "abandon" all of its lands, "reserving only the right of tithe." The attestation of Alix de Vergy, in 1232 (see chapter 1, note 7), is proof enough that the priory possessed vineyards in production at that time.

Following the deed of Hugues in 1131 (and with the exception of an insignificant exchange, in 1520, of some rents in return for two ouvrées of vines lying in an enclave within the Clos de Saint-Vivant), only four acquisitions of vines are recorded in the Saint-Vivant ledgers. All four fall within a fifty-year period at the heart of the thirteenth century, an especially prosperous moment in the history of Saint-Vivant, during which time two wealthy and influential members of the same family, Yves de Poisot and his nephew Yves de Chasans, both chevaliers de Vergy and Cluniac abbots, were succeeding priors of Saint-Vivant.

These acquisitions undoubtedly concerned terrains originally owned by Saint-Vivant and surrendered by emphyteutic leases, on which the priory claimed dues and tithes at the time that the properties were recuperated by donation or purchase. The selection was not random, for all of the acquired vines adjoined the already existing Clos de Saint-Vivant and were obviously chosen to complete the clos.

The earliest of the four transactions, Simon Clerc's donation to Saint-Vivant, in 1241, of vines "adjoining the clos of the monks of Vergy" again confirms the existence, before this donation, of vineyards at Saint-Vivant. Two of the three remaining transactions—sales by Jean de Vosne and by Perrin d'Arc of the lands belonging to each "in the *finages* of Vosne and Poncey"—both occur in October 1276.

The last acquisition, in March 1285, a "sale by Guillaume Forestier d'Argilly and his wife to the prior of Saint-Vivant," specifies, "three journaux of vines adjoining those of the aforesaid prior in Vosne." Three journaux is too small an area to be relevant to La Romanée. Because no precise surface measurements are mentioned in the entries concerning the three other acquisitions, it is impossible to know the extent of the vines possessed by the priory before these transactions occurred.

The wording of the two entries from 1276 suggests that they were of greater importance than the other transactions and their proximity in time suggests that the two sales were related. Without insisting too much, one might conjecture that on a single day in October 1276 Yves de Chasans (prior from 1275 to 1289) purchased

most of what was to be the Clos de Saint-Vivant, including the future Romanée.

The dukes of Burgundy did not levy taxes on property. In 1512, thirty-five years after the annexation of Burgundy by King Louis XI, the priory of Saint-Vivant was obliged for the first time to declare its holdings, describing boundaries and surface measures.

The priory's declaration begins, "This is the domain belonging to the Reverend Seigneur Monsieur le Grand Doyen of the church and monastery of St. Vivant les Vergey of the Order of Cluny in the villages of Vosne and Flagey that the said Sieur possesses in hand." A detailed description of an enclosure—measuring two journaux, containing the prior's house and others, cellars, courtyard, falconeries, orchard and gardens—finishes; "appurtenances of the said house are the vines of the clos called Les Cloux de Saint Viven."[15]

"Les Cloux de Saint-Vivant" consisted of four adjoining *cloux*, or clos; separate from these clos were ten ouvrées of vines in Les Maizières, in Flagey, the subject of the Alix de Vergy document of 1232, of which, after 1512, there is no further trace. The four clos were the Clos des Neuf Journaux, the Clos du Moytan (five journaux), the Clos des Quatre Journaux, and the Clos des Cinq Journaux. Separated from the Clos des Cinq Journaux by a footpath was a "parcel of vines containing three ouvrées." A century and a half later, the Clos des Cinq Journaux and the adjoining parcel were known as La Romanée; their boundaries were identical to those of La Romanée-Conti today.[16]

There are no further declarations of the property of Saint-Vivant until 1769. At some time between 1512 and 1584, the Clos des Cinq Journaux came to be known as the Cros des Cloux (Creux des Clos, in modern French).

The Perpetual Lease

At midday, 19 February 1584, before the Great Portal of Saint-Vivant de Vergy, the prior and grand doyen, "*Vénérable et scientifique personne*," Me. Jean Marguot, offered the Cros des Cloux and the small parcel of adjoining vines to the highest bidder, "on the terms of annual and perpetual emphyteutic dues, carrying all seigneurial rights." Berthier Bonnepoux, bidding in the name of and by procuration of Maître Claude Cousin, *sergent général* (king's bailiff) of Dijon, carried the day with his bid of twenty sols (one livre) in annual dues.

The document recording this transaction is, at the same time, the official emphyteutic lease and a lively, blow-by-blow report of the bidding, of the events leading up to it, and of the impossibility of finding a short-term-lease tenant. Both the Cros des Cloux and the adjoining parcel are defined as *toppes*, a specifically Burgundian word, meaning a vineyard which has been torn up and is lying fallow; as if to emphasize the meaning of the word, the Cros des Cloux is described as "a toppe that used to be in vines," and the small parcel as "two ouvrées of vineyard also in toppes next to the above-said toppe." The only conceivable explanation for this condition would seem to be the mysterious scourge which ravaged the vineyards of the Côte during the fifteenth and sixteenth centuries.[17]

The contract specifies that the tithe and the dues are payable "on next All Saints' Day to come and from this time forward each and every year perpetually without cease" and that "in these toppes, the said holder will be required to plant vines of a good strain and to keep them up so that they may be worthy each year of their dues, and also to rebuild the wall, which at present is in ruin, the length of the vineyard facing the community road which leads to the mountain [the Mount of Vergy]."

Claude Cousin died in or just before 1603. His widow and their nephew Germain Danon, inherited the property.

In 1621 Germain Danon sold the Cros des Cloux to Jacques Venot. Early in his career, Venot was a protégé of the duc de Mayenne, governor of Burgundy, who had succeeded his brother the duc de Guise as chief of the intransigent Holy League, dedicated to the eradication of Protestantism and a declared enemy of King Henry IV.

In 1594, through Mayenne's influence, Venot acceeded to the post of *maître extraordinaire* of the Chambre des Comptes of Dijon.[18] In 1595, after Dijon's surrender to the royal army and Mayenne's submission to Henry IV, Venot was relieved of his duties. However, as his allegiance had meanwhile been transferred from Mayenne to the Crown and his talents proven, he was appointed a month later, 23 June 1595, to the more solid and enduring position of *maître ordinaire* of the Chambre des Comptes.

His capacities were valued by Henry IV and Louis XIII, both of whom confided in him a number of important commissions. In 1611 he was given the commission of defining the boundaries of the duchy of Burgundy, and in 1612 he was elevated to the newly created office of charters treasurer of the Chambre des Comptes. In 1617 he retired from his post at the Chambre des Comptes, to be replaced by his son Pierre.

On 21 June 1619, and again the following year, Venot was elected *vicomte mayeur de Dijon,* an honorary title bestowed upon each mayor of Dijon from the time of the municipality's acquisition of the viscounty of Dijon in 1284 until the Revolution.

In 1621, the year of Venot's retirement from the mayoralty of Dijon, and the same year in which he acquired the Cros des Cloux from Germain Danon, he also bought, from the Crown, the Seigneurie de Vougeot, one of several seigneuries that had been detached that year from the vast Châtellenie d'Argilly and sold to feed the coffers of Louis XIII. This transaction, in itself unrelated to the purchase of the Cros des Cloux, was nonetheless allied to the destiny of La Romanée, for it brought Venot's great-grandson, the second Philippe de Croonembourg, into contact with the House of Conti fifty years before André, the last of the Croonembourgs, sold La Romanée to Louis-François de Bourbon, the prince de Conti in 1760.[19]

Ten years after the purchases of the Cros des Cloux and the Seigneurie de Vougeot, by a contract dated 28 August 1631, Venot and his wife transferred both possessions to their daughter Jeanne Venot and their son-in-law Philippe de Croonembourg.[20] The wine of the Cros des Cloux, subsequently La Romanée, was vinified in the village of Vougeot on their property, which Jacques Venot and his wife continued to inhabit.

FOUR GENERATIONS OF CROONEMBOURGS

The Croonembourgs were professional soldiers. Philippe de Croonembourg, an infantry regiment captain whose family had received letters of nobility from the archduke of Austria in 1610, was a native of the county of Mouscron (today in Belgium) in Flanders. Having resided for several years in Burgundy, he was granted naturalization papers by the king of France, 30 September 1631, a month before his marriage to Jeanne Venot. He died seven years later in the service of the king. Philippe de Croonembourg had arrived from Flanders bearing the title of seigneur de Saint-Genois; in the records of the priory of Saint-Vivant, Jeanne Venot is always designated as Mlle de Saint-Genois.

A 1631 entry in the Saint-Vivant records reads, "Me. Jacques Venot Sieur de Vougeot owes on All Saints' Day twenty sols in emphyteutic dues on two parcels of vines in the finage of Vosne at the lieudit sur les Cloux." A 1651 entry reads, "Mademoiselle de Saint-Genois in place of Mr. le Maître des Comptes her father owes around All Saints' Day twenty sols for two parcels of vines situated in the finage of Vosne, *lieudit en La Romanée* [my emphasis]." Between 1631 and 1651 there are no entries.

At some time in that twenty-year period, long enough before 1651 for the appellation to have been accepted as a lieudit, the Cros des Cloux became La Romanée. The impulsion may have sprung from Jeanne Venot but the source of the inspiration is not recorded.

Until 1694, nearly twenty years after Jeanne Venot's death, the entries for La Romanée remain in the name of "Mademoiselle de Saint-Genois, daughter of M. le Maître des Comptes Venot," but, in the margin of the entry recording the years 1685 to 1693, the Saint-Vivant collector wrote, "Received from François Niquet, farmer of M. de Saint-Genois [Jacques de Croonembourg]." The 1720 entry is the first in the name of Croonembourg (the second Philippe, son of Jacques).

It was under the Croonembourgs that La Romanée ascended to its superior position in both reputation and price. Until the last half of the seventeenth century, the *vins de primeur* from the Côte de Beaune—*oeil de perdrix,* or rosé, wines from Volnay, Beaune, and Pommard, in particular—enjoyed a greater reputation than the wines from the Côte de Nuits. Arnoux (1728) and Courtépée both attribute the initial fame of the Côte de Nuits wines (of which Arnoux wrote, "These wines are at first very hard, very astringent & very green; they want to be awaited until their second, third, fourth & fifth year") to Louis XIV's use of them; Courtépée credits a mysterious M. Jaquinot de Richemont with having been the first, around 1680, to recognize "the superiority of the wines of Vosne to the Nuiton wines." This period coincides with Dom Pierre Pérignon's experiments with strong glass and airtight corks; his goal was to imprison the bubbles in champagne, but his achievement also permitted still wines to be laid down and to improve with age, a concept which had disappeared with antique civilizations. During a millennium and a half, old wine had meant wine which remained in barrels for two or three years and, for the most part, it was less admired than the wine of the year.

By 1733, according to the 1794 expertise, La Romanée was fetching prices five to six times those of the next most distinguished growths of La Côte (with the exception of Montrachet, whose prices approached those of La Romanée): "The wine of La Romanée has always fetched a price higher than the others . . . In 1733 and in the following years, the price established by the proprietor [the second Philippe de Croonembourg] was 900 livres, 1,000 livres and 1,100 livres per queue, depending on the vintage. From 1750 until the time the vineyard was sold [in 1760, to the prince de Conti], the price of a queue was fixed, depending on the vintage, at 1,200, 1,300, and 1,400 livres and the proprietor [André de Croonembourg] sold it only in feuillettes." For this same period, from 1733 to 1760, Dr. Lavalle cites prices per queue, from the official registers, for the Clos de Vougeot and the leading growths of Nuits. The highest price paid was 320 livres [in 1748 and, again, in 1759], the lowest was 50 livres [1740], and the average was 200 livres.[21]

While his vineyards prospered, the second Philippe de Croonembourg died in or just before 1745, leaving his wife, Marguerite Vallot, and his son, André, La Romanée, the seigneuries of Vougeot, Chambolle, and Morey, and a large collection of debts. In 1745 Chambolle and Morey were sold for 48,000 livres to pay a portion of the debts. Fifteen years later André de Croonembourg was obliged to sell La Romanée to Louis-François de Bourbon to settle more than 70,000 livres of remaining debts.

THE PRINCES DE CONTI

An aura of intrigue shrouds the sale of La Romanée.

Louis-François de Bourbon, prince de Conti, bought the vineyard of La Romanée from André de Croonembourg, 18 July 1760, for 80,000 livres plus 12,400 livres *pot-de-vin,* a total of 92,400 livres, or 2,310 livres per ouvrée. The price astounded everyone at the time; distinguished neighboring growths were selling for less than 200 livres per ouvrée.[22]

The sale was imposed by Philippe de Croonembourg's creditors and by court order; the sum was settled upon by the creditors because it corresponded closely to Philippe de Croonembourg's legacy of debts to his son; André de Croonembourg was to pocket the *pot-de-vin,* the buyer was to reimburse the creditors and, after all debts were paid, André de Croonembourg was to collect the difference (he collected 6,000 livres plus interest, 2 April 1762).

None of which explains the prince's willingness to pay the price; the Croonembourgs had, after all, never paid him for the Seigneurie de Vougeot (see note 19) and he had no reason to care whether the Croonembourg debts were paid . . . The fact that he cared nothing about money may have led André de Croonembourg to approach him. It is true that Louis-François lived very grandly; the exclusive privilege of pouring the greatest wine of Burgundy for his fastuous suppers at the Palais du

Temple in Paris and at the Château de Bourbon-Conti in L'Isle-Adam may easily have justified the price in the eyes of the prince.

The identity of the buyer of La Romanée was concealed until after the contract of sale was signed. The 1794 expertise of La Romanée has preserved the rumor that La Romanée "was jealously coveted by La Pompadour, who failed to succeed in her intrigues." It has been inferred, from this wisp of gossip, that secrecy was essential for the prince de Conti to be able to acquire La Romanée without the interference of the king's favorite.

The prince de Conti believed that his military career had been sabotaged through Madame de Pompadour's machinations. Certainly, it was common knowledge that she detested the prince de Conti and felt threatened by his influence on Louis XV (with whom, during the ten years following his departure from the army, he shared regular and prolonged secret work sessions, from which even Mme de Pompadour was excluded). It was common belief that, in 1757, she had orchestrated a falling-out between the prince and the king.

The grounds for secrecy were obviously ample if, indeed, it was true that Mme de Pompadour coveted La Romanée, but no reflection of this intrigue has come to light in the memoires and chronicles of the period.

Jean-François Joly de Fleury, intendant de Bourgogne, made all of the official arrangements and stood in as the buyer of La Romanée.[23] All of the documents leading up to the sale, as well as the contract of sale itself, indicate the buyer to be Joly de Fleury "for himself or his friend of election" [pour luy ou son amy à élire].

For centuries, surface area was measured by an experienced eye without recourse to other instruments. In 1512 the Cloux des Cinq Journaux was represented as containing "five journaux or thereabout"; in different declarations, the parcel of vines to the other side of the footpath is described as "three ouvrées," "two ouvrées or thereabout," and so on.

André de Croonembourg declared La Romanée to contain five journaux, or forty ouvrées. It was not his intention to include the parcel across the footpath in the sale. However, in the procuration signed by his mother, Marguérite Vallot, 10 May 1760, she declares La Romanée to contain thirty-seven and a half ouvrées.

The surveyor's map of La Romanée dated 16 May 1760, which does not include the vines across the footpath within the boundaries, declares La Romanée to contain "thirty-eight ouvrées, fourteen perches and three-quarters." Joly de Fleury apparently thought it politic to retain the measure from Marguérite Vallot's declaration and to suppress the surveyor's figures.

André de Croonembourg was obliged to sign a procuration, 4 July 1760, stating that "although the little parcel of vines, called en Richebourg . . . containing two ouvrées . . . had been included neither in the proposition nor in the conclusion of the conditions of the sale . . . [Croonembourg] has conceived the intention of releasing it [to the buyer] with no augmentation of the price of the sale."

The contract of sale defines the property as "a vineyard called la Vigne de La Romanée, enclosed by walls to the south and to the east containing thirty-seven ouvrées and a half including the enclosing walls . . . [and] another little parcel of vines called Richebourg, contiguous to La Romanée . . . containing approximately two to three ouvrées without, nonetheless, any guaranty of measure."

In the deed of sale, the basic terms of the act of 19 February 1584 are reiterated: "twenty tournois sols in emphyteutic dues each and every year and other duties." The other duties were the *lods*, the annual tithe, and the responsibility of improving the property, which naturally increased the value of the production and therefore the sum of the tithe. Perhaps in the interest of tax evasion, the priory records never include the sums received for lods and tithes; only the symbolic twenty sols in dues are recorded.

The contract specifies that the "Seigneur purchaser or his elected friend will be permitted to make his wine from the following harvest and even, if necessary, that from the harvest of 1761, in the wine presses and vatting sheds of the said Seigneur vendor in Vougeot."

Before midday, after the signing of the sale contract, three other documents were signed in rapid succession: a receipt by which Jean-Jacques Dupin, representing André de Croonembourg by procuration, recognizes having received from Jean-François Joly de Fleury or his friend of election 12,400 livres *pot-de-vin*, above and beyond the principal of 80,000 livres paid for La Romanée; a transfer-of-property declaration, signed by Joly de Fleury, "au proffit du Très Haut et Très Puissant Prince Monseigneur Louis-François de Bourbon Prince de Conty Prince du Sang"; another declaration by Joly de Fleury to the effect that he has paid the 12,400 livres *pot-de-vin* and has declared La Romanée "au proffit de Son Altesse Sérénissime."

Jean-François Joly de Fleury continued to represent the prince for several months following the sale. In September 1760, he signed his approval to a list of expenditures made for the vendanges of La Romanée; the following year, he left his post as intendant de Bourgogne and his name does not appear again in the records of La Romanée.

In Vosne-Romanée today, there stands a house abandoned. Its name is La Goillotte. It is surrounded by a park gone wild, and beneath the house lie beautiful cellars. Local folklore attempts to link it to a legend drawn from Courtépée, who wrote that the dukes of Burgundy owned a hunting lodge in Vosne.

La Goillotte was built in 1763–64 by the prince de Conti on two parcels of land, originally planted to vines, each measuring two ouvrées, lieudit "aux Goillottes," one of which he bought in 1762 from the Renaudot family, the other in 1763 from M. Soucelyer du Charmes. The architect's plans are dated 1762; it was conceived for the double purpose of housing the cellars, wine presses, vats, and vinification material for La Romanée and of providing living quarters for the vigneron and the *régisseur,* or overseer.

Louis-François de Bourbon

When the prince de Conti bought the vineyard of La Romanée, the wines became legend, for the entire production was henceforth reserved for the prince's personal use.

Louis-François was an extravagant prince. He tried to transform life into art, with no small success. Mme de Genlis wrote, "M. le prince de Conti was the only prince of the blood who had a taste for the sciences and for literature, and who knew how to speak well in public. He was strikingly handsome, with an imposing figure and manners. No one was able to pay a compliment with more finesse and graciousness and, despite his success with women, it was impossible to discern in him the slightest nuance of fatuity. He was also the most magnificent of our princes." His acquisition of La Romanée coincided with the most luxuriant period in his life, when, after having withdrawn from the court of Versailles, he created his own court at the Palais du Temple in Paris, during which time he amassed one of the most important collections of paintings and objets d'art of his time and pensioned the most celebrated musicians of the capital so that they would always be on command for his concerts; the prince de Conti's orchestra was known to be the best of Paris. His mistress, the comtesse de Boufflers, "the Minerva of the Temple," famous for her beauty, her wit, and her passion for all things intellectual, received there.[24] Monday evening was open house (to a very closed society); the other days were reserved for intimate friends. In summer, "la Société du Temple" moved to the ancestral Château de Bourbon-Conti in L'Isle-Adam, twenty-three miles (37 km) north of Paris, where hunting, fêtes champêtres, and theatrical productions were added to the agenda.

Louis-François de Bourbon, comte de la Marche, was born 13 August 1717 to Louis-Armand de Bourbon, prince de Conti, and Louise-Elizabeth de Bourbon-Condé.[25] Ten years later, at his father's death, he became the prince de Conti.

When Louis-François was fourteen, there were three dowager princesses de Conti at court: his mother; his grandmother, widow of François-Louis; and his great aunt, widow of the first Louis-Armand; as well as a doting maiden aunt, Mlle de la Roche-sur-Yon—all of whom were anxious to see him married to perpetuate the race. Fifteen-year-old Louise-Diane d'Orléans, the youngest daughter of Philippe II, duc d'Orléans and regent of France, was chosen; they were married 22 January 1732 at Versailles.

In October 1733, Louis XV declared war on Austria and the prince de Conti received orders from the king to report for duty (The real reason for Louis-François's having been swept into the army at the tender age of sixteen was that, shortly after his marriage, he had inherited a mistress from his mother's youngest brother, the comte de Clermont, abbot of Saint-Germain-des-Prés, who was anxious to shed Mlle Quoniam for a dancer from the Opéra. The dowager duchesse d'Orléans got wind of her son-in-law's indiscretions and plotted with Cardinal de Fleury, Louis XV's acting prime minister, to distance Louis-François from this sphere of activity). He was ravished. He entered the army with the rank of *colonel de cavalerie* and left it, two years later, a lieutenant general.

Louis-François-Joseph de Bourbon, comte de la Marche, son of Louis-François and Louise-Diane d'Orleans, was born on the first day of September 1734. His mother died two years later.

In 1742, France was back at war again and Louis-François was thirsting for the warrior's glory and honor. The conservative old Cardinal de Fleury disapproved of the young prince's independence. He had been happy enough to send the sixteen-year-old off to punish him for his indiscretions, but he now refused to permit the proud twenty-four-year-old lieutenant general to take up arms. The cardinal's decision was the king's command. The young prince plotted for months in advance, confiding in his adoring mother and in his good friend Mme de Mailly (the first of three sisters to be king's mistress) his plans to run away, against the king's will, to join the army of his friend the maréchal de Maillebois, encamped in Germany. Louis-François slipped away at three o'clock in the morning, Monday 10 September 1742; the king did not learn of his disappearance until Wednesday, when he dispatched a messenger to the maréchal with orders to put the prince de Conti under arrest. Madame la princesse de Conti waited until Thursday to move into action. Her first plan, which was simply to fling herself at the king's feet, begging pardon and grace for her son, was met with the chilly response, "He has done a very stupid thing . . . I have sent my orders to M. de Maillebois." The masterstroke was accomplished two days later when she asked the cardinal to introduce her little grandson into the king's presence. Upon entering the king's office, the eight-year-old comte de la Marche said, "Sire, I have come to beg of you to pardon my papa." The king melted, and the prince's punishment was reduced to a symbolic eight days of arrest, applicable only when the army was not marching, after which H.M. permitted the prince de Conti to serve as a volunteer. Two months after his great folly, the volunteer was commanding eight squadrons of dragoons, sixteen of cavalry, and a brigade; the king reported at court that the prince had performed wonders charging at the head of the dragoons. In the years to follow, the duc de Luynes's journal contained nothing but eulogies.

On the first day of January 1744, by an agreement with the infante of Spain, the prince de Conti was declared commander-in-chief (*généralissime*) of the French and the Spanish armies in Italy. He insisted on having a personal company of guards, which at first the king refused him. The duc de Luynes's entry, 24 April 1744, reads,

> Since Mme de Châteauroux [the king's mistress] is a close friend of M. le prince de Conty, her influence removed all obstacles and the company has been formed according to M. le prince de Conty's desires. It is composed of fifty noblemen, with yellow uniforms trimmed in silver braid, blue bandoliers trimmed in silver braid, all handsomely fitted out and well made . . . This company was passed in review a few days ago *chez* Mme la princesse de Conty, in Paris, by M. d'Argenson [minister of war], and the company has gone to join M. le prince de Conty in Provence.

Mme de Châteauroux died of pulmonary congestion, 6 December 1744. In March 1745 Jeanne-Antoinette d'Etoiles became the king's mistress. In July of the same year Mme d'Etoiles was elevated to the title of marquise de Pompadour and 14 September 1745 the marquise de Pompadour was officially presented at court by the dowager princesse de Conti.[26] (In return for this favor, the king was said to have paid the princesse de Conti's gambling debts.) Luynes, 15 September, wrote, "The most unusual thing about the choice of Mme la princesse de Conty is that she says to whomever will listen that she doesn't know Mme de Pompadour at all; I believe, in fact, that she had never seen her before that moment."

In August 1746, the prince de Conti's army and that of the maréchal de Saxe were both in Flanders. Mme de Pompadour enthusiastically supported the fusion of the two armies but she was determined that the command should go to her friend the maréchal, on whose behalf she was also exercising her influence for the choice of his niece, Marie-Josèphe de Saxe, future mother of Louis XVI, Louis XVIII and Charles X, to become the new dauphine.

After taking Charleroi, the prince de Conti sent the comte de Stainville (future duc de Choiseul) to Versailles with the news of the victory and a letter to the king, emphasizing the necessity of joining the two armies in Flanders, while observing the impossibility of a general, prince of the blood, being subjected to the command of another general. The prince de Conti received orders from the king to return on 12 August; he left his army an hour later. His return coincided with his twenty-ninth birthday.

The king did his best to placate the prince de Conti. Although he never returned to the army, the prince received papers the following month conferring upon him the highest rank of *généralissime*, "enjoining all marechaux de France and other military officers to take orders from him wherever it might please His Majesty to send him in command." In addition, "M. le prince de Conty had permission from the king to keep the fifty guards whom he had fitted out in his livery at the time that he commanded the army. The king pays them and they cost 80,000 livres per year," wrote Luynes, who added, "One can imagine that Louis XIV would not have shown the same indulgence for a prince of the blood."

For the next ten years Louis XV and the prince de Conti worked regularly together in secret sessions, a subject of continuous frustration in Luynes's journals. The subjects treated were never divulged though conjecture was rife; thus the marquis d'Argenson, the demented older brother of the minister of war, was inspired to write, "M. le prince de Conti's prolonged and frequent work sessions with the king are devoted to the single purpose of making this prince king of Poland." (The fact that Louis-François's grandfather had nearly attained to the Polish throne gave credence to this theory; henceforth, the wicked old salon-keeper, Mme du Deffand, referred sarcastically to the prince de Conti as "His Majesty the King of Poland").[27]

The prince de Conti had always kept his distance from Mme de Pompadour.[28] Silly gossip circulated concerning the prince's unprincely conduct and language in Mme de Pompadour's presence, but Luynes's journals indicate only a coolness on the part of the prince and a mounting resentment on that of the marquise. 1750: "It is quite remarkable, in view of the intimacy of this mysterious work [with the king], far from being closely associated with Mme de Pompadour, he [Conti] never went to her apartments; it is only in the last year that he has begun to go, only occasionally and, so to speak, despite himself." . . . 1754: "He has no relationship with her. They see each other and that's all." . . . 1756: Mme de Pompadour "has openly broken with M. le prince de Conty."

By March 1756 the prince de Conti, "who enters [the king's study] by the back door," had been working daily with the king; this work "takes place sometimes without Mme de Pompadour's knowledge." In February 1757, "She is still on bad terms with M. le prince de Conty and she knows that the king fears him and hates him." It was Mme de Pompadour who "feared and hated" the prince; Louis XV had always treated his charismatic, headstrong cousin with a very special mixture of admiration, indulgence, and generosity.

There are plenty of versions of the split between the king and the prince de Conti. The comte de Broglie, who replaced the prince as chief of the king's secret correspondence (see note 27), indicates simply that "M. le prince de Conty retired from these occupations." During the last year of his work with the king, the prince had been acting also as go-between for the Parlement and the king, whose differences were too fundamental to be resolved.

In 1748 the grand prieur of the Order of the Chevaliers de Malte, the chevalier d'Orléans, natural son of the regent, was dying. In addition to an annual subsidy of 110,000 livres, the office of the grand prieur brought with it the use—in effect, a lifetime proprietorship—of the Palais du Grand Prieur in the Enclos du Temple, an extraterritorial city within the city of Paris, immune to French law, exempt of taxes, enjoying its own jurisdiction and possessing the right to grant asylum within its walls, a privilege bestowed upon the order by the kings of France since the fourteenth century.[29]

When not at the Château de Bourbon-Conti or in his apartment at Versailles, the prince de Conti lived in the Hôtel de Conti in Paris, a huge palace of which he was coproprietor with his sister, the duchesse de Chartres. The Hôtel de Conti was one of the sites under consideration by the city of Paris for a new Hôtel de Ville and the projected Place Louis XV with an equestrian statue of the king.[30] The idea, first conceived by his mother, of being made grand prieur, then selling the Hôtel de Conti and moving into the Palais du Temple, was very attractive to the prince. Of the princesse, Luynes wrote, "Mme la princesse de Conty formed the project of obtaining this position for M. her son. Practically insurmountable obstacles are incapable of stopping her."

Louis-François was not a member of the order—he refused to take vows of celibacy and had no intention of visiting Malta—but he had the support of the king. The dignitaries of the order begged the king not to interfere and offered the prince a townhouse in Paris and 50,000 livres yearly to withdraw his candidacy; the king declared that it was His Will that the affair be closed with no further opposition. The vows of celibacy were dispensed with. In April 1749 the prince de Conti became grand prieur de France and moved into the Palais du Temple.

In 1751 the comtesse de Boufflers became the prince de Conti's official mistress.[31] She was established in the Enclos du Temple in a townhouse which took the name of the Hôtel de Boufflers. It was not until 1757, after the prince had withdrawn from the court at Versailles and three years before he acquired La Romanée, that the "Société du Temple" evolved into a regular pattern of receptions, civilized conversation, concerts, suppers, and games over which the comtesse reigned.

The comtesse de Boufflers had met Jean-Jacques Rousseau at the Château de Montmorency near L'Isle-Adam. In the autumn of 1760, curiosity, fed perhaps by the comtesse's desire to lure Rousseau into the Société du Temple, led the prince de Conti to pay him an informal visit. Another visit soon followed; a spell was cast. Rousseau the republican, despite a nagging distrust, succumbed to a helpless adulation of the prince: "There is nothing about him that is not close to my heart, excepting his title; still, his person attracts me more than his rank repels me." . . . "Never has a prince done so much for a common mortal as he has deigned to do for me!" . . . "This great prince, richly endowed with intelligence and enlightenment and so deserving of not being placed on a pedestal, sensed, in effect, that I alone treated him like a human being, and I have every reason to believe that he was really grateful to me."

The prince became Rousseau's protector. His patronage was typically generous, though it resembled at times possession more than protection.[32] He was pleased to be able to show off his prize, but his admiration and affection for Rousseau, whom he called "mon ami, Jean-Jacques," were certainly genuine. In 1770 Rousseau decided abruptly that he had been badly used by the prince de Conti and never saw him again. However, it is thought that he was deeply troubled upon learning of the prince's death.

The comtesse de Bouffler's private role as the prince's mistress lasted for fifteen years, but she remained his close friend and continued to receive officially at the Palais du Temple until his death. On 20 September 1775, in a letter to Gustave III of Sweden, she wrote, "His health seems to be in such a precarious state that I dare not dwell on my fears." The sudden decline, accompanied by radical loss of weight and mysterious internal pains, would today probably be diagnosed as cancer. After refusing extreme unction, Louis-François de Bourbon died, 2 August 1776.

At the death of Louis-François de Bourbon, his son Louis-François-Joseph became prince de Conti.

Louis-François-Joseph de Bourbon

Glimpses of the comte de la Marche, accompanied by his tutor M. de la Clavelière, his father, or both are scattered throughout Luynes's journals over a twenty-year period: at the age of five, paying court to the king; at eight, begging the king to pardon his papa; at nine, at an official banquet, seated on a window ledge eating off his knees; serving the king at the ritual Maundy Thursday suppers (*les Cènes du Roi*); and so on. An attractive shyness and respectful good manners made him very popular at court (his anonymous detractor, author of *Vie privée et politique . . .*, noted sarcastically, "He received lessons in politesse which he never forgot, for it can be said of my hero that he is the most gallant and affable prince at the Court").

An imminent marriage and the propagation of the line was important to everyone close to the comte de la Marche; the king chose an apartment at Versailles to be reserved "for Mme la comtesse de la Marche, when M. le comte de la Marche is married." In 1759 he was recalled from the army by his father to meet and to marry, in person, Fortunée-Marie d'Est (daughter of the duc de Modène and Charlotte-Aglaé d'Orleans), to whom he had been earlier married, by procuration, in Milan. The chemistry was wrong; he fled to L'Isle-Adam to sleep alone.

The following year, the Italian actress Coraline, née Anne-Marine Véronèze, became Louis-François-Joseph's mistress; he established her in the Hôtel d'Harcourt, in the Enclos du Temple, and gave her the marquisate of Silly. In 1761 she bore him a son, Louis-François, "whom he loved tenderly. He couldn't make him a prince of the blood, so he made him a grand seigneur . . . he bought him vast seigneuries and gave him the title of chevalier de Vauréal [the property which he had inherited from Mlle de la Roche-sur-Yon] . . . The chevalier de Vauréal died, in the flower of his youth, four years ago [1786], in Melun." Anne-Marine Véronèze de Silly died, 6 February 1782, leaving all of her worldly goods to S.A.S. (Son Altesse Sérénissime) Monseigneur le Prince de Conti.

Shortly before Louis-François's death, he and his son patched up their differences (the prince had been upset at his son's refusal to produce an heir to the name; he had been cross with him for paying court to Mme de Pompadour, and crosser still to learn that, after the latter's death, the comte de la Marche was among the first of the courtiers to accept and pay court to the king's new mistress, Mme du Barry. Finally, in 1771, when Louis-François-Joseph had been the only prince of the blood to support Louis XV's abolition of Parlement, an outraged Louis-François had disinherited his son in favor of his nephew the duc de Chartres.33

Reinstated in his father's good graces, the new prince de Conti inherited an intimidating accumulation of debts. Father and son could not have been more different. Despite rents from vast land holdings, of which those in Burgundy were among the least important; a governorship in Poitou; pensions and gifts from the king; scattered palaces and châteaux; the Palais du Temple plus an annual subsidy of 110,000 livres offered by the Order of Malta, the famous mounted guard of fifty noblemen, completely subsidized by the Crown; and so on, Louis-François always lived well beyond his means.

By princely standards, Louis-François-Joseph lived modestly. He was meticulous about money matters and abhorred debts. On these grounds, the anonymous and otherwise inflammatory libelist's "biography" *Vie privée et politique* . . . does him justice: "He was not rich [as comte de la Marche], although he always practiced economy without avarice . . . there has perhaps never been a house in France, or in all the countries of Europe, more ordered, better managed than that of the prince de Conty . . . with less than twelve hundred thousand livres of income, he cuts a magnificent figure, worthy of a great prince. Every month he, in person, pays his staff and all of his tradesmen with exactitude and generosity. He owes nothing."

To put his new house in order, the prince de Conti began by selling the entire art collection from the Palais du Temple; the auction lasted from 8 April to 6 June 1777.[34] During the next few years, he sold a number of châteaux, townhouses, and landed properties. Finally, in 1783, he released practically his entire inheritance—forty-some marquisats, comtés, châtellenies, baronnies, seigneuries, and the like—for 11,000,000 livres to Monsieur, the king's brother. Included was the ancestral château and seigneurie in L'Isle-Adam, of which, however, the prince reserved the use and the rents for his lifetime. La Romanée was, at the same time, too small to make a dent in the sum of debts and too precious to sacrifice. Henceforth, the prince's budget balanced, with annual expenses being kept discreetly inferior to the income.[35]

Vignerons, Dues, and Tithes

Denis Mongeard cultivated the vines of La Romanée from 1735 until his retirement in 1782, when he was replaced by Etienne Magnien. The contract—the same as Mongeard's—was on a *moitié-fruits* basis, which meant, theoretically, that the vigneron received as wages half of the harvest; in practice, however, the prince de Conti kept all of the wine and the vigneron received twenty livres per queue above the top price paid for other Vosne wines, on half of the harvest.[36] In addition, he received seventy-five livres for work in the vineyard and a special gratuity on condition that no bean fodder be planted in the vineyard. In Mongeard's declaration for 1774, this gratuity is described as *arricots dédommagement* (beans compensation).

Margue was the prince de Conti's steward, "Contrôleur de la Maison . . . in charge of the wines, legumes and subsistance." The prince's observations and desires were confided to Margue, who then conveyed them to François Ligeret, the prince's *homme d'affaires* in Burgundy; the vigneron's needs were expressed to Ligeret, who relayed them to Margue, who presented the vigneron's case to the prince. Thus, after Magnien had applied to Ligeret for a raise and Ligeret had written to Margue, Margue carried the case to S.A.S. and reported back to Ligeret, in a letter dated 3 May 1786,

> I had the honor of presenting to Monseigneur your request for an augmentation of ten livres per queue of wine in the treatment accorded to the vigneron of La Romanée . . . Counting from the vintage of 1785: S.A.S. has the goodness to accord to Etienne Magnien, vigneron of La Romanée, an augmentation of ten livres, or a total of thirty livres per queue, on condition that he cultivate the vines with the greatest of care and that one is satisfied with him, for if he fails in any way to fulfill his duties and the obligations of his position, Monsiegneur will withdraw his magnanimity. Furthermore, S.A.S. desires not a large quantity of wine, but quality. You know that a vine overcharged with fruit produces only a mediocre wine. Please tell the vigneron to prune the vines accordingly. Such is Monseigneur's ultimate wish on this subject.

Margue's authority was unquestionable and his words, though polite, were never minced. He kept a regular correspondence with the Ligeret brothers, on whom he depended to keep him abreast of the prices being paid for Burgundy wines and to ferret out the best of them for the prince's cellars. He was not always satisfied; to François Ligeret, he wrote, "I am sending you two samples of 1781 wine, one Vosne and the other, Richebourg, shipped by your brother for Monseigneur's service—you can judge for yourself. All gourmets and connoisseurs say that they have more in common with the wine of Roussillon than with the wine of Richebourg or Vosne. As for me, I find in these wines a detestable aftertaste."

Magnien's declarations of the harvest of La Romanée exist for the years 1783–92.[37] It was a precarious métier. In this period, the prices paid for the wine of Vosne varied from 85 to 400 livres per queue; the harvest at La Romanée varied from 1 1/4 to over 22 pièces; and the vigneron's wages varied from 134 to 865 livres. The vintage which Margue describes as worthless, 1785, brought by far the lowest price of the decade. Still, because this year also saw the highest production, it was Magnien's next to most profitable. Nevertheless, it was following this vintage that Margue expressed the prince de Conti's desire for quality, not quantity, and cautioned the vigneron to prune accordingly.

Only the annual, symbolic dues of twenty sols, or one livre, were entered in

Saint-Vivant's accounting records; the tithes went unmentioned. The tithe on La Romanée was treated like a rent, an agreed-upon sum of money replacing a percentage of the annual production of wine, with periodic leases permitting an augmentation of the tithe.

Until 1766, there are no records of what tithes were paid. On 13 November of that year, a slip of paper signed by Bartellemi Fistet, farmer of the vines of the priory of Saint-Vivant and dues and tithes collector for the prior, and Jacques Grimelin, "supervisor for Son Altesse Sérénissime Monseigneur le Prince de Conty, in charge of making the wine of La Romanée . . . having authority from S.A.S. to negotiate with aforesaid Fistet the terms of the tithe in coin," declares them both to be satisfied with the sum of two hundred livres in coin, payable each year on Winter's Saint Martin's Day (11 November) for a nine-year period beginning in 1766.

Until 1775, the accounts for La Romanée listed tithe and dues at 201 livres (200 for the tithe plus one livre in dues); after the end of the nine-year agreement, "tithe and dues are listed at 301 livres.[38]

From 1775 the Ligeret signature appears often. "Charged with overseeing the culture of the vines of La Romanée and also with keeping the accounts of La Romanée and the Châtellenie d'Argilly," the Ligeret brothers, François and Jean-Baptiste, and later François's son Pensée Ligeret, kept offices in Nuits, inherited from their father and grandfather, Jean-Charles Ligeret, who in the 1740s and 1750s had been châtelain d'Argilly and agent for the prince de Conti's affairs in Burgundy.

The Revolution and the Nineteenth Century

The prince de Conti became increasingly aware of the inevitability of the Revolution in the face of Louis XVI's erratic government. Having attempted to communicate this to the king, by way of Monsieur, the king's brother, he was in effect told to mind his own business. ("M. le prince de Conty, like the other princes of my blood, should address himself directly to me and I will be happy to listen when they wish to tell me what they believe may be useful to me.")

Immediately after the taking of the Bastille, the prince de Conti, at the same time as the comte d'Artois (the future Charles X) and the princes from the House of Condé, left the country for Turin; Conti was disguised, according to the author of *Vie privée et politique . . .*, "alternatively as a peasant, a peddler, and a bourgeois" [en paysan, en marchand forain, en bourgeois]. Unlike his cousins, he returned a few months later.

It was his presence in France in 1790 that inspired the hastily written book of calumny, in which the author, who complains that the prince de Conti receives only aristocracy at his table, presents him as Public Enemy No. 1:

> That it is only since the return of Conty that the Patrie is in the greatest of danger, that it is menaced by a disastrous counterrevolution. His house is filled with plotters and conspirateurs . . . It is easy to see that Conty is the agent of all the princes, that he is their insidious mentor, that it is he and he alone who conceives and guides the aristocratic plots, that, more flexible and more deceitful than the others, he is the soul of their organization, the guiding force of their decisions, finally it is obvious that this prince is in charge of all their plots, that he is collecting money from rich aristocrats, which he disseminates in the capitol to prepare an inevitable counterrevolution.

In fact, it seems that, rather than live outside of his country, the prince de Conti had resigned himself to being a citizen of the new order, a decision which served him badly.

On 22 February 1793, a certificate of residence, valuable for three months, was granted by the officials of the Département de Seine-et-Oise to "Louis-François-Joseph Bourbon, age fifty-eight, height five feet, six inches, blond hair and eyebrows, blue eyes, large nose, large mouth, rounded chin, balding, elongated visage, living at present at la Lande, community of Villiers-sur-Marne, a house belonging to him in which he resides and has resided without interruption since 11 July 1792."

In April 1793 citizen Louis-François-Joseph Bourbon was arrested at his home, the Château de la Lande, and incarcerated, with his valet de chambre, Jacquelin, who had received permission to accompany his master, in the prison of Fort Saint-Jean in Marseilles.

In June, in response to a petition from the prince de Conti, the directory of the Département de Seine-et-Oise issued a declaration to the effect that he was not and had not been inscribed on any list of émigrés of the department and that his holdings had not been placed under sequester.

In August, Ligeret received instructions to have the coats of arms removed from the facade and the front door of La Goillotte; a stonemason was sent into the vineyards of La Romanée to efface the fleurs-de-lys on the borderstones.

In September, Etienne Magnien went to Ligeret with the troubling news that a sign had been surreptitiously posted in front of La Goillotte reading National

Property for Sale or Rent; the local authorities didn't know who was responsible.

The former prince de Conti, unaware in his prison cell, was declared to have emigrated, 22 September 1793, which officially justified the confiscation of his properties.39

The Republican calendar went into effect, retroactively, 5 October 1793 (14 Vendémiaire, Year II).40 It was abandoned fourteen years later; during that period, the Gregorian calendar did not officially exist; all documents were dated by the new system.

On 4 Nivose, Year II (24 December 1793), Margue was obliged to declare the harvest of La Romanée to the Bureau du Contentieux (litigation) des Emigrés: "Citizen Margue, responsible for the wines, legumes, and subsistence of the house of Citizen Bourbon Conty, declares having received the harvest of the vines of La Romanée for the year 1793, amounting to five pièces and one feuillette of wine on its lees. He observes that this wine is susceptible to diminution by the rackings which one must give it, as well as by topping it up every month for at least three years, the time which one must keep it in casks for it to acquire its optimum quality." A note scribbled in the margin at a later date indicates that the wine was "sequestered 10 pr." (29 May). The name Conti, joined to La Romanée, appears for the first time (as well as the spelling, Conti, instead of Conty) in an account "done by the undersigned, former supervisor of the vineyard called: Romanée-Conti" for the years 1789 through 1793, signed and dated, Pensée Ligeret, 6 Prairial, Year II (25 May 1794) and delivered the same day to the directory of the District de Dijon.

The Sale of La Romanée

In the course of 1794, a three-way, often inflammatory correspondence between the Commission des Revenues Nationaux, the Parisian bureau which supervised the sales of confiscated properties, the administrators of the Département de la Côte d'Or, and the local authorities, members of the directory of the District de Dijon, of which the municipality of Vosne was a part, illuminates the deep distrust and resentment with which the local authorities viewed their Parisian counterparts, and the locals' predisposition to undermine by any means the Parisians' authority and projects.

The local authorities, known as the District, were responsible for organizing the sales at auction of confiscated holdings; it was their job to appoint experts for evaluation estimates, to present these estimates to the Parisian authorities, to set the dates for the auctions, and to make certain that these sales were well publicized throughout the Republic.

Instead of which, the District, acting in collusion with its chosen experts, followed a policy of deliberate obfuscation, misrepresentation, underestimation, and suppression of publicity, in the interest of keeping Parisian speculators at arm's length and permitting local people to buy these properties at low prices. The administrators of the Département de la Côte d'Or regarded this subversive activity with a benevolent eye as long as the wrath of Paris was not brought down upon their heads, for it was they who acted as go-betweens for the Parisian authorities and the District.

The District appointed an expert, Vivant Moissenet, to prepare an estimate of La Romanée; the report is dated 24 Pluviôse, Year II (13 February 1794). The report is of interest only insofar as it is outrageous. There is no indication that the expert ever visited the vineyard; having heard Etienne Magnien's declaration that La Romanée contains forty ouvrées, Moissenet estimated that it could be broken up into forty lots worth 400 livres each or sold as a whole at 700 livres per ouvrée.

The District sat on the report; copies were sent neither to the Parisian authorities nor to the administrators of the Côte d'Or.

The Parisians claimed to have positive information that the prince de Conti had paid 96,000 livres for La Romanée, and that, having been much improved, it was now worth four times that; they demanded an expertise followed by an early sale with one hundred posters to be sent to them as soon as they were printed.

Posters were printed but none were posted in Paris, nor were any sent to the Paris bureau. The sale was composed of fifteen lots, of which the first twelve were scraps of pasture, fields, and second-rate vines. Lot 13 was La Tâche; 14 and 15, under the misleading title "Holdings from the émigré Capet," were listed in small print: "forty ouvrées of vines, called La Romanée-conty, estimated 26,000 liv. . . . a house, wine press, and dependencies, estimated 5,500 liv."

A month after the poster was issued and five days after first bids had been placed, a hundred posters announcing first bids were delivered to the Commission de Revenues Nationaux with no accompanying letter of explanation. The commission was incensed; they ordered the withdrawal of La Romanée from the sale, demanded to be sent a copy of the infamous estimate, and suggested, in restrained but sarcastic language, that the local administration might judge it wise to order a new estimate.

The Côte d'Or administrators crossly upbraided the District officials for their indelicate behavior; their disingenuous answer was, in effect, that they had no idea that they were supposed to send reports of estimates to Paris; that it would require so much more work that they would have to hire extra copyists; that the extra bulk of papers would be unmanageable; that, in any case, vineyards are not subject to improvement; and that even if it were true, which they doubted, that a vastly wealthy former prince had paid the fantasy price of 96,000 livres for La Romanée, that did not mean that Moissenet's estimate was incorrect or that the property was worth more than 30,000 livres. They were ordered to appoint new experts immediately.

The new report (which has since become a classic element in wine literature) is dated 18 Messidor, Year II (6 July 1794). The experts, Henry Renaudot and Joseph Durand, although respecting the unspoken local guidelines, however more discreetly than Moissenet, of falsifying values and mystifying the Parisians, brought a good bit more finesse to the composition of their essay—fourteen pages, which are at once suffused with a genuine reverential awe for the uniqueness and the reputation of La Romanée and a subtle slyness when it comes to communicating the facts of potential yield, the perils of inclement weather, and the difficulty of attributing a value to the vines.

The opening line is famous: "La Romanée. Is a parcel of vines famed for the exquisite quality of its wine. Its situation in the vineyard territory of Vosne is the most advantageous for the perfect ripening of the grapes; higher to the occident than to the orient, it receives the first rays of sun in all seasons, being thus imbued with the impetus of the gentlest heat of the day." And, later:

> We cannot disguise the fact that the wine of La Romanée is the most excellent of all those of the Côte d'Or and even of all the vineyards of the French Republic: weather permitting, this wine always distinguishes itself from those of the other climats of predilection, its brilliant and velvety color, its ardor and its scent, charm all the senses. Well kept, it always improves as it approaches its eighth or tenth year; it is then a balm for the elderly, the feeble and the disabled, and will restore life to the dying.

The District officials' seditious instincts led them down the same path they had followed five months earlier; again, they sat on the report, with the same predictable results. Three months later, the Commission de Revenues Nationaux exploded, threatening to expose to higher authorities this "reprehensible negligence in the execution of operations prescribed by the laws." A few days later, they received the report. Although they found the estimate to be much too low, they were seduced by the style of the new experts, "who appear . . . to have operated with all the intelligence that one could desire."

The posters announced the "Sale of Holdings Confiscated from Louis François Joseph Capet, called Bourbon" in a single unique lot; La Romanée and La Goillotte were estimated together at 53,000 livres.

At the final bidding, 4 Nivôse, Year III (24 December 1794), La Romanée, its buildings, and its dependencies were sold to "Nicolas Defer, cultivator, domiciled in Paris" [dom. à Paris] for 112,000 livres, signed *Defer de la Nouèrre*.

The price of 112,000 livres is misleading, above all because confiscated properties were not paid for in coin but with assignats, the paper money issued by the government, the devaluation of which became more dramatic as the assignats were churned out faster and faster.[41] At the time of the sale of La Romanée, a hundred-livre assignat was worth about twenty livres in real money, or less than one louis d'or gold piece.

Furthermore, the contract of sale extended incredible facilities of payment to the buyer, permitting him to profit from the progressive devaluation of the assignats. The first three clauses read: "First Article. The highest bidder will pay, within the week following the sale, the expenses of division, estimation, posters, publications and others legitimately related to the sale . . . ; II. Within the month following the auction, he will pay one-tenth of the total price of the sale without interest; III. Each year, dating from the day of the sale, he will pay one-tenth of the total price of the sale plus five percent interest on the remaining capital that he owes at the time of payment."

On the day of the sale, Defer paid 2,242 livres in expenses. A year later, a hundred-livre assignat was worth less than one livre, although it was still acceptable at face value as payment for confiscated properties; Defer paid no more than the equivalent of a few thousand livres in precious metal for La Romanée.

Defer died in 1805. His sister, Anne-Marie-Antoinette, wife of François Coilleau, was his sole heir. The Coilleaus put Romanée-Conti and its dependencies up for sale at auction, 22 September 1819; it was sold to Julien-Jules Ouvrard for Fr 60,050.

Julien-Jules Ouvrard

The year preceding his purchase of Romanée-Conti, nineteen-year-old Julien Ouvrard, thanks to some imaginative juggling on the part of his father, Gabriel-Julien Ouvrard, had acquired from the bankrupt bankers Ravel and Tourton the Clos de Vougeot vineyard and the seventeenth-century Château de Gilly, once the Cistercian abbots' country house.[42]

In 1822 Julien Ouvrard entered the Ministry of the Interior, a career which he abandoned two years later because of his father's conflicts with the government. In 1828, having declared domicile in Gilly on 19 May, Julien settled definitively in the Côte d'Or to manage his vineyards (in addition to Romanée-Conti and the Clos de Vougeot, he eventually owned parts of the Clos de Bèze, Chambertin, Latricières and Les Cazetiers in Gevrey, Les Amoureuses in Chambolle, La Perrière and La Vigne Blanche in Vougeot, and, in Aloxe, most of Corton Clos du Roi and part of Les Renardes). He fashioned an exemplary, active, and devoted civic life in Gilly; he seems, at the same time, to have been a rather taciturn, withdrawn, and very private individual by nature, perhaps in reaction to an unusually colorful parent, whom he nonetheless admired and loved.

Julien Ouvrard was elected mayor of Gilly on 28 August 1837, and, except for the year 1848, remained mayor of the community until his death in 1861. He was, from 1840 to 1848, Conseiller Général de la Côte d'Or and, at the advent of the Second Empire, in 1852, was elected Député de la Côte d'Or to the legislative corps of the central government. Reelected in 1857, he held the latter post until his death.

Ouvrard was a powerful figure in the Côte d'Or, generally respected, capable of intimidation, and, if one may read between Dr. Lavalle's lines, sometimes resented. Speaking of Romanée-Conti, Clos de Vougeot, and Chambertin, Lavalle wrote, "La Romanée excels in finesse; but by their all-over qualities, all three share the laurels and all three would sell for the same price if the first two, which belong to a single and unique proprietor [Ouvrard], were subject, like the last, to the competitive prices of other growers." The remark is unjust, for Dr. Lavalle knew full well that Ouvrard also possessed a good part of Chambertin and that his Chambertin and Clos de Vougeot sold for the same price, whereas the Romanée-Conti was more expensive.

The year that Ouvrard acquired Romanée-Conti, 1819, marked the beginning of an especially somber period in Burgundian viticulture that lasted until the early 1850s. Robert Laurent (*Les Vignerons de la Côte d'Or au XIXe siècle*, 1958) records a slump of 26 percent in the average price of fine Burgundy wines from the period of 1799–1818 (Fr 396 per queue) to that of 1819–51 (Fr 294 per queue). Although Romanée-Conti remained marginally more expensive than the next most exalted growths, it was fetching no more than a third to a half as much as a century earlier (and despite a currency that was stabilized in terms of a given weight of precious metal, the same weight in precious metal could not possibly represent the same buying power after a hundred years of progressive inflation).

The Comptoir des Propriétaires de la Côte d'Or, founded in 1850, acted as agent for Ouvrard's wines during the early 1850s. It listed the following prices per queue for Ouvrard's vintages of 1847, 1850, and 1851:

	1847	1850 and 1851
Romanée-Conti	Fr 500	Fr 450
Clos de Vougeot and Chambertin-Clos de Bèze	Fr 460	Fr 420
Corton Clos du Roi	Fr 400	Fr 320

In further refutation of Dr. Lavalle's claim, the Chambertin-Clos de Bèze of MM. Marion and Mongin and the Clos du Roi of MM. de Grancey and Monnet are listed at the same prices as Ouvrard's wines from those growths.

In 1858 Ouvrard signed a twelve-year contract with the Société Passier & Cie. in Beaune, conceding commercial rights for the entire harvest from his vineyards, beginning with that of 1858 and finishing with the harvest of 1869. The contract specified that he could reserve for his personal use, "without being able to commercialize them by sale, barter, or other means" [sans pouvoir les vendre ni en faire l'objet d'aucune espèce de commerce soit par échange, soit autrement], three and one-half pièces of Clos de Vougeot; one pièce of Romanée-Conti; one and one-half pièces of Chambertin . . . Camille Rodier wrote, "Toward 1860, the director of the Clos [de Vougeot] posted the prices of Ouvrard's wines at the entrance to the cellars, without anyone's objection: Romanée-Conti: 6 francs [per bottle]; Clos de Vougeot and Chambertin: 5 francs per bottle." Whether this sign was posted before or after the pact was made with the Société Passier is unclear.

Ouvrard's sister, the comtesse de Rochechouart, died in 1857 and the comte de Rochechouart died the following year, leaving two daughters, Comtesse Juliette de Montalembert and Marquise (Madeleine) de la Garde, and two sons, Comte Aimery de Rochechouart and Comte Louis-Jules-Emilien de Rochechouart. At Ouvrard's death on 22 June 1861, his nieces and nephews inherited his properties. The Château de Gilly was sold the following year. The new owner dispersed all the grand furnishings and transformed it into an unkempt farmhouse (today it is a hotel). The marquis de la Garde assumed the direction of the vineyards until they were sold.

Romanée-Conti and the Clos de Vougeot were advertised for sale at auction, 7 August 1869. Romanée-Conti went to Paul Guillemot, négociant and proprietor of the Buffet de la Gare in Dijon, for Fr 239,000.[43] The transaction was completed 18 September and two months later, 25 November 1869, Guillemot sold Romanée-Conti to Jacques-Marie Duvault-Blochet for Fr 260,000.

THE DOMAINE

III

WHEN, IN HIS eightieth year, Jacques-Marie Duvault-Blochet, négociant in Santenay, at the southern tip of the Côte de Beaune, crowned his vineyard empire with the acquisition of La Romanée-Conti, he was the most important proprietor of top growths in the Côte d'Or, with 329 acres (133 ha) of vines, all of which are classified today as Grands Crus and Premiers Crus.

JACQUES-MARIE DUVAULT-BLOCHET

J.-M. Duvault had his beginnings in the wine business in 1816, the year before his marriage to fifteen-year-old Sophie Blochet. The four vast, vaulted, double-tiered cellars that he built in 1843 at the Château du Passetemps in Santenay are testimony to a business that flourished in spite of the general deflation of wine prices during the second quarter of the nineteenth century.

He was a man of firm determination who could not suffer events turning counter to his will. His descendants cherish the anecdote of the time Duvault-Blochet took a business trip to London, unaware that a cholera epidemic was raging there. After a few days he fell ill, with symptoms diagnosed by the hotel staff as cholera. The terrified hotel manager had him transferred from his rooms to an isolated cellar and called a doctor. Duvault-Blochet, whose English was fluent, overheard the doctor muttering to the hotel manager, "He's done for—too bad, because he's got a constitution of iron." Outraged by the whispered message, he ordered a pail of boiling water, a stiff-bristled scrub brush and some soft soap, scrubbed himself all over until he bled . . . and was cured!

The year 1846 promised to be one of the great vintages of the century, but the wines had found no buyers. The cellars of the Côte d'Or were overflowing and commerce was dwindling. The 1847 vintage yielded one of the most abundant harvests of the century and no one had space in which to stock the new wine. With the fall of Louis-Philippe in February 1848, the market collapsed and Duvault-Blochet moved into action. Here, in the words of François Chambon, his great-great-grandson, is the tale of the audacious exploit which earned him a fortune:

> 1848—the Revolution. Business comes to a halt. Prices plunge. M. D.-B., an astute businessman, decides that the time has come to buy. But, although his business is in good shape, he doesn't have the funds available to match the extent of his ambitions. He therefore goes to Paris to borrow money from his banker, who is not opposed but asks to be first permitted to examine the state of M. D.-B.'s affairs. Several days later, two distinguished-looking gentlemen arrive and spend three days going through his books with a fine-toothed comb. Two weeks later, the banker writes that he is prepared to receive his client and M. D.-B. hastens to Paris. As soon as he arrives, he poses the question: "Well?" The banker answers, "Oh, Monsieur, for 4 million, there is no problem" and adds, imprudently, "and even a little more, if you like." M. D.-B. immediately ups the bid: "6 million?—yes, Monsieur—8 million?—yes, Monsieur—10 million?—yes, Monsieur—12 million? no, Monsieur . . . " And so it was that, with 10 million gold francs in his pocket, M. D.-B. swept up all the wine to be found in the cellars of Burgundy and waited . . . Not very long: 1852—the proclamation of the Second Empire. 2 December—confidence returns, business picks up, and, by releasing his wines parsimoniously to the market, he makes a fortune which permits him to buy up vineyards the entire length of La Côte. He was nervy, the old man!

In 1851 production was low; in 1852 it was so low as to be characterized, in records of the time, as null; in 1854, following a vintage of splendid quality and yet another meager harvest, prices soared.

Duvault-Blochet was an impassioned versifier. Inspired by Erasmus's unfortunate description of Burgundy as "the mother of men since, from her breasts, she provides them with such good milk," the last verse of Duvault-Blochet's hymn to La Romanée-Conti reads:

> *Mamelle unique en la nature!*
> *Inspire enfin l'humanité;*
> *Fais sortir de ta source pure*
> *La Paix, l'amour et l'unité.*

The brilliant Burgundian poet-politician-historian, Alphonse de Lamartine was a close friend of Duvault-Blochet and a great lover of his wines; his formula for ensuring a regular place at the Duvault-Blochet table was to lavish praise over his host's poetry.

For fifty years the harvest of Romanée-Conti had been vinified and raised in the cellars of the Clos de Vougeot, a few hundred yards distant from the vines. For forty years to come, the grapes of La Romanée-Conti, as well as those from Duvault-Blochet's other vines in Vosne and Flagey, were transported in wagons during the cool night hours, with a change of horses at the Relais de la Croix in Pommard, to the Château du Passetemps in Santenay.

Legacy

J.-M. Duvault-Blochet died 23 February 1874. His properties were assessed and broken down into 341 lots; on 18 December 1876, his two daughters, Claudine-Constance Massin and Henriette Dupuis, appeared before the notary to divide the inheritance. Each received a domaine in Santenay with habitation and vines; Claudine-Constance received the Château du Passetemps. Most of the remainder was divided by drawing lots. Romanée-Conti, however, was left in joint proprietorship.

At the death of her husband in 1883, Claudine-Constance divided her properties among her three daughters, in anticipation of their inheritance. The lot containing Claudine-Constance's half of Romanée-Conti went to her daughter Gabrielle Chambon. On 15 April 1885, Gabrielle Chambon ceded her half of Romanée-Conti to her aunt, Henriette, in exchange for her aunt's portion of "les Gaudichots ou la Tâche," parcels of Les Richebourgs, Les Echézeaux, and a number of lesser growths. Thus, Henriette Dupuis-Duvault was sole proprietor of Romanée-Conti until her death two years later (5 November 1887).

Having no direct descendants, Henriette Dupuis's possessions reverted to her sister and were divided, as before, among Claudine-Constance's three daughters. Gabrielle Chambon again received half of Romanée-Conti; the other half went to her sister, Cécile Guyot, who, in another gift of anticipated inheritance, transferred her property to her three sons, Emile, Jean, and Honoré. On 23 October 1912, the three Guyot brothers sold their half of Romanée-Conti to their cousins, Gabrielle Chambon's two children Jacques Chambon and Marie-Dominique-Madeleine Gaudin de Villaine, for Fr 125,000.

Edmond Gaudin de Villaine

During the thirty-odd years of shuffling properties back and forth among sisters and cousins, the vines themselves were neglected; they were in a deplorable state in 1911, when Edmond Gaudin de Villaine, five years after his marriage to Marie-Dominique-Madeleine Chambon, was appointed managing director (*gérant*) of the Domaine. Henceforth, for more than thirty years, he was the motivating force, engineering all of the changes and formulating the policies of the Domaine, in the name of his wife, his sons, and his brother-in-law Jacques Chambon. It was he, the following year, who orchestrated the purchase of the other half of Romanée-Conti from the Guyot brothers and subsequently registered the name "Domaine de la Romanée-Conti" as a trademark. (Until 1912, separate accounts were kept for Romanée-Conti, the expenses of which were shared by the Guyot brothers, who received half the harvest. In 1911, each brother received one barrel of Romanée-Conti.)44

Gaudin de Villaine had a vision, which progressively became a reality, of an edifice apart, answerable unto itself alone, composed of the most distinguished growths of Vosne—those which, a century and a half earlier, Courtépée had described as "the summit of the wines of Burgundy"—its cornerstone the most hallowed growth of all; a Domaine whose name would be an unqualified guarantee of tradition and authenticity. At a time when nearly all the wines of Burgundy were in the hands of négociants, twenty years before pioneers like the marquis d'Angerville and Henri Gouges launched the campaign for bottling at the property, Romanée-Conti, Les Richebourgs and Les Gaudichots were bottled at the Domaine de la Romanée-Conti.

In 1911 Gaudin de Villaine hired Louis Clin (1874–1953), a retired army officer, as *régisseur* (supervisor) of the Domaine. Clin had been recommended on the grounds of managerial experience and of exceptional probity, but he had no experience with wine; nonetheless, thanks to his passion for perfection, he rapidly became an authority and many came seeking his advice in the practices of viticulture and vinification.

Henri de Villaine remembers his father's strict sense of propriety, symbolized by the ritual of his arrivals at the Domaine: to appear a few minutes late would indicate laxity, but to arrive early would be an imposition on the Clins' privacy; he arrived in Vosne a few minutes early but never approached the Domaine until the stroke of nine, at which precise moment, Mme Clin would open the gates to greet him. Madame Clin is also remembered for having kept an eagle eye on the Domaine's border stones, checking them daily, lest an unfortunate neighbor accidentally displace one.

The Clins' daughter, Geneviève, was born at the Domaine in 1913. She was office manager from the age of eighteen until her retirement in 1983.

LA TÂCHE

In 1933 Gaudin de Villaine acquired another great treasure—La Tâche Joly de Bevy.

At the beginning of the Revolution, La Tâche belonged to Louis-Philibert Joly de Bevy, seigneur of Vosne and Flagey and president of the Parliament of Dijon. When he emigrated, his properties were seized by the government and sold at auction.

The expertise of La Tâche, 28 Brumaire, Year II (18 November 1793), was prepared by Joseph Durand, who eight months later was to co-sign, with Henry Renaudot, the revised expertise of La Romanée. He recognized La Tâche to be

> cultivated by Henry Grivot, who declares it to measure thirty-four ouvrées . . . it being understood that the wine of La Romanée is no longer on the market, the wine of La Tâche is accepted as the foremost wine of Burgundy and, ever since the time of the sale of La Romanée [to the prince de Conti], has always fetched 1,200 livres per queue with the exception of the years when the best wines are worth nothing . . . the wine of La Tâche is easily worth as much as the wine of Saint-Georges in Nuits and a parcel of fourteen ouvrées of this vineyard, which had belonged to the former Chapitre de Nuits, was acquired by Citizen Marey Cadet for 900 livres per ouvrée."[45]

After having in effect written that La Tâche was second only to La Romanée and that it was worth more than 900 livres per ouvrée, Durand proceeded to evaluate it, "if broken up," at 350 livres per ouvrée—11,900 livres in all—or, "if sold in a single parcel," at 650 livres per ouvrée, or 22,100 livres.

La Romanée and La Tâche were listed for sale on the same affiche, 2 Floréal, Year II (21 April 1794). The Commission de Revenues Nationaux ordered both to be withdrawn from the sale and the local officials of the District de Dijon, in a letter dated 6 Prairial, Year II (25 May 1794), claimed that this had been done. Only La Romanée, however, was withdrawn; La Tâche was sold at auction on 14 Prairial, Year II (2 June 1794), for 27,200 livres, to Jacques Jacquinot fils, mayor of Nuits, "for his friend of election." Through Jacquinot, it passed into the hands of Claude-François Viénot, négociant in Dijon—the same who three years later shared the purchase of the Lamy de Samerey vines, Aux Echanges.

To settle debts, Viénot's vines were put up for sale at auction, 24 Nivose, Year VIII (13 January 1800); Guillaume Basire bought La Tâche, which then passed to General Liger-Belair by marriage. La Tâche remained in the Liger-Belair family from 1815 until 1933.

Les Gaudichots or La Tâche

Throughout the nineteenth century, a large part of Les Gaudichots, the lieudit adjoining La Tâche, was known also as La Tâche. Duvault-Blochet bought parcels of vines in Les Gaudichots in 1834, 1839, and 1859, which were defined in the title deeds as La Tâche.

In 1853 a M. Morellet sold the southern half of his property in Les Gaudichots to M. Lausseure (J.-J. Lausseure was the champion of champagnization for the great growths of the Côte d'Or—from the red grapes of his Tâche, he produced a sparkling white wine). The title deed specifically identified certain parcels of the property as "Tâche," others as "Tâche Gaudichots" (or "Gaudichottée") and the remainder as "les Godichots et Rochottes."

In 1862 Morellet sold the other half of his property in Les Gaudichots to Duvault-Blochet; the deed bore identical precisions concerning the appellations. Finally, in 1866, Duvault-Blochet acquired Lausseure's property. These transactions are reflected in the two principal expositions on Burgundy wine of the period: Lavalle (1855) listed, as proprietors of La Tâche, MM. Liger-Belair and Lausseure; Danguy and Aubertin (1892) list Liger-Belair and the heirs of Duvault-Blochet.

USAGES LOCAUX, LOYAUX ET CONSTANTS

The concept of an *appellation d'origine*, a legally protected place-name, as an inviolate property right evolved in the early part of this century. Laws were introduced in 1905 and in 1919; a 1927 modification of the latter law proposed the phrase *usages locaux, loyaux et constants*—meaning local, oral and written traditions of usage, employed honestly without intention to deceive, that have been generally and continuously in use over a long period of time—which became a key element in the definition of an appellation d'origine.

On 15 February 1932 the Liger-Belair family launched court proceedings to limit the rights to the La Tâche appellation d'origine to "the wines harvested on the parcel designated on the cadastre of the community of Vosne-Romanée by the number 513, Section C [the Joly de Bevy vines], to the exclusion, above all, of those from parcels situated in the lieudit 'les Gaudichots,' for which the respondents have laid claim to the same appellation."

Initiated before the court of first instance in Beaune, the case was appealed by the Liger-Belair family before the court of appeals in Dijon which issued the definitive judgment only after the judge and his assessors had paid an official visit to Vosne for an organized tasting of "les Tâches." On 6 December 1932, the court confirmed the right of de Villaine and Chambon to the appellation La Tâche for their vines in Les Gaudichots.

To settle problems of inheritance, the ten children of Comte Liger-Belair were obliged by court decision to put La Tâche up for sale at auction, 31 August 1933. Edmond Gaudin de Villaine acquired it in the names of his sons, Henri and Jean, and of Jacques Chambon, who in his words "were declared to be purchasers in indivisibility of La Tâche, a vineyard clos situated in the community of Vosne-Romanée, measuring one hectare, forty ares, five centiares [3.47 acres], cadastre parcel no. 513, Section C, for the price of 138,000 francs."

It was on the basis of the appellate court's judgment of 2 December 1932, and of subsequent visits to the vines by surveyors and experts, that the present boundaries of La Tâche, incorporating a large part of Les Gaudichots, were defined and, on 11 September 1936, officially consecrated La Tâche Appellation d'Origine Contrôlée (AOC) by the newly created (30 July 1935) Institut National des Appellations d'Origine (INAO).[46] This was one of the most important—and certainly the most striking—of the series of court decisions, dating from the 1920s and '30s, whereby boundary limitations for appellations d'origine were determined by magistrates, employing the concept of *usages locaux, loyaux et constants,* in conjunction with the integrity of the terroir and the appreciation of the wine, thus laying the groundwork for the AOC laws of the Côte d'Or in 1936.

Henri Leroy

The 1930s were a somber period in Burgundy. The market was dead and, with the exceptions of 1933, 1934, and 1937, the vintages were reputed to be bad. There are many tales of vineyard proprietors who were obliged to empty their kegs of wine into the gutters to make space for the approaching vintage. The creation of the Confrérie des Chevaliers du Tastevin in 1934 (dedicated to the promotion of Burgundy wines), the INAO in 1935, and of the AOC laws in 1936, with their promises of rigid quality control, lighted glimmers of hope in the depressed spirits of the vignerons. The rewards, however, were not reaped until well after the war, by following generations. Meanwhile, most of the vines in Burgundy were for sale and could find no buyers.

By the late thirties the Domaine de la Romanée-Conti had for long been a drain to the proprietors, imposing heavy personal investments with no returns. Jacques Chambon wanted to sell.

Ever since he was a young man in the early twenties, Henri Leroy, a third-generation wine négociant from Auxey-Duresses, had been a loyal personal client of the Domaine and had become a close friend of Edmond Gaudin de Villaine. He shared Gaudin de Villaine's vision of a united domaine of great growths. Both men knew that were the Domaine to be sold it would inevitably be bought by a group and divided up; Romanée-Conti and La Tâche would run the risk of being fragmented like the rest of the Côte d'Or. Leroy promised that when the time came he would top the highest bid for Jacques Chambon's share in the Domaine.

The most important first step in preparing for the transaction was to transform the Domaine into a company, or *société civile,* composed of shares, thus permitting Jacques Chambon to sell his half of the shares, while ensuring the indivisible continuity of the Domaine de la Romanée-Conti. Gaudin de Villaine had papers drawn up by Maître Callier, notary in Saint-Pourçain-sur-Siole, 31 July 1942, incorporating the Domaine into a société civile. At the first shareholders meeting the same day, Henri Gaudin de Villaine, who was then a prisoner-of-war, was represented by his wife; his brother Jean, who had been assigned by the Vichy government to a *foyer de jeunesse,* was represented by procuration. Because the Gaudin de Villaine residences in Moulins-sur-Allier had been requisitioned by the Germans and wartime travel restrictions rendered the 102-mile (165 km) trip to Vosne impracticable, the official headquarters of the new société were established in the offices of Maître Callier. After the war they were moved, first to Moulins, and in 1953 to the offices of the Domaine, in Vosne.

Henri Leroy, whose professionalism and financial support infused new blood and vitality into the Domaine, also invested in it an unbounded and lifelong passion. Although he preferred to remain officially in the background, with Edmond Gaudin de Villaine retaining the office of gérant, the two friends worked together in a spirit of complete mutual confidence until the death of Gaudin de Villaine on 24 November 1950. Henri de Villaine described this close-knit collaboration as, "in a word, two succeeding destinies which overlapped for barely eight years but which were bound to the same ideal: it is remarkable." The same atmosphere prevailed with Henri de Villaine, who replaced his father as gérant of the Domaine.

It was under Henri Leroy's impulsion that the failing vines of Romanée-Conti and the pre-phylloxera Richebourgs were torn up in 1945 and replanted in 1947 to grafted young vines; a rotating system of gradual reconstitution was imposed on the other vines of the Domaine; parcels of Montrachet were brought into the fold; and Romanée Saint-Vivant Marey-Monge was acquired on a long-term lease, thus paving the road to its purchase. After the dismal prewar and war years, old markets had to be renewed and new markets created. The United States, in particular, which had been released from the bondage of Prohibition during the depression of the thirties, remained an unknown quantity. As late as 1949, Edmond Gaudin de Villaine was obliged to declare maintenance expenses two to three times in excess of sales, always with the observation that, given the quality of the wines and the accumulation of stocks, there had to be better times ahead.

In 1954 Henri Leroy divided the Leroy half-interest in the Domaine equally between his two daughters, Pauline and Marcelle (Lalou), while he and his wife became usufructuaries and retained full rights of representation at the shareholders meetings.

André Noblet

André Noblet, whose name was to become indissociable with that of the Domaine de la Romanée-Conti, was born to a family of vignerons at the Domaine. In July 1940, when Louis Clin hired him to work in the cellars, he was sixteen years old. His vivacity, his dedication, and an intelligence grounded in a sure intuition inspired Clin to groom him for the eventual role of *chef de cave* (cellar master). Noblet vinified his first wines, under Mr. Clin's supervision, in 1946. In the same year, he married Madeleine Adnot, whose family were also vignerons at the Domaine. In illustration of the traditional Côte de Nuits claim that women are superior pruners to men, Madeleine Noblet was the only person to prune the vines of Romanée-Conti for many years.

At Louis Clin's death on 26 January 1953, André Noblet became chef de cave and *chef de culture*; no one was named régisseur in Mr. Clin's place—Noblet and Geneviève Clin, who officiated in the offices, shared the responsibility of day-to-day management.

I met André Noblet in 1961 with my brothers James and Byron. Our visit to the Domaine had been arranged in advance and reconfirmed by telephone half an hour before our arrival. Perhaps because our bearing was less worldly than that of the usual guest to the Domaine, Mlle Clin received us coolly, with the observation that, if we wanted to taste wine, there were establishments in Beaune that specialized in that sort of thing. Happily, André arrived at that moment and swept us off to the cellars. The magic of tasting the Domaine's new wines from the barrels was reinforced by Mlle Clin's change of mood, for she was awaiting our return from the cellars, smiling and bearing the guest book to receive our signatures.

André thought of his wines as his children, and he was a proud and jealous parent. He loved receiving in the cellars and was famous for his discussions of wines, upon all of which he bestowed feminine attributes. I only once saw him angry; it was the result of a misunderstanding, fortunately, for I was the object of his wrath. One morning, while tasting in the cellars, Aubert de Villaine mentioned to André that the previous evening we had drunk a bottle of Grands Echézeaux from another grower. Aubert's sentence was cut short as André, thinking that it had been a Domaine wine, turned, beaming, to me and asked how I had liked it. I said that it was disappointing . . . He flushed deeply and there was a moment of silence before the explosion. His words were: "Young man [André was three years older than I], you deserve a good spanking!" When he realized that the wine in question was foreign to the Domaine, he was more embarrassed than I.

THE DOMAINE TODAY

In 1974 the new bylaws of the Sociéte Civile du Domaine de la Romanée-Conti established a Conseil de Surveillance, or Board of Supervisors, shared by Henri Leroy and Henri de Villaine, while their children, Lalou Bize-Leroy and Aubert de Villaine, became co-directors of the Domaine. Because the wines are marketed in the third year following the vintage, Lalou's and Aubert's signatures first appeared on the 1971 labels, beneath the title "Les Associés-Gérants."

Henri Leroy died on 21 February 1980. One day, while tasting an extraordinary Richebourg 1952 from the Domaine, he had said, "The day I am buried, you will drink this wine and you mustn't be sad." On the day of his funeral, in accordance with his wish, his family drank the Richebourg 1952, united with him in thought and in spirit. In June 1980, Leroy's eldest daughter, Pauline Roch, replaced her father on the Board of Supervisors.

Geneviève Clin retired in 1983. André and Madeleine Noblet retired in 1984; André died only two years later, 30 May 1986.

With succeeding generations, the management of the Domaine continually evolves. Bernard Noblet has replaced his father as chef de cave and Gerard Marlot, who joined the Domaine in 1982, replaced André Noblet, at his retirement, as chef de culture. Jean-Charles Cuvelier is assistant director, while Chantal Jovin, André and Madeleine Noblet's daughter, works in the offices, along with Madeleine Jayer-Haegelen and Françoise Juillet, who succeeded her mother there in 1986.

It is, moreover, a mere symbol, but it is just that the house built by the prince de Conti, in which to vinify and raise La Romanée and to lodge his vigneron and his régisseur, should, after more than a century and a half of separation, be rejoined to La Romanée-Conti.

After Ouvrard bought Romanée-Conti and its dependencies in 1819, La Goillotte passed into other hands. It was transformed into a comfortable bourgeois residence by Dr. Chanut, one of the important proprietors in Vosne during the last century (an engraving of La Goillotte, entitled "Domaine de M. le Docteur Chanut," appears in *Les Grands Vins de Bourgogne*, Danguy and Aubertin, 1892). The Chanut family sold the property in 1907; it eventually fell by inheritance to Mlle Groffier, who died in 1977. The Domaine acquired it in 1979 from her heirs.

MONTRACHET

At the shareholders meeting of 11 September 1963, Henri Leroy announced to his associates that he had the possibility of acquiring, from the comte de Moucheron, a parcel of vines in the lieudit "Le Montrachet" and that it seemed to him "to be of the greatest possible interest that vines benefiting from the greatest white wine appellation in Burgundy should be attached to the Domaine de la Romanée-Conti." The Domaine bought these .85 acres (.3419 ha) of vines, situated in the Chassagne sector of Montrachet; in 1965, .41 acres (.1670 ha), acquired from M. Roizot, were added to them and, finally, in 1980, another .41 acres (.1670 ha), acquired from M. Roland Thévenin.

ROMANÉE SAINT-VIVANT

From 1584, when the future Romanée left the fold, until the Revolution, the exterior boundaries of the Clos de Saint-Vivant remained unchanged. Around 1750 a portion of the prior's garden and courtyard area, which in 1512 was declared to contain two journaux, was planted with vines. The property declaration of 1769 "in conformity with the Saint-Vivant property records of the year 1512" describes the buildings and courtyard as "enclosed by walls containing a half journal." The next item is "a parcel of vineyard . . . called Laplante containing a journal and a half adjoining the courtyard, buildings, and hemp patch of the said priory." In this declaration and in that of 1774, the last before the Revolution, the descriptions of the Clos des Neuf Journaux, the Clos du Moytan, and the Clos des Quatre Journaux are identical to those of 1512.

Ecclesiastical properties were confiscated and declared *biens nationaux* on 13 February 1790.

The surveyor's report of "the vines called Le Clos de la Romanée," 12 December 1790, reveals the Clos des Quatre Journaux to contain four journaux; the Clos du Moytan, five journaux and a quarter; the Clos des Neuf Journaux, seven journaux and a half; and La Plante, one journal and a half. In the expertise dated three days earlier, the first three items are evaluated at sixteen livres per ouvrée, with the observation that these vines "are estimated 20 sols more per ouvrée than the vines of Citeaux because they are in better condition and better cultivated" (the expertise of the Clos de Vougeot—"the vines of Citeaux"—is dated a month earlier). Finally, "the fourth and last article, designated under the name of Plante, is not in the same class as the others although the said Plante is over forty years old . . . estimated because of the slight quality of the wine . . . at three livres 15 sols per ouvrée." The global estimate for the vines, buildings, wine presses, and the rest was 54,256 livres. The property was sold at auction, 22 January 1791, to Nicolas-Joseph Marey ("Charles-Nicolas Marey le jeune" in the sale record, elsewhere often designated as "Marey cadet") for 91,000 livres.

Marey separated La Plante, a growth of inferior quality, from the other vines of Saint-Vivant; he renamed it the "Clos Saint-Vivant" (it was later sold—today it is called La Croix Rameau). The other three clos he called simply La Romanée. Between 1791 and 1807, he acquired fourteen small parcels of vines in the lieudit Au Plans lying within the square containing the Clos du Moytan, to enlarge and clean up the boundaries of his Romaneé. Finally, in 1821, Nicolas-Joseph Marey's widow, Jeanne-Charlotte Monge, acquired another two ouvrées and a half Au Plans, making a total of about thirty ouvrées incorporated into the Marey Romanée which, thanks to the persistence of *usages locaux, loyaux et constants*, continued, despite the owner's efforts, to bear the name of Saint-Vivant.

In 1898, heirs of the Marey-Monge family put the Clos des Quatre Journaux up for sale at auction. Louis Latour's great-grandfather bought it for Fr 60,200. The Latour label reads, "Romanée Saint Vivant Les Quatre Journaux."

The remaining three-quarters of the original Clos de Saint-Vivant, the Domaine Marey-Monge, was farmed out to the Domaine de la Romanée-Conti in 1966 by Mlle Marey-Monge, the last to bear the name. Excepting the absence of the Clos des Quatre Journaux, the wheel has now turned full circle: in September 1988, the Domaine de la Romanée-Conti purchased the Domaine Marey-Monge from the Neyraud family, Mlle Marey-Monge's heirs. After four centuries of separation, the Clos des Neuf Journaux, the Cloux du Moytan, and the prior's buildings and courtyard have been gathered into the fold of the Cros des Cloux, today Romanée-Conti. In addition to the holdings of the Domaine and of Louis Latour, there are today 6.59 acres (2.67 ha) of AOC Romanée Saint-Vivant vines which lie outside of the original property of the priory of Saint-Vivant.

The vineyard holdings of the Domaine de la Romaneé-Conti, at present, are as follows:

	Area Held by the Domaine	Total Area of Cru	Average Production (1971-1991)
BOTTLED AND SOLD BY DOMAINE			
Romanée-Conti (*monopole*)	4.46 acres (1.8050 ha)	4.46 acres (1.8050 ha)	6,000 bottles
La Tâche (*monopole*)	15 acres (6.0620 ha)	15 acres (6.0620 ha)	20,000 bottles
Richebourg	8.67 acres (3.5110 ha)	19.85 acres (8.0345 ha)	11,000 bottles
Romanée Saint-Vivant	13 acres (5.2858 ha)	23.32 acres (9.4374 ha)	17,000 bottles
Grands Echézeaux	8.7 acres (4.6703 ha)	22.60 acres (9.1445 ha)	11,500 bottles
Echézeaux	11.5 acres (4.6703 ha)	93.14 acres (37.6922 ha)	15,000 bottles
Montrachet	1.67 acres (.6759 ha)	19.76 acres (7.9980 ha)	3,000 bottles
Total			83,500 bottles
SOLD TO NÉGOCIANTS			
Bâtard-Montrachet	0.43 acres (.1746 ha)	29.32 acres (11.8663 ha)	
Suchots	2.52 acres (1.0190 ha)		
Petits Monts	1 acre (.4050 ha)		

Production is extremely variable. The year 1982, despite all precautions, was a runaway vintage, the most abundant in recent years—Romanée-Conti produced about 9,000 bottles and La Tâche more than 32,200; in 1987, there were about 2,900 bottles of Romanée-Conti; in 1984, 3,000; and in 1979, 3,350.

To help finance the 1988 purchase of the Romanée Saint-Vivant vines from the heirs of the Marey-Monge family, most of the Echézeaux vines and a very small portion of Grands Echézeaux were sold, but they continue to be farmed by the Domaine on a thirty-year renewable lease, and to be bottled with the Domaine's labels.

As a matter of principle, only Grand Cru wines are bottled and commercialized by the Domaine. The AOC village appellations (Vosne-Romanée Premier Cru) Suchots and Petits Monts, are sold to the négoce. Because of the slight quantity, the Bâtard-Montrachet, although a Grand Cru, is either sold to the négoce or bottled at the Domaine for personal use. Finally, in difficult vintages, when the Domaine decides that one or several of its Grand Cru wines are not up to its standard of quality, these wines are sold anonymously to négociants, as AOC Vosne-Romanée. Thus, in 1950 and 1951, only La Tâche was bottled at the Domaine; in 1960, only La Tâche and Romanée-Conti; in 1963 and 1965, there was no Echézeaux and, in 1968, none of the red wines were bottled at the Domaine.

At the end of 1991, Lalou Bize relinquished her post as co-director of the Domaine to her nephew, Charles Roch, eldest son of Pauline Roch. After his tragic death in an automobile accident, 10 March 1992, Charles Roch was replaced by his brother, Henry-Frédéric Roch, who, since April 1992, shares with Aubert de Villaine the responsibility of co-director, or associé-gérant, of the Domaine.

Until Lalou Bize's resignation, the distribution of the Domaine's wines depended on three distributors, one for the United States, one for Great Britain and, for the rest of the world la Maison Leroy, the family firm of which Lalou is director, which acted, from 1964 to 1991, as exclusive agent. At present, the distribution outside of

France (which counts for about 25 percent of the sales) is assured by some thirty distributors, each with exclusive rights. About 30 percent of the Domaine's wines are shipped to the United States, where they are distributed by the firm Wilson & Daniels, Saint Helena, California. Similar arrangements exist with Corney & Barrow for Great Britain and Suntory, Ltd. for Japan, each of which represents approximately 10 percent of the sales.

The Genius of the Terroir

IV

TERROIR MEANS SOMETHING more than mere soil—a fugitive something that is almost mystical in concept. Of all the aspects of a climat, the terroir is the most difficult to define, for its definition must embrace the elusive elements responsible for a wine's personality, whatever it is lying hidden there that makes a wine from a given climat different from all its neighbors. What lies hidden there—a chthonic mystery—has a name; it is called *le génie du terroir,* but the science of oenology can no more explain it than can that of art history explain Michelangelo. The aspects of a terroir responsible for quality, in an abstract sense, can pretty well be defined; the mystery of a wine's personality remains intact.

Romanée-Conti's destiny was cast by terrestrial upheavals during the Jurassic period, 160 million years ago, more or less, at approximately the same time that the first mammals and flowering plants appeared on the earth. Out of this chaos rose the Côte d'Or.

In Vosne, the vineyards begin at 754 feet (230 m) above sea level and there are no vines higher than 1,150 feet (350 m). The AOC Grands Crus lie between 820 feet

(250 m; the eastern boundary of Romanée Saint-Vivant) and 984 feet (300 m; the western boundary of La Tâche); Romanée-Conti rises from 853 feet (260 m) at its eastern wall to 902 feet (275 m) at the western boundary. By a subtle shift in the slope's structure, the shallow basin described by the vineyard's surface (for which, four centuries ago, it was named the Cros des Cloux), whose exposure is to the east, tilts slightly to the south to collect a maximum of heat throughout the day; these particularities provide protection against spring frosts, encourage a precocious growing season, and hasten the ripening of the grapes.

The bedrock base is a very hard skeletal limestone composed of the calcareous appendages, or *entroques,* by which primitive crinoid sea creatures, cousins to the sea urchin and the starfish, affixed themselves to the sea floor.

The soil of Romanée-Conti reposes directly on another layer of limestone, a layer which surfaces between the Côte de Nuits and the Côte de Beaune, at Prémeaux and Comblanchien, and is quarried in the form of a light beige, delicately pink-veined marble.

Between the beds of hard limestone and pink-veined marble lies a vein of crumbly limestone and clay, called *terre à foulon* (fuller's earth), or *marnes* (marls) *à Ostrea acuminata,* because of the abundance of tiny oyster shells in its composition. Speaking of this precious material, as well as of red clay deposits, Dr. Morelot noted that "when vignerons discover such a treasure, they dig deeply to extract all of it; it is left, for a year, exposed to the air; after which it is spread among the vines, where it improves remarkably the initial soil." Geologists and oenologists alike have for long felt that the presence of this substance in the soil is an important quality factor.

Schema of the Jurassic Structure of the Côte at Vosne-Romanée

I. Bathonian Series

1. White, oolitic limestone
2. Pink-veined limestone

II. Bajocian Series

3. Crumbly clay and calcium marl formed from oyster deposits
4. Hard limestone formed from the articulations of primitive sea animals (crinoids)
5. Mixed deposits of limestones and clays from later periods

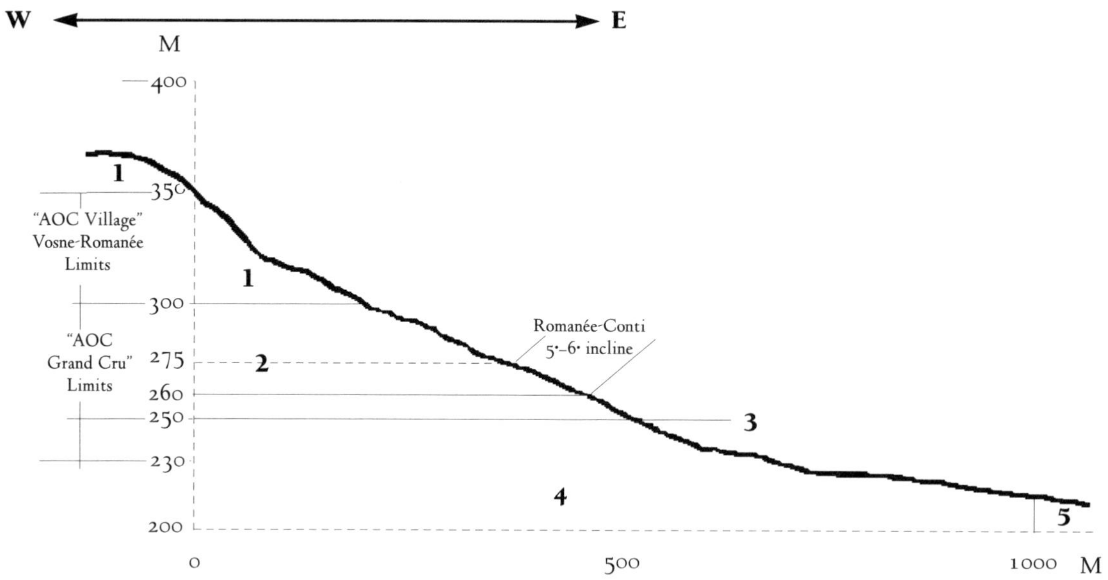

Rolande Gadille, a geologist, whose study *Le Vignoble de la Côte Bourguignonne* (1967) is unique of its kind, wrote, "8 to 10 meters thick, these marls, characterized by innumerable tiny oyster shells, bluish in color at the moment of extraction, turning yellowish in contact with the air, have an unquestionable influence on certain growths in the Côte de Nuits, at least when they surface on the lower third of the slope, that is to say, on the part of the hillside where vines are grown, which is the case between Gevrey and Nuits."

These oyster marls are certainly chanced upon less frequently than in times past; although fragments of oyster shell are often turned up when the soil is dug, no vein of pure oyster marl has been struck on any of the Domaine's properties in recent memory. Professor Leneuf, who holds the Chair of Geology at the University of Burgundy, confirms the position of this strata of marls at the base of Romanée-Conti, but, he adds, "The base level of these marls is most often buried beneath erosional clay and gravel deposits, washed down from above by rains. The age-old labors, which have reshuffled the upper layers of the soil, must also be taken into account, as well as the transports of earth, of undefined origin, particularly during the last century, destined to compensate the disastrous effects of erosion."

Higher up the slope from Romanée-Conti, superimposed on the pink rock and punctuated with crevices containing red clay, is a white, oolitic limestone, so-named because of the egg-shaped pebbles, or oolites, cemented into its composition. It lies beneath the soil of the highest vineyards and, higher still, often surfaces, its erosion enriching the vineyards below.

The soil is a testimony to centuries of labor, incorporating into it from beneath fragmented bedrock, fissured and decomposed by the perennial penetration of vine roots; washed down from above is eroded top soil, veins of red clay, and smooth pebbles, liberated by winter freezes from the mass of oolitic rock.

Since the early nineteenth century, in the belief that all things can be understood, men have sought to explain the miracle of a climat by analyzing the composition of the soil. Dr. Morelot was the first to publish an analysis of the soil of Romanée-Conti; others followed suit. The analyses varied greatly, but so do those from different laboratories today. A synthesis presents a soil about one-quarter of whose bulk is composed of pebbles and small gravel; of the remaining fine soil, about 40 percent is clay, 2 percent is organic material, a high iron oxide content colors it a deep, reddish brown, and there are traces of nitrates, phosphates, potassium, magnesium oxide, and aluminum oxide.

Professor Leneuf wrote, "The soil of Romanée-Conti, in addition to its content of fragmented limestone gravel, contains a certain amount of fine, slightly sandy, alluvial clay, composed of polyhedral aggregates [a crumbly mixture of minuscule grains with multiple flat surfaces], which lends to the soil a stability and a fine, porous structure, permitting it, at the same time, to breath and to retain a healthy humidity."

In the Côte d'Or, hillsides are not terraced, as they are, for instance, in the northern Côtes du Rhône, nor does their structure permit artificial installations of drainage, as in parts of the Bordelais. A pebbly, crumbly texture, in combination with an incline which is neither too shallow nor too steep, are primordial requirements for a perfectly drained, healthy soil not impoverished by erosion. At the base of the Côte, the rise is hardly perceptible and the degree of incline—three degrees or less—is insufficient for perfect drainage. Going up the hillside, the incline becomes progressively steeper, and at the upper limit of vines erosion is a problem. Above that point, from 984 feet (300 m) to the summit, the bedrock often surfaces.

At Romanée-Conti, a five-to-six-degree incline provides perfect drainage, while remaining sufficiently gentle to not only avoid serious erosion but also to collect valuable elements washed down from steeper slopes by rains. Soil which collects at the bottom of the vineyard after violent rainstorms is brought up and redistributed among the vines during the winter months.

Pacottet (*Viticulture*, 1905), after noting that in all of the great growths the soil is at least twenty inches (50 cm) deep, wrote, "In the Romanées, for instance, as a result of the repeated accretions of decalcified red earth brought down from the plateau over the centuries, the soil has a depth of no less than 1.5 to 2 meters [4.9–6.7 ft.]." Aubert is more circumspect: he observes that the cartloads of earth brought down from the mountaintop by André de Croonembourg and by the prince de Conti could not possibly have a noticeable effect on the overall depth of the soil; he also believes that, in those parts of Les Richebourgs and La Tâche that share with Romanée-Conti the same level and degree of incline, the soil is of about the same depth. He writes, "The soil of the hillside at the level of La Romanée-Conti is certainly deep: the bedrock has never been struck while working it. The vines' roots certainly wind their way easily to a depth of several meters."

Amendments at the Domaine are discreet and rare—once every four or five years, depending on the soil's needs as determined by careful analysis. The purpose is not to enrich the soil, but to maintain a balance. Manure is brought in rarely and irregularly; a number of years ago, a bit of sheep manure was spread in the alleys between the rows.

Since 1985, the Domaine has been experimenting with organic cultivation—soil amendment by the introduction of natural products based on decoctions of algae and trace elements and the suppression of pesticides, with the exception of traditional sulfur and copper sulfate treatments—with excellent results.

The concept of amending the soil in any way except for the addition of virgin soil, would have shocked the vignerons of the first half of the nineteenth century. The 1845 report on the Clos de Vougeot reads, "The clos produces an average of 13 hectoliters per hectare, somewhat less than that generally obtained in the region. Despite malicious gossip to the contrary, it can easily be seen, it is obvious that the vineyard is never fertilized; only a bit of humus and pomace are brought in, uniquely for provignage. . . ."

This deep distrust of the introduction of any foreign element to a vineyard's soil is not recent; in 1395 Philippe le Hardi forbade the transport of manure and composts to the vineyards. Dr. Lavalle, in the middle of the last century, was categorical: "Any animal matter [that is, manure] brought into a vineyard, even in moderate doses, greatly alters the quality of wines of the first order. If this sort of fertilizer is employed in quantity, it can rob a harvest of all its quality, compromising the conservation and producing third-class wines in the most renowned of climates."

At the end of the last century, Durand and Guicherd wrote, "It was only around 1860 that the use of manure became more or less generalized; the increase in production was immediate. Since the invasion of phylloxera, things have changed a great deal: all of the old vines were manured [to give them more strength to resist phylloxera], in very modest doses in most cases, it is true. We were all the better off for it, for the quality of the wines was not diminished as a result."

The Croonembourgs and the prince de Conti amended the soil of La Romanée by the transport of virgin soil from the plateau at the summit of the Côte, the only method considered correct at that time, since it was the same soil that naturally washed down the slope by erosion. Today, the situation is reversed: everyone is expected to fertilize—the wisest use discretion—but the transport of soil from outside the vineyard is forbidden, except in cases of extreme soil impoverishment, when special permission may be given upon request.

The Climate

The microclimate of the vineyard Côte is warmer and less humid than the climate of the department of the Côte d'Or in general. The east-southeast exposure ensures a maximum reception of sun throughout the long, northern summer days, as much as sixteen hours if the skies are not gray. Above the village of Vosne, the summit of the Côte reaches 1,312 feet (400 m) above sea level; behind the Côte to the west, "the Hautes-Côtes de Nuits" (once known as *l'arrière côte*, a usage now discouraged) rise to over 1,970 feet (600 m), protecting the Côte from western winds. The weather is unpredictable from one year to another. An ideal vintage is preceded by a rainy winter, warm, sunny weather and gentle breezes at the time of flowering in early June, a hot, dry summer and a few rains in late August or early September. Good weather during the month preceding the harvest can make up for an imperfect summer. By midsummer 1978, for instance, everyone assumed that the vintage would be a disaster;

June and July were cold and the flowering was late and interminable. From August onward, however, the weather was unusually hot and dry. The grapes were picked in fine weather during the last half of October, and the wines are glorious. In 1989 and, again, in 1990, after unusually hot, dry growing seasons, picking took place during the last half of September; the drought was so extreme in 1990 that despite the heat Lalou and Aubert worried lest the grapes not ripen for lack of nourishment from the vines. Euphoria has now replaced all that worry.

The Côte d'Or is hail-prone. A hailstorm usually centers on a very restricted area and lasts no more than a few minutes, during which time it beats the vines mercilessly, stripping them of leaves and bark and scattering the ground with broken branches and grape clusters. The vines often take several years to completely recover. In 1979, just before the flowering, over half the potential harvest of Romanée-Conti and La Tâche was destroyed by hail. Hail again struck Romanée-Conti and parts of La Tâche, Richebourg, and Romanée Saint-Vivant in late July 1983. During the following two months, the Domaine's vignerons combed the vineyards, removing with typographer's tweezers the dried-out damaged grapes from the clusters that remained on the vines.

PINOT NOIR

The great red wines of the Côte d'Or issue from the pinot noir grape alone. The conjunction of *climat* and grape variety must be considered as a single phenomenon for, without the one or the other, the magic would be lost.

From the handful of noble varieties (perhaps twenty or so among several thousand) of the European wine-grape vine *Vitis vinifera*, pinot noir is the most erratic, one of the smallest producers, the least adaptable to other soils and climates, and the least stable. It is singularly susceptible to mutation within the individual plant buds, often producing on a vinestock a branch whose fruit differs from that of the other branches. Ampelographers, whose business is the science of vine identification, speak of "the family of pinots," which includes pinot gris and pinot blanc, as well as a number of atypical red varieties, all originally mutations of pinot noir. Dr. Lavalle wrote, "In the Côte d'Or, all of the pinot noirs are known by the name of *noirien*." More than a neatly definable variety, pinot noir is, perhaps, an unruly family, in which there nonetheless exists an ideal type.

In the past, *pinot* was often spelled "p-i-n-e-a-u"; the spelling p-i-n-o-t was made official at the end of the last century to protect its pronunciation, the Burgundian patois pronunciation of *pineau* being "peen-yo." Today, *pineau* designates only the Loire Valley white chenin grape.

Pinot noir fin, or noirien (known also as *franc noirien, plant à bon vin, plant fin, plant noble, franc bourguignon, franc pinot, petit pinot,* and, outside of the Côte d'Or, as *morillon, auvergnat,* and so on), is classified as an early-ripening grape. It is a slender and willowy-branched, not especially vigorous vine. The leaves of a healthy vine are nearly round, three-lobed but only slightly indented; they are thick, the color is dark viridian green with a mat finish on the upper surface, lighter and grayer beneath; the leaves' characteristic, irregular surface is described as bubbly or waffly. The ripe grape cluster is unusually small, compact, and more or less cylindrical with no wings; its smaller-than-average, round or imperceptibly oval grapes contain an abundant, colorless juice and usually no more than one or two seeds; the skins, beneath a violet-hued bloom, are of a blue so deep that it is called black. Pinot is thought by many to have been so-named because the form of its grape cluster resembles that of a pine cone.

Dr. Morelot wrote in 1831, "The skin [of the noirien grape] is thin [and] presents only a small dose of coloring matter by comparison to that which adheres to the skin of the common grape." Thirty years later, Vergnette-Lamotte described the skin as "thick and rich in coloring matter." The same discrepancies occur today from one author to another. Perhaps changing tastes and criteria for judging the red wines of the Côte d'Or were accompanied by an evolution, through selection, from a thinner-skinned pinot at the beginning of the nineteenth century to a pinot with thicker skin and more pigmentation by the 1860s. In any case, these are variable qualities: older vines produce thicker-skinned grapes with more coloring matter than young vines; after a hot, dry summer, the grapes may be smaller than usual, the skins thicker and the pigmentation more intense. Given a similar growing season and vines of the same age, pinot skins are no doubt thinner and contain less color than, for instance, those of the cabernet sauvignon grape, the most tannic of the Bordeaux varieties.

According to Jean Siegrist, oenologist at the Station Oenologique de Beaune, "Pinot is a moderately colored varietal. Its content in anthocyanins [soluble botanical pigments in the blue-to-red range] can be as little as one-tenth that of a hybrid variety [Seibel] and approximately half that of Syrah [the variety responsible for the tough, long-lived wines of Hermitage and Côte-Rôtie]."

During the flowering season, pinot noir is especially susceptible to accidents of fecundation, caused by rains or radical temperature changes: imperfect pollination causes *millerandage,* the grape clusters containing a portion of stunted grapes that never grow to normal size and ripen later than the other grapes on the cluster; pollination failure causes *coulure,* in which the embryo fruit falls, unfertilized, to the ground. Millerandage and coulure often go hand in hand. A partial coulure, while compromising the importance of the harvest, can bring greater concentration to the remaining grapes and, because its effect is to produce less tightly packed clusters, it can repel gray rot, which often attacks the unaerated heart of a ripe, compact grape cluster during rainy vintage seasons. Among recent vintages, cold spring weather and rains have caused millerandage and coulure in 1981, 1984, and 1987, severely reducing the harvest.

Almost nothing is known of Burgundian viticulture before it fell to the great monasteries of the Middle Ages to develop it. A few wisps of straw in the wind have led those who clutched at them to formulate conflicting theories concerning its origins and those of pinot noir.

Columella (A.D. first century) described three grape varieties grown in Gaul during his time; of the third, to which he gives no name, he wrote, "The smallest and the best of the three is very readily recognized by its leaf, for it bears the roundest leaf of all of them; and it is praiseworthy because it endures drought best of all, because it bears cold if it is free from humidity, because in some regions its wine is racked off for long keeping, and especially it alone gives a good name to even the poorest soil by reason of its own fertility." Dr. Lavalle wrote, "These characteristics are so close to those of our own pineau that it is almost impossible not to recognize it."

Roger Dion (*Histoire de la vigne et du vin en France . . .*, 1959) suggested, by tenuous inference, that pinot noir is an extra-Burgundian creation of the Celtic Allobroge tribe, whose territory was, during the Roman occupation, the Dauphiné, with Vienne as its capital and Grenoble at its center. In their efforts to improve the agriculture of their region, he wrote, the Allobroges "used the vine as one of the principal instruments of this progress, after having succeeded in conferring upon one of the varieties of this plant—we don't know by what method—properties which permitted it to ripen in colder climates than those in which it had until then been cultivated." He paraphrased a text of Pliny the Elder, writing in the year A.D. 71, to the effect that, in the course of the preceding ninety years, "a new species of vine had appeared for which Vienne on the Rhône, the Allobrogian capital, had become famous. Thus, it is called allobrogica. It is adapted to cold climates and ripens at frost time. The grapes are black." He added, "It was necessary for the vine to acquire this resistance to rough winters in order to succeed on the slopes of the great alpine valleys. And it is perhaps for this reason that, only a century ago, the vignerons of Vienne still gave the name of 'montagnard' to our modern pinot, whose traits resemble, in more ways than one, the allobrogica of ancient times."

Today, most people are willing to concede that pinot noir is probably indigenous to Burgundy, that it originally evolved from a local wild grape and that it has been, over the centuries, progressively refined by the careful choice of vines selected for regeneration through layering or *provignage*.

The earliest existing document concerning specifically the vines of the Côte d'Or dates from A.D. 312. Known as the *Panégyrique d'Eumène*, it is a transcription of a discourse delivered to Emperor Constantine by a professional rhetor from Autun, capital of the Celtic Eduens' territory, of which Arebrignus, which included the Côte de Beaune and most of the Côte de Nuits, was a part. After describing a luxuriant agricultural paradise from a distant past, the speaker presents a picture of desolation in which the former garden land of irrigated plains has become useless swampland and, on the hillsides,

> the vine is no longer cultivated except at one point; beyond are only unapproachable forests and rocks, harboring savage beasts . . . the vines, admired only by those who are unaware of their condition, are so worn out from old age that, even though cultivated, they are nearly barren. The roots of these vines, whose age we no longer know, because of their bulk, endlessly piled upon one another, prevent trenches from being dug deeply enough [for provignage] and the unprotected *provins* are exposed to drowning rains and the burning sun.

Gaston Roupnel pleaded an eloquent case for the "immemorial antiquity" of these vines, basing his argument on the fact that, when the vineyards of the Côte were reconstituted with grafted vines, mostly at the end of the last century, the old vines, which had been renewed by provignage for centuries, were by no means in the pitiable condition of those described by the orator. For the soil to have become that congested with old wood, tangled roots, and layered vinestock, he figured, the vines would have had to be subjected to several more centuries of provignage than those which had been torn up during his own lifetime. He concluded in a whisper of awe, "Hesitating on the threshold of History, and after feeling our way cautiously, we may perhaps be able to fix this period around the 6th century B.C."

Dion, who for reasons of his own was determined to prove that vines cannot have existed in the Côte d'Or before the third century A.D., took Roupnel to task, but he was hardly more convincing in his claim that "the real age of these old vines 'whose age we no longer know' was not much more than that of a long human life." He concludes that "nothing in the discourse addressed to Constantine obliges us to place the beginnings of the vineyard of the Côte d'Or earlier than the 3rd century of our era."

Pierre Forgeot (*Origines du vignoble bourguignon*, 1972), employed a circumlocutional logic, impossible to capsulize, which led him to deduce that the first vines in the Côte d'Or were planted between 200 and 150 B.C., precisely where the vineyards of Monthelie and Auxey-Duresses lie today, and that those who planted them experimented first with cuttings brought from Italy before finally succeeding, after a long and progressive selection, with native wild grapes.

However ancient the fourth-century vineyard may have been, the panegyric clearly depicts the last gasp of a once flourishing culture; henceforth, the chronicles of the vines of Burgundy are silent for two and a half centuries. Grégoire de Tours, bishop of Tours during the last quarter of the sixth century, mentions the delicious wine from the vines covering the slopes to the west of Dijon. At about the same time, around 587, according to Dr. Lavalle, Gontran, king of Burgundy, gave vast land holdings, including vines, to the abbey of Saint-Bénigne, in Dijon (founded in 536). Lavalle listed, from church charters, a number of other gifts of vines in the Côte d'Or over the five centuries to follow. Cluny was founded in 910, at about the same time as the priory of Saint-Vivant; Citeaux was founded in 1098 and, in 1110, received the first of many donations that would eventually make up the Clos de Vougeot.

The word *pinot* first appeared in 1375 when Philippe le Hardi, duc de Bourgogne, preceding a diplomatic visit to Bruges, had "six queues and one poinçon [pièce] of vermilion pinot wine" [vin de pinot vermeil] sent there for his receptions.

Dion was convinced that the appearance of a new word signified the unveiling of an improved grape. He wrote,

> Is it not possible that the duc Philippe le Hardi, whose vigilant and authoritarian protection of quality in the Côte d'Or vineyards is well known [a reference to Philippe le Hardi's ordinance, twenty years later, that all gamay vines—"a very bad and very disloyal plant named gaamez . . . very noxious to human creatures . . . full of great and horrible bitterness"—be torn up], initiated, himself, the selection by which was obtained this improved black grape which, from 1375 on, he judged to be worthy of himself. Did he not even personally contribute to the creation of the word, pinot, of which no mention is known before 1375?

Pinot was, in any case, called noirien long before someone called it pinot (*vin de noirien* occurs in a document from the reign of Hugues IV, mid-thirteenth century) and, in the Côte d'Or, it remained noirien. In the last century, pinot was a word used by scientists and foreigners; the *plant à bon vin* was noirien.

THE VINES

V

LA VIGNE CROÎT à l'ombre du vigneron
[The vine flourishes in the shadow of the vigneron]

From the dawn of Burgundian viticulture until the onslaught of phylloxera during the last quarter of the nineteenth century, the vines had perpetuated themselves underground, on the hillsides of the Côte d'Or, by a system known as *provignage*. A vine was never torn up unless it was degenerate or dead; a vineyard was never torn up unless it had succumbed to a catastrophe akin to the mysterious scourges which ravaged the Côte during the fifteenth and sixteenth centuries (see chapter 2, note 17).

French dictionaries define *provignage* as "vine layering" (*marcottage de la vigne*). One must not, however, confuse layering, in the usual sense of the word, with provignage. Layerage consists simply in placing a supple branch of a plant in contact with earth until it forms roots, after which the newly rooted shoot is severed from the parent plant. Provignage was a very different process: the entire vinestock, or parent plant, was buried, with only selected tips of the year's growth protruding above ground; the parent stock became part of a complex root system which was never ruptured and which continued to nourish the newly-rooted young vines for years to come. New vineyards were planted in rows, with vine cuttings ("a thousand cuttings per ouvrée," that is, 9,717 (or approximately 10,000) vines per acre [24,000 vines per hectare], wrote Dr. Morelot), but because of the impossibility of extending high-quality vineyards beyond the narrow strip of Côte d'Or slopes, new plantations had been for centuries a rarity. Beneath the earth's surface lay a dense web of roots and chains of layered vinestocks, the gradual disappearance of the oldest wood permitting the system of provignage to eternalize, the process of perpetual renewal and decomposition going hand-in-hand. Meanwhile, above ground, ordered rows of vines had long since vanished; there were from two to three times as many vines per acre as today—8,000 to 13,000 (20,000 to 30,000 vines per hectare), the average estimate falling around 10,000 (24,000)—and the vines grew at intervals of approximately 1-1/2 to 2 feet (50–60 cm) in all directions. Horses and plows were out of the question; the vineyards could only be cultivated by hand, with hoe and pickax. It was called plantation *en foule*—in a mob.

PROVIGNAGE

In late February or early March, each vine was radically pruned to leave only its most vigorous single cane, or branch, which was, itself, pruned back, depending on the vigor of the vine, to from two to four eyes (the nascent buds which form during the growing season at the crotch of each leaf-stem base at its attachment to the branch and which, the following spring, will unfurl into the new branches which will bear that season's fruit). Under normal circumstances, the most vigorous cane was always the outermost, the farthest removed from the old wood, which meant that the trunk of the vine, or vinestock, easily gained 3 inches (7.6 cm) in length each year and that a vine fifteen-to-twenty years old could have a trunk nearly 5 feet (1.5 m) long.

During the growing season, the vines were attached to stakes, or *paisseaux*. New paisseaux were something over 5 feet (1.5 m) long. A stake was planted by each vine in early April, following the second labor, and, after the grape harvest, the stakes were pulled up (*dépaisselage*), resharpened, and stored until the following spring. When stakes became too short from repeated sharpenings, they were put to other uses. Thus, the stakes rose 3 feet (1 m), more or less, from the earth, at 1-1/2-foot (.5 m) intervals, more or less, in all directions. The old vines whose trunks were longer than the stakes, had to be laid along the ground for most of their length before being staked, further encumbering the already crowded vineyard.

Provignage had quasi-numinous overtones, since it involved the sacrifice of a vigorous vine, in the full flower of maturity and perfection of its fruit, to create two or, ideally, three new vines. It was a ritual annual sacrifice, meant to ensure eternal life to the noble noirien vine. Central to the concept was the fact that the newly created vines were never severed from the buried parent vine which, in turn, had never been severed from its parent, and so forth.

The healthy, fifteen-to-twenty-year-old vines chosen for sacrifice had to be growing near spaces to be filled or close to dead or declining vines which would be torn up in order to maintain a balance in the plantation. Speaking of these healthy vines, whose elongated trunks complicated the culture of the vineyard, Durand and Guicherd wrote, "Provignages caused them to disappear, but slowly, for according to the vignerons, it was these old trunks which gave the good wine." From this observation, it seems clear that many were spared, that others grew to a riper old age before being provined, and that sometimes younger vines were provined in order to save those that gave the best wine.

The vines could be provined any time after the first *labour* (which took place as soon as the stakes were pulled up, following the harvest) until the end of March, on condition that the weather be clement and the soil moist and workable. They were chosen just before the harvest, when the qualities of the new wood and the fruit were most in evidence, and each vine was marked with a fragment of hemp, tied around the vinestock. The requisite qualities were two or preferably three sturdy, equally strong and perfectly lignified branches, the tender green, supple year's growth having been transformed into stiff but bendable young wood sheathed in a thin, smooth, dark reddish-brown husk, each branch bearing one or two clusters of typically noirien small black grapes. The marked vines which had not been provined before pruning were left untouched by the pruners.

A *provin* was the individual operation of provignage, the ensemble of the trench and the vine or vines layered in it; by extension, it could mean the trench itself. In the Côte de Nuits, often two and sometimes three vines were layered in a trench to form a provin (in the Côte de Beaune, each provin was composed of a single vine).

When the time came to lay the marked vines beneath the ground, each vine was first cleaned up. All growth was removed except for the two or three branches destined to form the new plants, which were left intact in their entire length. The trench was begun beneath the vine itself. Its length depended on the length of the vinestocks and on the number of vines to be incorporated into the provin; its serpentine direction was commanded by the placement of the new plants and the position of the other old vines, if more than one were to be accommodated. The trenches were about 1-1/2 feet (45 cm) deep and some 14 inches (35 cm) wide.

The earth was dug away from the vine's roots and the exposed section of root was trimmed free of all superficial roots and rootlets to render it more supple; it was gently curved downward and laid along with the rootstock and the branches, along the bottom of the trench; at appropriate intervals, the branches were curved upward and supported against one of the walls of the trench, their extremities projecting well above the level of the earth's surface. The layered vines were covered with fine earth, a thin layer of compost, and another layer of earth. The trenches were often not completely filled with earth until the year following the provignage. The earth dug up from the trenches was spread in the vineyard, which meant either that virgin soil was brought in or that eroded soil was carried up from the bottom of the vineyard for filling the trenches.

The protruding extremities of the branches were pruned back to two or three eyes; these future vines were called projections, or *saillies*. The following year, the lower branches would be removed and the uppermost branch pruned back again to two or three eyes. There was some production the first year, and the second year these new vines produced abundantly. This exuberance gradually attenuated; by the fifth or sixth year, they were producing grapes of good concentration.

Rolande Gadille writes, "The rhythm of these provignages accelerated greatly from the Middle Ages [5 per ouvrée each year in the Dijonnais] to the nineteenth century [30 per ouvrée each year]." At first, the figures are surprising but, upon reflection, they are possible if that of the nineteenth century indicates the maximum number of provignages per ouvrée in the Côte de Beaune, where each provin took only one vine; there is no way of knowing how many vines were incorporated into a provin in the Dijonnais during the Middle Ages. The observation, in any case, holds true for La Romanée from the eighteenth to the nineteenth century, where the number of annual provignages increased by about a third in the space of seventy years. The prince de Conti's contract with his new vigneron, Etienne Magnien, in 1782 (see note 36) specified that "the vigneron assigned to cultivate the vines of la Romanée will be held responsible . . . to practice each year twelve or thirteen provins per ouvrée and as many more as may be judged necessary." The instructions, spelled out by Julien Ouvrard's chef de culture for his vignerons and cited by Dr. Lavalle, in 1855, read, "Twenty provins will be prepared per ouvrée, or one hundred sixty per journal. Vignerons who exceed this number without authorization will only be paid for twenty. Since, however, there may be areas in the vineyard where more are necessary, the vigneron, in that case, will inform the manager, who, after verification, will tell him how many he should prepare." It is also specified that the provins "will be composed of no more than two or three vines, each of them having two or three *saillies;* the number of saillies should never be more than six nor fewer than three."

Twenty provins, in each of which were layered two or three rootstocks, added up to approximately fifty provined vines per ouvrée, or one-twentieth of the population. A vineyard was said to be provined by twentieths (*provignée par vingtièmes*) and, therefore, theoretically, completely renewed every twenty years.

BEFORE PHYLLOXERA

With more than twice as many vines per acre, the system of plantation en foule, provignage, and single-branch short pruning nonetheless limited production to about half the amount which is thought today to represent a rational, restrained production. Because each vine bore so little fruit, the "glucometer" readings (measuring sugar level, or alcohol potential) were, except in disastrous years, generally higher than those today.

In 1869, a couple of months before he acquired La Romanée-Conti, J.-M. Duvault-Blochet published his vintage notes from over a period of forty-seven years, from 1822 to 1868. On the basis of these notes, he built a case for late picking and the use of the glucometer to determine the right moment for picking (instead of depending blindly on the *ban des vendanges*—see chapter 6).

He wrote, "So many years, during which I was only four times a loser (and I won forty-nine times in fifty-three years) by picking late." The figures are impressive: out of the forty-seven years which are noted, the natural sugar counts for nineteen vintages were 13° or more (several reached 14° and 14-1/2°; 1868 reached 15° and 1856, 16°); thirteen vintages fell between 12° and 13°, eleven between 11° and 12° and four between 10° and 11°. The four vintages in which Duvault-Blochet claimed to have been a loser counted no winners: in both 1828 and 1836, the glucometer descended from 11 1/2° to 11° because of late picking and, he noted, "rain and rot" [pluie et pourriture]; in 1853, by picking late in Santenay, the reading fell from 11-1/2° to 10-1/4° (but rose elsewhere); in 1866 the reading in Vosne rose from 9-1/2° to 10-1/2°, but he noted that the increase was due to rot and that they were the worst wines of Burgundy.

To bring all of these figures into perspective, Duvault-Blochet defined quality in terms of glucometer readings:

> At 11°5 one makes barely passable wines, at 12° one makes decent, marketable wines, at 12°5 above average, at 12°3/4 they are lively, firm and ruby; at 13° and 13°5 one makes great wines; at 14°, 14°5, 15°, and 15°5, one makes altogether exceptional, incomparable wines." He recommends picking when the glucometer reaches 13°, "when the season is not advanced, when there is no rot and when the grape clusters are not tightly packed . . . for if picking is begun at 13° one is certain to make very good wine; and the following day and the day after, if the weather is good, the must may reach 13°1/4 to 13°1/2, which will produce remarkable wines, whereas, upon waiting, one runs the risk of the must's losing rather than gaining in degree.

Dr. Jules Guyot's official study of all the vineyards of France, commissioned in 1861 by the Second Empire government and first published in 1868, lambasted the Burgundians for their stubbornness and blind loyalty to the costly and unproductive traditions of plantation en foule, single-branch short pruning, and provignage, which, he claimed, was nothing more than underground long pruning. He exclaimed, "The vigneron hides beneath the earth that which he dares not do in the open." Furthermore, he said, "Everyone knows that the grapes from provins, quite plentiful in the first year and very abundant in the second, are of inferior quality. Therefore, unless they are separated out, which is not done for they often make up half the harvest, they are responsible, every year for a loss of quality, a drawback which does not exist for independently rooted vines." (According to Lavalle, grapes from the young vines were separated out at the Clos de Vougeot, where Romanée-Conti was vinified.) As to production, Guyot wrote, "But gamay, at 50 or 60 hectoliters to the hectare, is at its maximum potential, and pineau, at 15 hectoliters, is at a third of its average potential, which would be easy to achieve without in any way altering the quality."

Guyot conceded only that "this provignage, which bestows eternal life upon the original vines, although it has serious drawbacks, has had at least one great merit for the Côte d'Or, that of having preserved the same varietal, pineau, which might, perhaps, have long since disappeared if the vineyards had been planted to individual vines which were torn up and replaced by new vines every forty to sixty years." The Burgundians lent a deaf ear to Dr. Guyot's criticisms and recommendations—that is until the infestation of phylloxera forced them to abandon provignage; today, the grafted vines of the Côte d'Or are pruned by Dr. Guyot's method.

No doubt, provignage was a sacred concept; to relinquish it must have seemed like tearing out the heart of the Côte. So sore was the need, the yearning to recapture the past that the distinguished oenologists, Durand and Guicherd, even attempted to provine the new vines, which had been grafted onto American roots: phylloxera thwarted their experiments.

OIDIUM, MILDIOU, AND PHYLLOXERA

During the last half of the nineteenth century, thanks to incautious scientific curiosity, three scourges—two fungi and a louse, all from North America—devastated the vineyards of France: the fungi, *oidium* or powdery mildew, which appeared in 1847, and *mildiou* (mildew), which arrived in 1878, are both capable of destroying the harvest if the vines are not treated; mildiou, which hibernates in the dormant buds, can destroy the vine as well.

From 1853, oidium has been controlled preventatively by *soufrage*—blowing sulfur powder onto the vines. Mildiou spread destruction for years before a preventative treatment—spraying a solution of copper sulfate and slaked lime, known as *bouillie bordelaise,* on the vines—was perfected. Today, whether or not this treatment is alternated with other fungicide sprays, the process is always called *sulfatage.* Treatments for oidium and mildiou also hold in check many of the insect pests which caused damage to the vines and the grapes in centuries past.

Phylloxera, the mortal enemy of *Vitis vinifera*, is a minuscule insect whose complicated biological cycle embraces several different forms, aerial and subterranean, winged and wingless. The winged phylloxeras—the spreaders—consist only of inherently fecund females. They lay eggs on the undersides of vine leaves, from which are hatched, in late autumn, males and females with no digestive organs. The male and female couple at birth, the male dying immediately thereafter, the female after having deposited, beneath the split bark of year-old vine wood, a single, small, winter egg. The following spring an inherently fecund, wingless female emerges from the winter egg and creates a leaf gall in which to lay hundreds of eggs. The hatched young, all female and fecund, continue to form leaf galls in which to lay eggs until, at high summer, their progeny go underground, where reproduction continues. A part of the population, on which wings have begun to form, returns above ground to fly off and lay male and female eggs beneath distant vine leaves, relaunching the cycle of annual males, winter eggs, and spring and summer generations of inherently fecund females.

In phylloxera's deadly, subterranean phase, colonies of insects attach themselves to the vine's roots and suck out the lifeblood, leaving poisoned and unhealable wounds; the leaves wither and fall and the vine dies.

Phylloxera was introduced to the South of France during the early 1860s with immune American wild grapevine hosts, presumably for purposes of research. Reports of its spread and its ravages reached the Côte d'Or long before the scourge itself arrived. Burgundians hoped that they would be spared; when its presence was reported in Meursault in 1878, they hoped that it would go away; it arrived in Vosne in 1882.

The reconstitution of vineyards, by grafting vinifera cuttings onto phylloxera-resistant American rootstock, was already well under way in the South of France but, in the Côte d'Or, there was tremendous resistance to grafting, in particular among the proprietors of the greatest vineyards, who were deeply attached to the system of provignage, who knew that, from time immemorial, great wine was only produced by old vines and who were convinced that vulgar, wild vine roots would nourish the noble noirien with a coarsened sap. Grafting onto American rootstock was, in fact, officially forbidden until 1887, when the gravity of the situation imposed its authorization.

The only alternative to grafting, at least on the slopes of the Côte d'Or, was to treat the soil with carbon disulfide (*sulfure de carbone*), an expensive and dangerous insecticide applied through a complicated process. It did not eliminate phylloxera but, when rationally employed, it kept it at bay. Bitter quarrels divided the Américanistes (in favor of grafting) and the Sulfuristes (champions of carbon disulfide).

Liquid carbon disulfide is heavier than water, it boils at 115°F (46°C) and, at normal temperatures, is transformed rapidly into a gas. The vapors are highly inflammable and a spark can cause an explosion; it was recommended that the sealed metal drums in which the liquid was delivered be stored far away from living quarters and that smoking be forbidden in their proximity.

The vines were treated twice a year, in October after the harvest and in either May, before the flowering, or midsummer, when the roots were most infested. The soil had to be loose enough to permit the penetration and the dissemination of the gas, but, to prevent its escape, the soil's surface had to be compact, from the trampling of pickers or as a result of a recent rain. The vineyard could not be hoed for at least two weeks following the treatment.

Four or five points of insertion per square yard, equidistant from the crowded vinestocks, were first traced in the vineyard where, by means of a giant syringe called a *pal*, the liquid carbon disulfide was injected to a depth of about one foot (30 cm), rapidly transforming itself into a gas which penetrated the soil in all directions. The sulfurers were followed by men carrying heavy, roundheaded sticks with which to plug the injection holes with packed earth to prevent the gas's escape.

Beginning at the turn of the century, all of the vines belonging to the Domaine de la Romanée-Conti, with the exception of Romanée-Conti itself and a portion of Richebourg, were gradually and progressively reconstituted with young vines grafted onto American rootstock, while the old vines in each climat continued to be provined and treated with carbon disulfide.

In 1942, at the time that the Société Civile du Domaine de la Romanée-Conti was formed, Edmond Gaudin de Villaine wrote:

> [Romanée-Conti] is still planted to the old French "Pinot Noir Fin" vines, rescued from phylloxera. Their renewal has always been and is still effected by

> provignage . . . a third of les Richebourgs belonging to us is still planted to old French vines . . . consequently, our Richebourgs form two cuvées . . . [one] sold under the appellation "Richebourgs Vieux Cépages," [the other] "Richebourg" . . . [the other growths belonging to the Domaine] are reconstituted on American rootstock, but the remarkable thing is that all of the grafts have always been chosen among the vines of la Romanée-Conti . . . It must, therefore, be emphasized that at present, we are the only proprietors in Burgundy who still possess old French vines, and furthermore, the only ones whose reconstitution is based on grafts of such unusual quality.

In February 1584, when Claude Cousin acquired the Cros des Cloux from the priory of Saint-Vivant, the vineyard was lying fallow. One of the conditions of the perpetual lease was that it be replanted with vines of good quality; this would have been done that spring or, at the latest, in the spring of 1585. Romanée-Conti remained on its original roots from that time until 1945. Because carbon disulfide was unavailable during the war years, the vines declined; the 1945 harvest produced only two pièces (608 bottles) of Romanée-Conti. Romanée-Conti and the pre-phylloxera vines in Richebourg were torn up in October 1945, the soil was manured, plowed, disinfected, and left fallow until 1947 (an accident in the preparation of the grafts retarded the new plantation by a year), when it was replanted to grafted vines whose cuttings were chosen in La Tâche (whose cuttings had been chosen in the old Romanée-Conti). The first vintage from the young vines was 1952.

The Vineyards Today

With the uprooting of Romanée-Conti, provignage became definitively a thing of the past. Today, the vineyards are planted in neat rows of grafted vines trained on wires, with excess growth trimmed, keeping the alleys between rows unencumbered to facilitate mechanical cultivation. Since the late fifties, after a period of cultivation with horse and plow, most of the back-breaking work of the past is accomplished by the small, high-perched, versatile *enjambeur* tractors which straddle the rows of vines. The *psou*, a short-handled, wide-bladed hoe and the *meille*, a heavier, sharply incurved, or swan-necked, two-pronged pickax are still used for shallow summer hoeing.

A vine must be made to suffer to give its best. A hectare planted to 10,000 vines and another planted to half as many will yield approximately the same quantity of grapes, but the crowded vines, which are forced to send their roots deeper in search of nourishment, will produce fewer grapes of greater concentration per vine. Legislation imposes a minimum of 10,000 vines per hectare (4,050/acre) in the Côte d'Or, which, although less than half the number cultivated under provignage, is near the maximum that can be cultivated by mechanized means. Plantations at the Domaine measure 43 inches (110 cm) between rows and 32 inches (80 cm) between vines within the rows, or approximately 11,250 vines per hectare (4,550/acre).

In order to preserve the old vines as long as possible, missing vinestocks within the rows of the Domaine's vineyards are replaced each year by grafted young vines from the nursery. When too many vinestocks are missing—usually among vines over fifty years old—the process of reconstitution begins, in limited areas and at prolonged intervals. For example, in recent years two-fifths of an acre (.16 ha) of La Tâche (which contains just over 15 acres [6 ha]), or something less than 3 percent of its population, has been replaced every four years. In Romanée-Conti, the occasional dead vinestock is torn up and replaced and, a few years ago, several rows in the parcel to the Richebourg side of the footpath were reconstituted.

AOC legislation doesn't permit grapes to be vinified for AOC wines until the vines are three years old; at the Domaine, until the vines are at least ten years old, their wine is vinified apart.

Vines to be replaced are torn up by tractor after the harvest, the soil is composted, plowed deeply, and fumigated by injections of disinfectant gas as a preventative measure against viral diseases. When time permits, the soil is leveled, the rows and the placement of the new vines are traced, and stakes against which the young vines will be trained are planted.

Among the vigneron's worries of recent years is an insidious fungus infection whose symptoms do not appear until several years after contamination. It is called eutypiose and there is no cure. It enters the vine through open cuts, usually at pruning time, when it is transferred to a healthy vine by pruning shears which have been used to prune an invisibly infected subject. Spores are also carried by wind and rain to infect fresh cuts. Visible symptoms begin with a slowing of growth while the leaves become increasingly stunted, deformed and yellow; the vine dies within a few years. At the Domaine, infected vines are marked, torn up, and destroyed during the growing season to ensure their not being inadvertently pruned in winter. Torn-up vinestock and dead fruitwood, nests of potential infection, are burned before pruning begins.

Clones and Grafts

The pinot population, confined within the boundaries of the Domaine, excepting the recent acquisition of Romanée Saint-Vivant, is the product of four centuries of evolution through selection, in combination with the ongoing process of mutation. Pinot gris and blanc mutations are most often cited as an illustration of the genetic instability of pinot noir, but in fact most mutations are invisible and much more subtle in character. Some disappear; others, whose qualities reinforce the typicality of the pinot noir ideal, are inevitably among those eventually chosen for reproduction.

If one accepts the definition of a clone as a group of genetically identical individuals reproduced by asexual means, it follows that, to the degree that the buds of the grafted vinifera cuttings are not mutant, all the vines in Burgundy are cloned. However, "clonal selection," as the term is commonly used, refers to varietal strains, developed by specialists in laboratory nurseries for specific characters—level and constancy of production, size of grape clusters, disease resistance, freedom from viruses—and reproduced on a large scale for the repopulation, alone or in combination with other selected clones, of entire vineyards. Clonal selection, in this sense, is not practiced at the Domaine de la Romanée-Conti, whose proprietors are opposed to a leveling uniformity of quality within the Domaine and to the intrusion of pinot strains from without. To explain this point of view, Lalou likens a vineyard to a village made up of many individuals with varying personality traits, all of which are essential to the complexity of the whole; no doubt, Romanée-Conti is a rather special village, whose population can only be compared to that of Versailles under the Ancien Régime, where each resident was required to trace a noble lineage back four centuries.

Until the early eighties, the Domaine practiced *sélection massale*—essentially a more homely form of *sélection clonale*—in which the origin of the parent vines lay within the vineyard of Romanée-Conti itself.

At present, the menace of viral diseases imposes a more rigid control of the vines selected for propagation, lest healthy-appearing vines be carriers. Viral diseases are not new, but it is only recently that a number of viruses have been identified, not all of which are thought to have a noticeable effect on production or quality.

The most insidious of the lot is called *court-noué*, or "short-noded," because the nodes on the vine's branches appear abnormally close together. Its English name is fanleaf virus because another of its visible characteristics is the deeply indented, fan-like form of the diseased leaves. The vine is rendered sterile and goes into decline.

For new plantations in all of the Domaine's vineyards, about fifty vines from the vineyard of Romanée-Conti have been chosen, for the perfection of their fruit and their health, for restrained production, and regularity of performance from one year to another. Each of these vines is marked with a number, and the cuttings, then the grafts, and the young plants are all marked with the number of the parent vine so that their evolution and performance in the vineyard may be followed and studied. Every autumn after the harvest, a section of a branch from each of the parent vines is sent to a specialized laboratory in Colmar for analysis to ensure its being virus-free. With the passage of time, the number of vines tested for virus and used for propagation will increase.

The American wild vines—mostly varieties of *Vitis riparia, V. rupestris,* and *V. berlandieri,* from which hybrids have been developed to create rootstocks on which to graft vinifera cuttings—come from different soils and climates, none of which resemble those of the Côte d'Or. Their adaptabilities to other soils and their affinities to pinot noir are variable. While pinot noir retains its essential qualities, the period of flowering, the vine's vigor, its susceptibility to coulure and rot, the size of its grapes, its level of production, and its moment of ripening can all be affected by the choice of rootstock. All of the wild vines are naturally more vigorous than pinot noir, a quality which, when combined with too perfect an affinity, can lead to an exuberance of foliation at the expense of fruiting. Of the three, riparia has the least affinity to vinifera vines, which imposes a restraint on the grafted vine's vigor.

Rupestris transfers the most vigor to the vinifera grafts; berlandieri tolerates soils with higher calcium content.

At the beginning of this century, most pinot noir in the Côte d'Or was grafted onto a riparia ¥ rupestris hybrid, 3 309, obtained in 1880 by Georges Couderc, one of the early researchers in hybridization. Now the Domaine prefers a more recent Couderc hybrid, 161–49 (riparia ¥ berlandieri), whose principal qualities are calcium tolerance, restrained vigor, moderate productivity, and precocious maturity.

In the winter, the Domaine receives canes of American grafting stock, guaranteed to be virus-free, in bundles of 39-inch (1 m) lengths, from specialized growers. They are soaked in water for a couple of days and layered in damp, fine, slightly earthy sand until ready for use. At about the same time, pinot canes are taken from the chosen vines in Romanée-Conti. They are cut above the first couple of eyes, and tendrils and imperfectly lignified extremities are removed. The canes are then tied into small bundles and layered in nearly dry sand at a constant temperature, much cooler than that of the American canes, to prevent any awakening of growth urges. At the moment of grafting, the rootstock canes are ready to spring into growth, whereas the vinifera canes are still dormant.

Before grafting, in early spring, the bundles of vinifera canes are stood up with their bases immersed in running water for a couple of days to recuperate any loss of moisture incurred during their stay in the sand. The rootstock canes are sectioned into approximately one-foot (30 cm) lengths. Because the roots will spring from the bottom cut, as well as from beneath each eye, the base of each section is cut directly beneath an eye to create a concentration of root growth at the base; the eyes are removed to discourage any aerial growth from the rootstock. The vinifera canes are cut into short lengths, each bearing a single eye. The base of a vinifera cutting and the upper end of a rootstock cutting of exactly the same diameter are stamped in an omega grafting press, one in the female contour, the other in the male form of the Greek letter so that, when joined, they are locked together.

The grafted cuttings, held by the rootstock ends, are dipped in disinfectant-treated melted grafting paraffin to seal the grafts before being embedded in cases of damp sawdust, which are first held at 104°F/40°C for eight to ten days, then lowered to 86°F/30°C until the graft has taken, roots begin to appear and the first leaf opens out from the vinifera bud. Before being planted in the nursery for a season's growth, they are again dipped in melted paraffin; the leaf withers and falls, but no damage is done.

V-shaped trenches, about one foot (30 cm) apart and one foot deep are dug in the nursery. The cuttings are stood, at approximately two-inch (5 cm) intervals, leaning against one side of the trench, the eyes lined up at the level of a cord stretched just above earth level. The trenches are filled with fine earth, which is packed down to the level of the graft and watered generously, and fine, sandy earth is mounded up to completely cover the grafted vinifera tips. In August this soil is dug away to the level of the graft, and any roots that may have formed above the graft are removed.

In late February or early March the plants are dug up from the nursery and their roots are trimmed. The young vines are planted, with their grafts at earth level, in holes plunged next to the stakes in the vineyard and they are mounded up in *buttées*; in their first year, they are not pruned except for the imperfectly lignified extremities of the branches.

The individual stakes, to which are affixed metal plaques stamped with the number of the parent vine, are left in place for several years to protect the young vines. After their second year in the vineyard, the vines are trained on wires during the growing season. Within the rows, after every eighth vine, stakes measuring 4-1/2 feet (1.35 m), first dipped in a protective copper sulfate solution, are planted with three feet (1 m) remaining above ground; the stake at each end of a row is planted at a bias, leaning outward from the row. The wires are attached at three levels, the lowest at one foot (30 cm) from the ground; the middle level, consisting of double wires which may be lowered or raised, at two feet (60 cm) from the ground; the top wire is attached to the tops of the stakes. After their attachment to the biased stake, the wires are joined, twisted, and attached to a heavy stone, buried well underground.

Works and Days

Taille tôt,
taille tard,
rien ne vaut
la taille de mars.
["Early pruning, late pruning,
none can equal March pruning"]

Burgundian folklore credits Saint Martin with having taught the vigneron to prune his vines (by unleashing his ass in the vineyard to eat them). Saint Martin's Day—11 November—is the age-old symbol of season's end and the beginning of a new viticultural year: the vines' leaves have fallen or are falling; the sap is descending and the vines will be dormant for four months; the wine is finished. It was on the day of Saint Martin, each year, that the vigneron of La Romanée declared the harvest to the prince de Conti and, in the following century, when Romanée-Conti was vinified in the cellars of the Clos de Vougeot, Saint Martin signaled the removal of the barrels of new wine from the vinification shed to cool cellars. On Saint Martin's Day, vignerons' contracts are issued or renewed. Winter chores begin: the first *façon,* when the earth of the vineyard is plowed between the rows and the vinestocks are mounded up; *remontage,* when eroded soil is transported to the top of the vineyard and respread among the vines; and *démontage,* when the vines are pre-pruned.

Pruning is perhaps the most exacting of vineyard chores. On the way and the care with which it is done depend the formation and the health of the vinestock, or *cep*—the gnarled and twisted trunk from which springs each year's growth—and the level of production. A good pruner joins creative intelligence, intuition, and decisiveness to an intimate familiarity with the vines, each of which must be treated as an individual.

The style of pruning is called *Guyot simple;* in the middle of the last century, Dr. Guyot recommended it to the vignerons of the Côte d'Or, who at that time rejected it. All of the year's growth is removed except for one *baguette,* or cane, which, at the Domaine, is normally pruned back to six eyes (or fewer, if the vine is lacking in vigor), and a *courson,* or spur, pruned to two eyes. After pruning, the baguette is curved outward and attached horizontally to the lowest wire. The following winter, the baguette, bearing most of the season's growth, is removed, and the two branches which have grown from the courson are pruned to a new baguette and a courson. In the interest of reforming a vine, a vigorous *gourmand,* or sucker (a branch which sprouts from an invisible eye on the rootstock, is sterile in its first year, and is usually removed during the growing season), may be saved to form the following year's courson; in this instance, only the branch chosen for a baguette is retained from the old courson.

This style of pruning keeps the rootstock low and permits the grapes to ripen close to the ground, profiting from the heat absorbed by and emanated from the earth. Fixing the baguette horizontally frustrates the rush of sap to the vine's extremities and encourages both fruiting and ripening. In principle, each branch of the baguette will bear one or two grape clusters. The vine, however, does not always respect principles; in some years, one or both of the courson's branches may bear fruit and, in others, a vine may be nearly or altogether barren.

Nowadays, pruning is accomplished in two stages. The *démontage,* or pre-pruning, may be tucked in whenever time and clement weather permit, from Saint Martin's Day until March; the démonteur uses a *sécateur coupe-cep*—long-handled pruning shears, manipulated with both hands—to remove the previous year's baguettes; at the same time, unwanted suckers which earlier may have been overlooked are removed. Another worker follows, clipping tendrils and attachments to free the branches from the wires; the pruned wood is burned and the ashes are scattered in the vineyard.

Weather permitting, the *taille,* or final pruning—the creation of the new baguette and the new courson—begins the first of March. The traditional *gouzotte,* or small billhook, which vignerons still carry and use for innumerable cleansing and trimming tasks, has been replaced by small sharp-bladed sécateurs. The important thing is a clean cut; it is usually given a slight bias—enough to direct the flow of liquid away from the bud as the sap begins to rise, but not so much as to noticeably extend the surface of the cut and increase the loss of sap.

When pruning is finished, the *enjambeur* tractor again plows between the rows of vines, but the *débuttage*—hoeing around the vinestocks to spread out the mounded-up earth—is done with the *psou.* Within the rows, used stakes are replaced and the wires are tightened.

The first *soufrages* and *sulfatages*, both effected by mechanisms attached to the enjambeur, begin in May. Their frequency throughout the summer depends on the weather and the state of the vines' health. Except for the young plantations, which are especially susceptible to mildiou and whose grapes are not picked at harvest, treatments are arrested at the beginning of August. One or two *bouéchages*—shallow digging with hand tools to weed and break up the earth's surface—are given in the course of the summer.

The Vine's Seasonal Cycle

Coinciding approximately with the spring equinox, the sap begins to rise, and the first sign of the rebirth is seen: the pruning cuts shed tears; they are called *les pleurs de la vigne*. In a year that is neither unusually precocious nor retarded, the vine's development unfolds usually in the following pattern: *débourrement* (budding), last half of March; *feuillaison* (leafing), early April; *sortie* (flower budding), late April; *floraison* (flowering), second week of June; *nouaison* (setting of the fruit), mid-June to mid-August; *véraison* and *aoûtement* (beginning of ripening of the fruit and lignification of the branches), second week of August.

As the sap rises, the latent eyes formed during the previous season begin to swell. Each protective husk splits open and the bud emerges; the first leaf opens out. As the tender shoot unfurls, a leaf appears, first to one side, then to the other, with a tendril forming to the opposite side of the node. At the axil of each leaf stem, an embryonic latent eye forms. A secondary latent eye, called a replacement bud, because often it develops only if the primary latent eye is destroyed by frost or otherwise injured, sometimes develops at the same time as the primary eye, causing two branches to sprout from the same axil the following year. Finally, a non-latent eye, or prompt bud, often opens out during the immediate growing season, issuing a sterile, parasitic branch from the same axil which harbors the primary and secondary eyes.

The first tendrils to appear are sterile. It is usually at the appearance of the fourth and fifth leaves that their opposite tendrils form flower buds, resembling minuscule grape clusters, on the fruiting branches.

A gentle breeze encourages correct pollination. If during the flowering the air is still, nature is given a helping hand by a soufrage, the breeze caused by blowing sulfur powder onto the vines. If, in addition, the weather is warm, with no extremes of temperature, no rains or violent wind, the flowering should pass rapidly and well; in difficult weather, it may drag for weeks and there is usually a high percentage of coulure, millerandage, and *grappillons*—grapes which, because of tardy flowering, will not ripen in time for harvest.

For two months the vine continues to luxuriate, thrusting forth leaf after leaf, and, with no noticeable alteration in their chemical structure, the green grapes grow, their chlorophyll permitting them to feed on the air as well as from the soil. Suddenly, growth comes to a near halt, and, from one day to another, scattered grapes begin to turn color; at the same time, the supple green branches begin to show signs of hardening and darkening in color at their bases. Henceforth, all of the vine's energies are devoted to ripening both the new wood and the grapes, whose acidity diminishes as their sugar content rises; the leaves, from which the grapes draw their sugar, often curl and partially wilt under the strain. About six weeks after the first violet blush, around the autumn equinox, the grapes are ready to be picked.

The tasks specifically related to the cycle of the vine are: *ébourgeonement* or *évasivage* (spring pruning), in May, after flower budding but before flowering; *accolage* (attaching the young branches to wires), in June, after the flowering; *rognage* (summer pruning), late June to mid-August; removal of grappillons, July to September.

A vine's general structure and comportment is determined by winter pruning, but the vine is always in revolt against the constraints imposed upon it. From invisible eyes, beneath the bark of the vinestock, spring parasitic shoots; nearly imperceptible eyes at the bases of the baguette and the courson can sprout other unwanted, sterile shoots. The secondary latent eyes sometimes cause double-budding, producing unexpected branches, which are often fertile and overload the vine. All of this growth robs the predetermined fruiting branches of precious nourishment and must be removed while the shoots are sufficiently tender to be easily snapped off at the nascent points without harming the vine.

At the Domaine, it is felt that six to eight grape clusters represent the ideal load for a mature vine; in certain years—1982, for example—when the number of flowerbud clusters promises an unusually heavy load, the terminal, or sixth branch on the baguette is also snapped off during spring pruning.

Except for a possible soufrage, all work in the vineyard is suspended during the flowering. The sweet, delicately acrid fragrance of the flowers loosens tongues, inspiring a lyrical eloquence in all whose lives are bound up in the vineyard.

After flowering, the vine's growth becomes increasingly rapid, the branches often lengthening by two or three inches (5–8 cm) daily; they are then long enough and strong enough to be directed without snapping. They are first trained between the double, middle wires; those that refuse to stay in place are attached with fragments of rush, first soaked in water to render them more supple. After a few days and a few more inches' growth, each branch is tied loosely to the top wire with rush; the tendrils begin immediately to wind round any wire or neighboring growth that they touch, fixing the branches firmly in place.

The vine's tendency is to nourish its extremities at the expense of the fruit. By the end of June, the constantly unfurling branches begin to clutter the alleys and to tumble from above the top wire. The large, fully developed leaves will furnish sugar to the grapes as they begin to ripen, but the newly formed and forming leaves drain the vine of sap which can more profitably serve the grapes if its trip to the extremities is cut short.

Rognage consists in cutting back the new growth to a height of about four feet (1.2 m) and trimming it to the sides to free the passage. The first rognage is executed by hand with a *cisaille* (long-bladed shears); during the following month and a half, the enjambeur, fitted with horizontal and vertical blades, passes three or four times, trimming back the growth. For aesthetic reasons, the enjambeur's work is completed with a cisaille, refining the clean, rectangular hedge shape of the rows.

When flowering is prolonged for several weeks because of difficult weather, the last flowers to be pollinated produce grapes that will not ripen in time for the harvest. Sometimes, also, a freakish scattering of flowers occurs, after the main flowering is finished, from which issue small straggly clusters of grappillons. When time permits, from mid-July until a week or so before the harvest, the vignerons pass through the vines, picking and discarding verjus clusters and grappillons and, if the harvest promises to be too abundant, normally maturing clusters as well.

THE WINE

VI

THE PRINCE DE Conti's Romanée was quite different from today's Romanée-Conti. A very short *cuvaison,* or vatting, and a proportion of white grapes—about 20 percent pinot blanc—were considered fundamental to its finesse. The prince's steward, Margue, was sharply critical of La Romanée 1780 for having been vatted too long, which, at that time, could have been no more than a few days. Margue raised La Romanée in barrels for at least three years before bottling, after which he figured that one should not begin drinking it for another fifteen to eighteen months; today, the sacrifice of a bottle of four-or-five-year-old Romanée-Conti is condemned as infanticide.

The principle, then, was to obtain a brilliant vermilion color while vatting the grapes for the shortest possible time; the fermentation was finished in the barrels. On the day of picking, the vat was filled with the uncrushed bunches of grapes, the surface was leveled and they were left overnight. An eighteenth-century manuscript, cited by Vergnette-Lamotte (*Le Vin,* 1868), described two ways of proceeding. In one method, a nude man entered the vat early the next morning, and trampled the grapes for an hour or two. Eventually, a mass of skins and stems would be forced above the surface of the fermenting must, and held there by the pressure of escaping carbon dioxide. When this cap, or *chapeau,* was formed and the liquid beneath was a rich red, the pomace, or marc, was brought to the wine press and its juices were poured over it. The preferred method, however, was to send two strong, vigorous men in to trample for four or five hours, without respite. "It is up to them to crush every single grape . . . they don't leave the vat until all of the grapes are reduced to liquor." As soon as the chapeau was formed, the grapes were sent to the press. The author noted that these instructions would be for a hot year; in a cold year, instead of leaving the grapes for from twelve to fifteen hours in the vat, two or three tramplings would be necessary and the grapes would have to remain in the vat for up to thirty-six hours. Were it not for the prolonged trampling, this would be a rosé vinification.

Fifty years later, Morelot wrote:

> The most important thing for our wines is to seize the precise instant of *décuvage* [devatting], so that the wine is fermented no more than absolutely necessary . . . if the season has been hot, the fermentation begins after a few hours and the vat is ready to be emptied within twenty-four to thirty-six hours; on the other hand, when the weather is cold, fermentation doesn't begin until the third or fourth day and the wine is drawn off on the sixth day. Years have been known when the grapes remained in the vats until the eighth and even the tenth day: fortunately these years are rare, for this is always a bad omen for the quality of wine.

In the mid-nineteenth century, according to Guyot, the wines at the Clos de Vougeot, where Romanée-Conti was vinified, were drawn off the vats after four or five days, "troubled and hot" [troubles et chauds], to finish their fermentation in new barrels. A couple of decades later, eight to twelve days were a normal vatting period.

Ouvrard's reign in the Côte d'Or spanned a period during which the red wines deepened in color and gathered more tannin. He was the first to begin progressively eliminating pinot blanc from his vineyards. By 1845, the pinot blanc population had been reduced from one-fifth to one-fifteenth. (Dr. Lavalle lamented the disappearance of pinot blanc and pinot gris from the top growths, in the interest of obtaining wines that were "more deeply colored and harder." However, he asked, "Is it not at the cost of finesse and bouquet?"

At this time, the wines at the Clos de Vougeot were aged in barrels for as long as four or five years. Vergnette-Lamotte, observing that, in Belgium, the same wines were bottled after fifteen months in barrels, wrote, "This wine leaves a very light prickle on the palate, known in Belgium as a fermentation taste; this taste is not disagreeable to the Belgians. It must be admitted that, in that condition, the wines have a very remarkable bouquet and, since, furthermore, they retain a pronounced fruit, it is certainly in Belgium that one finds the finest and the most highly scented of wines." Of the bottling practice at the Clos de Vougeot, he admits that the wines, after four years in barrels, are "cleaner . . . But, they are also drier, possess less finesse, less vitality above all, and have a less developed bouquet than the wines treated by the Belgian method."

The Wine Today

Burgundy wine has always been defined in terms of finesse. The following figures emphasize a changing concept of finesse and the radically different methods used to obtain it:

	Proportion of white grapes	Ideal cuvaison period	Barrel aging period
The Prince de Conti's Romanée	20%	12–36 hours	3 years
Ouvrard's Romanée-Conti	6%	4–5 days	4–5 years
Today's Romanée-Conti	0%	2–3 weeks	1 1/2–2 years

The way in which wine is made depends on the potential of the terroir and on the kind of wine one wants to make. In the Côte d'Or, stemmed grapes and short cuvaisons often produce supple, fruity wines which may be pleasant to drink when four or five years old, but which, on the whole, lack dimension and do not age well. It is the Domaine's intention to produce the longest lived and the most complexly structured wines of Burgundy, which express perfectly their terroirs of origin. Their philosophy of winemaking sounds deceptively simple: after first extracting the maximum of the grapes' and the stems' constituents through a prolonged cuvaison, it consists in protecting the wine from harmful influences and permitting it to make itself, with as little manipulation as possible; racking, or *soutirage*—drawing the clear wine from one barrel to another to separate it from its lees—is kept to a minimum and filtering is avoided. Because each vintage is different, and the weather and the balance of structural components are variable, the wine's requirements change from year to year. The conductor's experience must be complemented by sensibility and intuition.

THE VENDANGES

Grapes are considered to be physiologically ripe when their stems and pips turn from green to brown and the plant ceases to nourish the grapes, each of which can then be detached from the stem with no resistance. In a hot year, the grape sugars may continue to concentrate by dehydration; the grapes wither and are said to be *figués,* like ripe figs that wither on the tree. A proportion of *raisins figués* is a good thing, on condition that the acid balance does not fall too low. Different degrees of ripeness, the result of a difficult and prolonged flowering, can produce wines of greater complexity.

THE BAN DE VENDANGES

For the six centuries before the Revolution, the imposition of the *ban de vendanges,* or picking ban, was a seigneurial right. Its principle purpose was to ensure a maximum quality to the wine by preventing grapes from being picked too early (each year, the date was determined from reports following official visits to the vineyards to check the degree of maturity of the grapes). A proclamation, published several days in advance of the date before which it was forbidden to pick, would serve to notify the pickers, who descended on the Côte in hoards from outlying regions. The Seigneur, whether a person, a municipality, or a house of prayer, as well as proprietors whose vineyards were enclosed within walls, had the right to harvest on the day preceding the ban and to pay lower wages to the pickers. Others who attempted to pick early were severely punished.

With the Revolution, seigneurial rights disappeared, but the councillor general of the commune was granted the right to impose a ban de vendanges on all vines which were not contained within walls. (To escape the strictures of the ban, many vignerons enclosed their vines within "walls" built of old stakes, branches, and similar debris.)

Under the Consulate and the Empire, and until the end of the Restoration, the ban de vendanges was reinstated in full force and strictly policed, the seigneurs of old being replaced by the most important vineyard proprietors of the Côte. Despite the attempts of the owners of the greatest growths to maintain the ban, the system declined into a more democratic process after 1830. By the end of the century, it was an optional formality. Today, in the Côte d'Or, the ban de vendanges, applicable to AOC wines, has returned in the form of an annual prefectural decision published a week or so before the opening dates (usually earlier in the Côte de Beaune than in the Côte de Nuits). A grower who picks without authorization before the published date theoretically risks losing his right to the AOC.

Following in Duvault-Blochet's footsteps, the Domaine normally begins picking, depending on the vintage, from several days to a week later than the official ban de vendanges. (Twenty and thirty years ago, it was not uncommon for the Domaine to begin picking when most other growers had finished. Today, many pick later.) Picking most often begins the first week of October, occasionally earlier or, in difficult years, it may fall as late as 20 October; it lasts from six to twelve days.

Three weeks to a month before the opening of the vendanges, the cellar staff begins to prepare the *cuverie*, or vatting shed, which houses ten oak vats and eight of stainless steel. (Although Lalou and Aubert both confirm the perfect performance of stainless steel, Romanée-Conti has its own oval, thirty-pièce wooden vat, partly because the stainless-steel vats are too large to be practical for such a small harvest, but no doubt also because of an underlying sentiment that Romanée-Conti should be permitted to contact only traditional material.) The wooden vats, which, following the last year's vintage, had been simply scrubbed out with the wine remaining in them, leaving a protective layer of tartar, are washed out each morning with strong jets of cold water and emptied each evening; this is the *abreuvage*. On the day before receiving the grapes, they are cleansed with jets of hot water; the apparition of Bernard Noblet emerging, radiant, amid billows of steam, from Romanée-Conti's vat, the image of a benevolent deity, presages the excitement of the vendanges, the elation of partaking creatively in an age-old mystical ritual, which infects the entire staff.

In addition to the Domaine's twenty permanent vignerons, some fifty vendangeurs arrive. About thirty, from horizons more distant than the immediate villages, are lodged at the Domaine. Most return every year.

The day before picking begins, the caterer arrives from Dijon to set up the kitchens and to make up his menus for the week or so to come. At lunch each day, there will be approximately a hundred people, including the men from the cuverie. Those who are lodged at the Domaine are also served the evening meal, and each morning at nine o'clock the kitchen sends cold cuts, cheeses, bread, and wine to the vines for the pickers' morning *casse-croûte* snack break. Lunches are hearty, rustic, and bounteous. Before the shuffle of the arrival en masse at the stroke of noon, the tables are laden with platters and terrines of pâtés, sausages, ham, salads, and crudités; the wine matches the food and is drunk *à volonté* from tumblers. Next, simple roasts and their garnishes alternate with *daubes, estouffades, bourguignons, coqs-au-vin*. Most beautiful of all is the *grande potée,* symbol of abundance. The women file into the dining room from the kitchen bearing huge platters heaped high with everything, cured or fresh, that is most succulent in a pig—sausages, petit-salé, shoulders, hocks, and ears—steaming, straight from the great marmites. More women follow with mountains of braised and quartered cabbages, root vegetables, and beans. Green salads, cheese platters, pastries, puddings, or ice creams and fruits precede the coffee. The atmosphere in the dining room is high-spirited, often boisterous. On the last menu, La Paulée, a celebration of vendanges' end and the birth of the new wine, the chef lavishes special care, adding more elaborate preparations.

The grapes may be more or less advanced in a given growth, depending on the vintage; there is no hierarchy to the order in which the growths are picked. Romanée-Conti is picked in a half-day and the day of picking is often a last-minute decision.

The pickers, or *coupeurs,* are limited to sixty, the number necessary to ensure a regular but not too rapid flow to the cuverie. Each coupeur is equipped with a small basket, or *vendangerot,* and a small sharp-pointed *sécateur,* which serves both to clip the grape cluster from the vine and to clip out any imperfect grapes. Any grappillons which may have been overlooked in previous *tris,* or selections, are left on the vines.

The vendangeurs are separated into groups, composed of a leader, a dozen coupeurs, the tractor driver, and two men on, or beside, the tractor platform. As the vendangerots are filled, the coupeurs pass them from one to another, across the rows, to the two tractor attendants. The *enjambeur* tractor is fitted with a high platform on which are piled large baskets which, when filled, will be stacked in a criss-cross fashion to make certain that all the grapes arrive intact and uncrushed at the cuverie. The size of the baskets permits an even distribution of the grapes on the conveyor belt for the final tri. (On average, eight or nine of these baskets, or approximately 660 pounds (300 kg) of grapes are necessary to produce one pièce of wine—over 2 pounds (1 kg) to a bottle.) The two attendants empty the vendangerots into the large baskets and pass them back.

The sight of these slow, measured processions, interspersed among the vines, of tractors surrounded by workers in multicolored accents of dress, touches chords of emotion which cannot be explained by the mere beauty or the folkloric charm of the thing.

Before entering the cuverie, the large baskets are transferred to a dray, on which the empty baskets had been previously weighed, and they are wheeled onto the village scales to record the weight of the grapes. In the cuverie, the two attendants gradually tumble the grapes from each basket onto a slow-moving, white conveyor belt, twenty feet (6 m) long and lighted overhead, to either side of which five or six men, each with a bucket to his side and a sécateur in hand, perform the final tri, removing stray grappillons and leaf fragments and clipping damaged grapes or those affected by gray rot from the healthy bunches. The grapes pass onto a troughlike escalator which feeds them into the vat through a crusher with widely separated, dentate, stainless-steel rollers sheathed in rubber, leaving a large proportion unbroken. They are not stemmed, except in rare instances when, for instance, the stems have been damaged by hail.

Vinification

All of the color and many of the aromatic elements in the pinot noir grape, as in any noble red variety, are imprisoned within the cellular structure of the inner lining of the grape skin; they are released, progressively, as the cellular structure is broken down by the combined actions of carbon dioxide, the mounting degree of alcohol, and the heat generated during the fermentation process. Pinot noir is jealous of its color and requires greater attention to temperature than most grape varieties for a maximum extraction.

Tannin forms the architectural skeleton of any red wine whose vocation is to evolve beyond the stage of a fresh, fruity drink; it holds the wine together. Because tannin is an antioxidant, it permits a wine to remain fresh and age with grace, unveiling hidden complexities. It combines with the pigmentation to fix the color, much of which is, otherwise, unstable, and it is a clarifying agent, helping to precipitate solids out of suspension during the wine's sojourn in barrels.

The grapes' tannins are drawn from the stems, the skins, and the pips. Initially, the tannin from the stems is the most astringent of the three, but as a wine ages, the molecular structure of the tannins becomes more complex and the astringency disappears. A maximum extraction of these tannins demands a prolonged maceration, which in turn imposes a slowed-down fermentation at relatively low temperatures. The Domaine's system of vinification is conceived to satisfy the contradictory requirements for maximum extractions of color and tannins.

THE FERMENTATION

Among the microorganisms clinging to the bloom—the misty, waxlike film which veils the skins of ripe grapes—is a dense population of indigenous yeasts; they also inhabit the cuverie. It is the action of these yeasts which will turn sticky, sweet grape juice into an ethereal nectar, whose weight, for an identical volume, is diminished by one-tenth.

The alcoholic fermentation, in simplified terms, consists in the transformation of the grape sugars—as the yeasts feed on them (eliminating a small portion) and rapidly multiply—into approximately equal parts of alcohol and carbon dioxide, plus minute quantities of glycerol and several different acids.

At 50°F (10°C) the yeasts are dormant; at 59°F (15°C) they are sluggish. Up to a certain point the intensity of yeast reproduction and the rapidity of the transformation of the sugars into alcohol increase with the temperature; beyond that point, the yeasts stop reproducing, the fermentation slows down, and it may stop before all of the sugars have been transformed into alcohol. The danger point is considered to be 95°F (35°C); the safe point beyond which it is unwise to venture, 90°F (32°C).

The course of the fermentation in each vat is charted on a graph on which is recorded, three times daily, the temperature and the density of the must. The density of a liquid is defined in terms of its weight per liter, 1,000 grams representing a liter of water at 59°F (15°C). Unfermented must is heavier than water; the finished wine is lighter. Seventeen to eighteen grams of sugar are necessary to produce one degree of alcohol in a red wine. Must with an alcohol potential of from 11.5° to 12.5° will contain from 210 to 225 grams of sugar per liter and its density will be from 1,090 to 1,096; the density of the finished wine, containing two grams or less of sugar, will be about 995.

The fermentation is conducted in an open vat "with floating cap" (*à chapeau flottant*). If the vat is of wood, its inside surfaces are sterilized by splashing a bucket of heated eau-de-vie de marc about and igniting it before introducing the grapes. The vat is filled to within 1-1/2 feet (45 cm) or less from the brim, thus leaving space for volume increase during fermentation and for a protective layer of carbon dioxide to hover over the surface. An antiseptic solution of sulfur dioxide, a protection against acetic bacteria, is added. It is also an antioxidant, it eliminates some of the less useful yeasts, leaving the field open for the resistant and prolific sugar yeasts (*Saccharomyces*), and, in collusion with the large proportion of uncrushed grapes, it slows down the early stages of fermentation. A *remontage* is practiced immediately, in which the juices are pumped up from the bottom of the vat over the surface, mixing up, equalizing and aerating the mass. Each remontage lasts for about ten minutes.

Whenever possible, the grapes are first macerated for five or six days at less than 59°F (15°C), with twice-daily remontages, to supply the yeasts with oxygen and to protect the surface from bacterial alteration. In the climate of the Côte no particular control is necessary to maintain the vats at this temperature in most years; grapes picked in October rarely surpass 59°F (15°C) and, at this temperature, a five-to-six-day period before active fermentation sets in is normal. In hot or very cold years, a *drapeau*—a serpentine construction of stainless-steel tubes through which cold or hot water can be run—may be thrust into the heart of the vat's contents to lower or to raise the temperature. In a hot year when the vendanges are precocious, the yeasts' activity often cannot be easily restrained and the fermentation must be permitted to run its course, the temperature rising rapidly after the second day.

As the temperature rises, the tough, spongelike chapeau swells above the turbulent liquid and the remontages are replaced by *pigeages*, in which, traditionally, men break up and immerse the chapeau by a combination of trampling and ramming with plungers during the first days. Later, when the must has reached 60°F (27°C) or so, and the chapeau is less resistant, nude men enter the vats, trampling and treading, often sinking in up to their chests. Romanée-Conti and the other growths which are fermented in wooden vats are still treated in this way. In 1989, the Domaine introduced mechanical pigeage, which, insofar as possible, imitates the actions of the human foot, for use in the stainless-steel vats where, because of their size, traditional pigeage was difficult to realize. The pigeages take place twice daily and last for fifteen to twenty minutes in each vat. Like the remontages, these repeated churnings and immersions protect the surface from acetic bacteria; they aerate the mass, reactivating the yeasts, while equalizing and dispersing the heat; they thrust the solids back in to be macerated; and the kneading friction exercised on the grape skins helps to extract the color.

When the temperature beneath the chapeau approaches 90°F (32°C), the contents of the vat are cooled back to about 80°F (27°C) and the temperature is again permitted to rise, this time leveling off usually at around 90°F (32°C) and gradually descending as the last sugars are fermented out. It is at this point that the first intervention to prolong the fermentation takes place.

CHAPTALIZATION

The addition of sugar to the must to raise the degree of alcohol, *chaptalization,* takes its name from Chaptal, Napoleon's minister of the interior, who recommended the procedure. It was a controversial subject during the last century. Today, in the Burgundian climate, it is considered to be necessary in most years, when practiced with discretion, to produce a stable, well-balanced wine with finesse, a potential for longevity, and a resistance to the fatigue of long journeys. To the winemakers of the Domaine, it is an integral element in the system of vinification, considered not at all as a necessary evil but as a positive virtue, for it permits them to control the last stages of fermentation, prolonging the maceration to extract a maximum of tannins. The law permits the addition of sugar to raise the alcohol content by two degrees; the Domaine, whose natural sugar readings tend to be high, thanks to privileged climats, the age of the vines, limited production, and late picking, usually chaptalizes to the extent of about one degree. About a barrel of must is drawn from the vat into a rectangular container, then refined white sugar is pushed back and forth in it by two men, with flat wooden spades, until the sugar is dissolved. The sweetened must is pumped into the heart of the vat's contents, and it is further dispersed by a remontage. The sugar is never added until the density of the must has descended to between 1,010 and 1,000; it is then added in small amounts, at spaced periods, to tease the yeasts two or three times into renewed activity.

Finally, as the temperature declines, the chapeau disintegrates, skins and stems settling to the bottom of the vat, and a tarpaulin is thrown across the top to prevent the escape of the protective layer of carbon dioxide during the last couple of days. When the fermentation is completely finished and the density has stabilized at 995 or less, the wine is drawn off, still warm (about 73°F/23°C) into another vat (maceration is never prolonged after the end of the fermentation, because of the danger in an open vat of contamination by acetic bacteria). The residue, or marc, is given a single, light pressing in a horizontal, pneumatic press exerting two kilograms of pressure per square centimeter. The pressed wine, richer in tannin but lower in alcohol content, is assembled with the free-run wine in the vat and drawn by gravity—the gentlest way of displacing a wine—into the new barrels, which have been installed in one of the two cellars lying beneath the cuverie (the alternate cellar harbors the wine of the previous vintage). The wine will remain in barrels for from eighteen months to almost two years, depending on the vintage's natural inclination to evolve and to clarify.

The Barrels

The wines of the Domaine are raised in new oak barrels. The barrels contact no wine except that of the growth for which they are destined. After the wine is bottled, they are sold to other growers. In a solidly built wine with depth and a future, the taste of new oak never dominates, and it vanishes completely in the wake of an expanding bouquet and palate long before the wine is ready to drink. For the wines of the Domaine, the virtues of new oak are simple: noblesse oblige; virgin oak carries no memories of other wines; the oak's tannin lends support to the grapes' tannins and, at the same time, it acts as a precipitant of impurities in suspension, hastening and improving the natural clarification of the wine and stabilizing the color.

The wood comes from France's finest oak forest, the Forêt de Tronçais (Allier), where the combination of terroir and close plantations produces tall, slender trees with an especially fine-grained wood. Each winter, the cooper, François, visits the splitter in La Charité-sur-Loire to choose the hand-split staves (*merrains*), which are transported to his atelier in Saint-Romain, near Meursault, to be dried by weathering outdoors for three years before being formed into barrels. When the barrels are made, the staves are heated no more than necessary to permit their being forced into shape; they are not "toasted." Before receiving the new wine, the barrels are rinsed out with tepid-to-hot water, to which has been added a bit of coarse salt, which draws out superficial tannin.

The wine needs oxygen to evolve normally and to gain strength for a long bottle life. This is furnished by a slow breathing through the pores of the wood and, eventually, by the deep breath of a racking. Direct contact with air at the wine's surface exposes it to the dangers of oxidation and bacterial attack; the barrels must always be kept filled to the precise level of the bunghole.

Wines from the different growths to be used for topping up are kept in small stainless-steel tanks fitted with adjustable lids which prevent air from contacting the wine's surface. During a wine's first four months, the barrels are topped up twice weekly, henceforth once a week. Barrels from which wine is drawn for tastings are marked by placing a pebble on each barrel and topped up immediately afterward. Before a barrel is topped up, it is struck several times with a wooden mallet to chase out the carbon dioxide with which young wines are saturated. The barrels are kept hermetically sealed by placing a circle of jute canvas over the bunghole and pounding the wooden bung into it; each time a barrel is topped up, the canvas circle is replaced by a new one.

THE SECONDARY FERMENTATION

The wine is not stable and apt not to age correctly until it undergoes a subsequent bacterial fermentation, known as malolactic fermentation, very different in nature from the alcoholic fermentation. It is, in effect, a natural deacidification in which the malic acid contained in the wine is broken down by the action of lactic bacteria into lactic acid and carbon dioxide gas. The bacteria are fragile and capricious: they can support no trace of sulfur dioxide, their activity is frustrated by the presence of yeasts, tartaric acid, and alcohol but their requirements are not well understood. In some years the malolactic fermentation takes off spontaneously and is finished by the beginning of December; in others, it may come to a standstill and pick up again in the spring, or its beginnings may be retarded until spring. It is often recommended that cellars be heated to hasten the malolactic fermentation. However, because heating alters the natural humidity of a cellar, drying out the surfaces of the barrels, and because, in their experience, finer wines are produced when the malolactic fermentation follows a natural evolution without provocation by heat, the winemakers of the Domaine eschew that path. The wine is always left on its lees and never treated with sulfur dioxide until the malolactic fermentation is finished, which can be best verified by laboratory analysis.

The wine is kept on its lees for as long as possible. It is tasted weekly to check its progress. Usually a single racking, which may take place in the spring or, often, in the autumn following the vintage, is all that is necessary.

COLLAGE

Collage, or fining, is done six to eight weeks before bottling. The red wines are fined with egg-white: for each barrel, about four very fresh whites (an average of some 1,200 eggs in all) are whisked—with a pinch of salt and some of the wine—until foamy, poured into the barrel, and whipped into the wine with a *dodine*—a long-handled stainless-steel device with, at a right angle, an elongated, perforated, blade-like foot. Slowly the albumin of the egg whites attracts any solids in suspension and they fall, together, to the bottom of the barrel.

BOTTLING

In the past, the wine was drawn from each barrel, directly off its *colle,* or fining agent (which now lies at the bottom of the barrel along with the solids drawn out of suspension), into bottles. Since 1985, in order to eliminate the slight variations which sometimes evolve from one barrel to another, as well as the variations which may exist at different levels of an undisturbed barrel, five or six barrels at a time are first drawn off their colle—gently, by atmospheric pressure—into a small stainless-steel vat. From here the wine is drawn, again by gravity, into bottles.

The Domaine's classic, old-fashioned, slope-shouldered and rigidly straight-sided Burgundy bottle is instantly recognizable by the solidity and the dignity of its form: it stands three-quarters of a centimeter taller than other Burgundy bottles today, its punt is slightly deeper and its weight varies from 29 to 30 ounces (820–840 g), in contrast to the standard modern Burgundy bottle, whose weight is about 21.7 ounces (620 g). The color is a deep earth green, designated professionally as *feuille morte antique* (the Montrachet bottle is a much clearer version of the same color). A bottle contains 25.5 fluid ounces (75 cl). There are no half bottles. An average of 8–10 percent of the red wines exist in larger formats: magnum (double bottle), jeroboam (double magnum) and methuselah (eight bottles). In addition to 5,852 bottles of Romanée-Conti 1988, for instance, there were 149 magnums, 36 jeroboams, and 18 methuselahs. About 5 percent of the Montrachet harvest is put into magnums.

The best cork comes from Spain or Portugal; it is in short supply and great demand. The Domaine maintains a continuous search to obtain the finest-quality corks available. During the bottling of the 1988 Romanée-Conti, I spirited one away for further study: it is a lovely object, a minor work of art, compact, with a smooth, velvety surface and a hardly perceptible grain—the natural perforations in the structure of the cork bark are mere pinpoints. It measures 2-1/8 inches (53 mm) in length and 1 inch (25 mm) in diameter (which will be compressed to 3/4 inches [20 mm] within the bottle neck). An engraving of the vineyard of Romanée-Conti and the cross which stands as its symbol embellishes the brand.

At the time of bottling, the corks are first soaked in hot water—not so hot that one may not dip a finger in it. If the water is not hot enough, it will not render the corks sufficiently supple to be compressed in the corking machine; if it is too hot, it will impair the cork's resilience. The corking machine is designed to create a vacuum in the neck of the bottle before forcing in the cork, leaving no trace of air.

The bottles are not labeled and capsuled until they are brought up from the cellars for expedition, when each is wrapped, first in a protective sheet of fine tissue, then in an insulatory sleeve of excelsior, before being packed into wooden cases.

THE WHITE WINE

The chardonnay grapes are nearly always among the last to be picked. The Montrachet and the Bâtard-Montrachet harvests are picked in an afternoon; to keep the grapes intact, they are transported in small crates from the vineyards to the cuverie in Vosne, pressed immediately, treated lightly with sulfur dioxide to protect them against acetic bacteria, and left to settle for several hours before being run into barrels to ferment. The barrels are not completely filled, a certain amount of space being necessary to nourish the yeasts with oxygen and to prevent the fermenting must from overflowing; as the fermentation slows down, the barrels are progressively filled. Chaptalization doesn't provide the extra benefits that it brings to the red wine vinification; because chardonnay has a naturally higher sugar content than pinot noir and, in most years, the glucometer readings indicate a potential alcohol content of 13° or more, the white wines are rarely chaptalized. Because heat loss is much greater in barrels than in large vats, the temperature never rises above 64–68°F (18–20°C) and need not be controlled. The alcoholic fermentation may last for as much as a month or more and the malolactic fermentation for up to a year. The lees are said to nourish the wine; they are periodically churned up with a dodine, facilitating both the alcoholic and the malolactic fermentations. Once the malolactic fermentation is finished, the Domaine considers that nothing is to be gained by keeping the white wine in barrels. The wines are racked, then fined: instead of egg whites, the white wines are fined by the addition of milk, whose casein acts as a precipitant to the lighter sediment of a white wine. Bernard Noblet picks the milk up from a nearby farm, fresh from the cow and separated from its cream, to be used immediately. A small amount, three to four fluid ounces (9–12 cl) per barrel, is injected by force into the wine with a *pompe à colle*—a long, conical tube, perforated at the tip and fitted with a plunger. Three to four weeks later, the wine is drawn off its colle, assembled five or six barrels at a time, and bottled.

FROM CELLAR TO TABLE

VII

THE DOMAINE'S WINES are cellared until approximately thirty months after the vendanges before being released, that is to say, six months to a year after bottling the red wines and about a year and a half after bottling the Montrachet; the 1992s were shipped in January 1995 and the '93s will be released early in 1996.

However exhilarating it may be to taste the wild, dense fruit of these wines when young, they need, depending on the growth and on the vintage, eight, ten, fifteen years or more in a good cellar to tame down—to reveal civilized bouquets whose dimension and nuance will unfold with the passage of time. Often, before beginning to open out, a wine closes up, fresh fruit waning to reveal, undisguised, the uninviting tannic skeleton while no hint of future opulence is apparent; in some instances, this dumb period can persist for several years. Wines evolve more slowly and more perfectly in a cold cellar. The Domaine's cuverie and the cellars beneath it—the *caves d'élevage*, in which the wines are raised in barrels—are a couple of blocks of houses distant from the courtyard and the other buildings of the Domaine, beneath which lie the *caves de vieillissement* (aging cellars), which house the most recently bottled vintage, remaining stocks from previous vintages and the private reserves in the *vinothèque*, whose treasures span eighty years.47

Serious wine merchants have good cellars; for the private individual who intends to lay down these wines, it is nonetheless wise to obtain them as soon as possible after they have left the Domaine's cellars and to offer them a home of similar quality for the years or decades to follow. A good cellar should be relatively humid and it should smell clean; a vent and a chimney will provide the necessary circulation of air. The ideal temperature is said to be 53.6°F (12°C), which, according to many, should be absolutely constant. In my experience, a gradual and circumscribed temperature variation from winter to summer, falling approximately within the limits of 50-57°F (10-14°C), is not a serious fault—may, in fact, be a good thing, for I believe that wine lives with and reacts to the seasons.

WINE SERVICE

It is a mistake to serve the wines of the Domaine at room temperature. Wine should be refreshing. To be so, it must be cooler than room temperature; how much cooler depends on the color, the origin, the vintage, and the age of the wine, the stage of its evolution and the time of year. Too cold, a wine is paralyzed, the tannins of a red wine harshened; too warm, it falls out of balance, acidity and alcohol becoming aggressive, and one has the impression of smelling and tasting the different components separated out from one another.

Complex wine of a certain age should perhaps be drunk less cool than simpler wines, drunk younger—but, a wine served somewhat cooler than its ideal temperature will rapidly warm up and open out in a glass, whereas a wine poured too warm will never cool down. A wine served at 60°F (16°C) of a summer evening may seem cooler than the same wine served at 57°F (14°C) in a comfortably heated room during the winter. For lunches at the Domaine, Bernard Noblet brings the wines up from the cellar just before the meal is served. Montrachet is served at cellar temperature; by the time the red wines are poured, they are, at a guess, close to 57-59°F (14-15°C).

Because capsules are damaged and labels disintegrate in the humidity of a good cellar, bottles are never labeled and capsuled until just before their expedition; those served at the Domaine arrive at table undressed, their only identification being that of the cellar bins or racks from which they are taken and the brands on the corks. There are no cradles and no decanters; Burgundians do not decant their wines. A wine needs to breathe for its bouquet and its palate to expand, but red Burgundies, especially old red Burgundies, are more rapidly subject to oxidation and alteration, in prolonged contact with air, than any other wine. It is safer to wait for the wine to open out in the glasses than to risk alteration or fading through decantation. Old bottles, which are expected to contain sediment, are set upright in the cellar the preceding day so that the sediment, which has collected on the bottom side of the horizontal bottle, will slip down into that side of the punt. To serve, the bottle is held from the opposite side and the wine poured with a minimum of back and forth movement, no flourish and no twisting.

Except for a half-dozen tulips at each place setting, prepared to receive a half-dozen of Burgundy's most magical wines, there is no outward indication that these lunches are in any way extraordinary; they are, essentially, informal work sessions, concentrated on tasting wines. The menu is always simple; its most important role is not to interfere with tasting. The meal often opens with a Montrachet and there is often a red wine theme—a "vertical" tasting of a number of different vintages of a single growth or a "horizontal" tasting of all the Domaine's red growths in a single vintage, with a venerable Romanée-Conti, La Tâche, or Richebourg to accompany the cheeses. The formula depends, to a certain extent, on the guests.

Any wine glass is good, provided that the circumference of its rim is slightly smaller than that of its midsection, its stem is long enough to take hold of, and its total capacity is at least eight fluid ounces (25 cl), so that when filled to between one-third and one-half—or less than one-third if the glass is larger—the wine may easily be swirled and the bouquet captured in the space above. A number of variations on the tulip form are practical and attractive. The huge, stemmed bowls called *verres à Bourgogne*, into which one must sink not only one's nose but one's entire face to sip, undoubtedly throw a bouquet into relief; one should, nonetheless, be able to lift a glass effortlessly. Baccarat's Burgundy glass, baptized "Romanée-Conti," is among the lightest of this style and its contour, a slightly depressed sphere, cuts an elegant line. A table set with differently shaped glasses for each wine reflects the ritual form of a meal and the drama of the progression to come. Each wine should be poured before its accompanying course is served.

It is not possible to accurately predict the evolution of the Domaine's wines. "Drink up before 1997" or "Begin to drink after 2009" are vain conceits. The Domaine enjoys a well-deserved reputation for producing great wines in generally disparaged vintages. They are usually lighter-bodied—less fleshy—than those with high ratings on the vintage charts, they often express with greater fidelity their terroir of origin, and they may take longer to achieve that expression. The 1975 vintage, for example, is usually written off as a disaster in Burgundy. However, in October 1989, Peter Thustrup, Paris rare wine merchant, organized a tasting of fifteen vintages of Romanée-Conti, 1985-1929, and the Romanée-Conti 1975 was lean, clean, and finely drawn, a delicate wine with a firm, steely skeleton and an unclouded future. It will show better drunk alone with a dish of sautéed chanterelles, for instance, than in a comparative tasting, where light-bodied wines are usually at a disadvantage. 1956 is regularly dismissed as the worst vintage of the decade, but at the Domaine's dream tasting in March 1991 (see chapter 8) the Romanée-Conti 1956 was lyrical. Moreover, 1938, 1936, and 1922, vintages with no reputation, were lovely wines which displayed an awesome resistance to the ravages of time, and 1921, which is classed in wine literature as a good but not unusual vintage, received unconditional praise from all tasters—a timeless perfection outside of the realm of normal human experience.

One evening in the autumn of 1961, my brother James and I stopped in a half-empty restaurant on the outskirts of Paris. The wine list was uninspired until it revealed La Tâche 1954 at thirty francs a bottle and Romanée-Conti '54 at thirty-five. The patron explained that they had been left in the cellar by a former proprietor. We ordered both; both were beautiful, but the Tâche was the more exciting of the two. Some of the food was banal, some was bad. I returned several times to wash down boring food with a divine Tâche. Twenty-four years later, Aubert arrived in Solliès-Toucas, in the South of France, bearing a bottle of La Tâche 1954 which, drunk that evening, was irreal, unearthly. It made one hold one's breath lest some of its message or distant melody be lost. Its color had faded, its flesh vanished; it was all spirit, finesse, and nuance, a fragile lacework akin to the music of the spheres. Within the following year, I drank it twice again with Aubert and his wife, Pamela, at their home in the village of Bouzeron, a few steps beyond the southern tip of the Côte, each time in awe before the same ethereal presence. In November 1990 (see menu, page 129), La Tâche '54 had returned from its celestial voyage: the color was deeper, more ruby, less tile-tinged, it had filled out, bones and flesh appearing from nowhere; the scents had come back to earth also; it was bigger, more youthful—and, perhaps, less magical. Incomprehensible.

While turning the pages of the *livre d'or* at the Domaine, I discovered these lines, written in reverence: "Divine Romanée-Conti: Diamond of the *aigrette*—without which *la haute cuisine française* could not attain its perfection. A. Dumaine de Saulieu 20 Feb. '58." Alexandre Dumaine, who fashioned some of the most beautiful and the purist food in France during his thirty-three years (1931–64) in the kitchens of the Hôtel de la Côte d'Or in Saulieu, worshipped the wines of the Domaine above all others. My first visit there was in 1954. To accompany his *poularde à la vapeur Lucien Tendret,* a truffled Bresse chicken, placed on a plate and a tripod and steamed in the vapors of a double consommé within a hermetically sealed earthenware marmite, he had chosen a Beaune Dames Hospitalières 1947, a fine wine which, however, was not of a breed to engrave itself indelibly in one's memory. My friends and I, with more enthusiasm than experience, were determined to scale the summits and I asked him to choose something very special for the cheeses; he sent to table a cool bottle of La Tâche 1951, barely three years old and from a despised vintage. It was explosive—I had never tasted anything so wonderful. On my next visit there, I placed La Tâche '51 on the truffled chicken. The marmite was always unsealed at table, its fragrant vapors released at the last minute; the chicken was served with the juices collected in its plate while steaming and accompanied by creamed morels.

Tasted twenty years later at a "theme" tasting—"A Half-Century of Great Vintages from Vosne-Romanée"—at Lalou's home, La Tâche 1951 had grown up, its youthful exhuberance had yielded to a velvety texture, the color was still intense but warmer, and wild fruit had given way to an intricate bouquet. Today, its pale tile color retains no memory of its deep purple youth, the wine is frail but healthy and present, rich with souvenirs.

Simple Food for Great Wine

Simple wines can sometimes support complicated food. The wines of the Domaine de la Romanée-Conti—i.e. complex wines of great finesse—require simple food. This quality can be sought in the nature of the virgin product, as with a roast, whose goodness then depends on heat-control and timing, or, as with braised meats and traditional meat and game sauces, in a sort of distillation of many elements to create a single new essence or unity of flavor. The mechanics may be complex—the simplicity resides in the purity of the finished preparation; thus, a partridge chartreuse is simple.

Red meat and game roasts are among the most perfect accompaniments to these wines: rare beef; semi-rare saddle or leg of lamb or unmarinated venison; unmarinated saddle of young hare, rare; young game birds, just done (because the breast of wild duck is best quite rare, the legs are still bloody when the breast is right—they are usually removed after roasting, grilled until done, and served as a separate course, after the breast).

Truffles are good for Burgundy. If I had to choose a preparation certain to exalt a Romanée-Conti, high on the list of choices would be young hare fillets, shaved free of their outer membranes, filets mignons inserted into slits in the fillets, which are twisted into crescents, seasoned, thickly encrusted with chopped truffles, laid side by side in a shallow buttered oven dish, sprinkled with cognac and melted butter, covered loosely with foil, and baked at high heat for eight to ten minutes; to accompany them, a fine purée of lentils, generously buttered, with diced crisp celery heart stirred in at the last minute. Or, simply, a ragout of truffles—peeled truffles, cut into wedges, gently warmed in a buttered poêlon with a few drops of cognac, salt, and freshly ground pepper, combined with a sauce composed of demiglace—a strained reduction of red wine and mirepoix and the pounded truffle peelings—and served in individual bread cases, first painted with melted butter, turned crisp and golden in the oven and stroked lightly with a peeled garlic clove.

Serena Sutcliffe wrote, "One of the greatest gastronomic partnerships I ever experienced was in the company of that respected burgundy man, Harry Yoxall, at what was to be our last dinner together. We had roast grouse, *bien faisandé*, with a bottle of Grands Echézeaux 1952 from the Domaine de la Romanée-Conti. What was incredible was that the Grands Echézeaux had the rich, gamey smell of the grouse!"

Stamped in Aubert's memory is "a Tâche '49 drunk chez Lucas-Carton with a woodcock which was an extraordinary alliance." This was during Alex Allégrier's time at Lucas-Carton when, in season, woodcock was always on the menu. The rarely roasted birds were finished at table, split, and emptied, a voluptuous little sauce prepared with their livers and entrails, mashed with foie gras and flamed with a bit of cognac.

The alliance of the Domaine's wines with cheeses is not necessarily—like that with certain truffled preparations or with a pinkly roasted partridge—of the sort that inspires each, in the presence of the other, to soar to new heights of eloquence. Romanée-Conti is most often poured with the cheese course, not because it is a marriage made in heaven but simply because, in the context of a traditional modern menu, the climax of a suite of red wines coincides with the cheese service (there is, obviously, no reason that a truffled game terrine cannot replace the cheese course). In the unfolding of a menu, this is also the first moment of complete relaxation, when hunger is sated and the wine becomes, more than ever, the star. Everyone appreciates a handsome cheese platter, tastefully presented, but few guests will serve themselves more than two or three slivers of cheese to nibble at while examining, tasting and discussing the wine; a sliver of maroilles or livarot, however, can wreak havoc with a Romanée-Conti. Very strong cheeses should be as scrupulously avoided as bland, anonymous industrial cheeses; blue cheeses and old cheeses with a sharp bite, such as aged cantal, are dangerous. Very fat cheeses, like Brillat-Savarin, seem to me to have no particular affinity with the Domaine's wines, but if fresh, they are innocent. On the other hand, although many people firmly reject goat cheeses in the presence of any red wine, well-drained, still soft, and mild-flavored *chèvres fermiers* (two weeks in a humid cellar, turned daily on straw mats) do not offend my palate. A cheese platter, well balanced in terms of flavors and textures, might consist of one of the milder, soft bloomy-rind cheeses (brie de Meaux, coulommiers), a soft washed-rind cheese (Cîteaux or another of the Trappist cheeses, reblochon, vacherin), one or two semi-hard cheeses (Beaufort or Fribourg, farmhouse cheddar or one of the *tommes de montagne*) and some chèvres fermiers or simple, semifresh cow's-milk cheeses, prepared in the same way. Saint-Nectaire fermier and tomme de Savoie are also good choices. All of the soft cheeses should be "fermier," which ensures traditional fabrication with unpasteurized milk from cows which have been to pasture; on the quality of the pasturage depends the finesse of the cheese. When these cheeses are perfectly ripened, the rind is supple, never dry or cracked, the inside is uniformly soft, no chalk at the center and never runny (vacherin is the exception—it must be served with a spoon); when cut into, a creamy belly begins discreetly to distend. Once, pont l'évèque was transcendental; for many years, I have not found a pont l'évèque which recalled the sublime bouquet and flavor of those which seduced me forty years ago. Among widely available soft cheeses on the market today, reblochon fermier is the most consistently inspired, provided that it be raised in a good cellar and cut into at the right moment.

Cheese needs bread. A rustic, firm-crumbed sourdough bread is best; whole-grain breads are too strongly flavored. With cheese, a walnut bread is sometimes an interesting supplement to the sourdough. The amount of bread eaten with the cheese can affect very noticeably the relationship of the wine to the cheese.

Lalou and Aubert, at my request, made up a short list of cheeses—possible accompaniments to a Romanée-Conti—and then proceeded to eliminate all but one! Aubert wrote,

> The only cheese which we can really accept is Cîteaux, the pressed cheese made by the Cistercian monks in their monastery [who else could have created THE fromage des Grands Crus] . . . Until a few years ago this cheese was distributed by the brothers of the monastery, who traveled all over the department selling their cheeses to a well-established and loyal clientele. But then, the Father Superior feared that these worldly contacts might be harmful to his brothers' vocation of spirituality and the door-to-door sales were stopped. Today, the cheeses must be searched out at the Cistercian abbey unless one is lucky enough to have a cheese merchant who furnishes himself there.
>
> If memories can possess an odour, those of my childhood are permeated with Cîteaux—the scent of the cheeses which, after Brother Joseph's visit, my father brought home to ripen in the stairway leading to the cellar. When I was sent there to bring up a bottle, it was nearly always with instructions to collect a Cîteaux also.
>
> Somewhere, in the far reaches of my childhood memory, I find the souvenir of a white tablecloth, reflections of wine playing in the glasses and of the intoxicating combinations between the sumptuous bouquets of the first great wines of my life and the rustic flavor and firm texture of these Cistercian cheeses.
>
> Is it surprising that we find no better companion for a Romanée-Conti—or any other wine from the Domaine than a perfectly ripened Cîteaux?
>
> Reblochon, on the other hand, is not suitable: it has too pronounced a flavor. Other pressed cheeses, as well as certain cooked cheeses, made from cow's milk, can provide acceptable support, as can, with a young Richebourg, a fresh cow's milk cheese.

Later, both Lalou and Aubert relented somewhat; Lalou willingly includes Saint-Nectaire, Coulommiers, and fresh Brillat-Savarin among her choices and Aubert concedes that a *fresh* Reblochon is admissible.

PERFECT HARMONIES: EIGHT MEMORABLE MENUS

Intuition and fantasy can successfully order the placement of wines on a menu only if one is familiar with each wine from recent experience. Without this intimacy, the growth, the vintage, and the age must determine the choice of wines and the order of their service, moving progressively from relatively light-bodied wines to those of greater depth and complexity and, usually but not necessarily, from younger to older. Within each category this is true of white and red alike if more than one white wine precedes the reds, but the transition from white Burgundies to red Burgundies, which is one of contrast rather than of mounting intensity within a similar mode of expression, poses no problem.

Among the Domaine's red growths, Echézeaux is usually the least complex, the most direct, and the most precocious in its evolution. On a menu to be accompanied by a selection of the Domaine's wines, it is a natural choice for the first and the youngest of the red wines. Grands Echézeaux and Romanée Saint-Vivant, although of different temperaments, share a similar complexity and, in the same vintage, are pretty much interchangeable in relation to the other wines. In the stratosphere of ultimate nuance, the same can be said for Richebourg, La Tâche, and Romanée-Conti.

Generalized theory cannot replace personal experience and the choice of wines, after all, depends on the wealth of one's cellar and not on that of the Domaine's vinothèque. Choosing wines for a menu is always an adventure, but a misjudgment is never a disaster. Practical illustration, historical curiosity, and sentimental memories have all played a part in the choice of the following menus.

Dream Menu

This menu, conceived for the month of November, when sea urchins (*oursins*) are fullest and Caesar's mushrooms, white truffles, game, and vacherin cheese are in season, is, in fact, only a menu of dreams. The dream element is heightened by the presence of the Domaine's Montrachet 1966, a honeyed, voluptuous miracle, which, on my only encounter, left me breathless in admiration. No dessert is included because the real purpose of the menu is to serve as a tailor's dummy on which to fit the Domaine's red wines for purposes of illustration. *Violets* are small Mediterranean sea creatures with a tough, leathery exterior, which when cut in two reveal a tender yellow flesh, sweet and sea-flavored with a light lemon accent. *Oronges* (Caesar's mushroom/*amanita caesarea*), the loveliest of all mushrooms, are anointed with olive oil, seasoned only with salt and pepper, grilled over fruitwood embers, and sprinkled with a few drops of lemon juice. The sweetbreads are braised on a bed of mirepoix with demiglace, white truffles shaved generously over the surface before serving. The terrine will profit from being prepared several days in advance; it is best accompanied by a trembling, chopped jelly made from the ducks' carcasses, moistened with veal stock.

§

Vioulets et Oursins
Montrachet 1966

§

Oronges Grillées
Echézeaux 1978 (DRC)

§

Ris de Veau Braisé aux Truffes Blanches de Piémont
Grands Echézeaux 1972 (DRC)

§

Terrine de Canard Sauvage aux Truffes
La Tâche 1962

§

Fromages: Reblochon, Vacherin, Saint-Nectaire, Fribourg, Chèvres
Romanée-Conti 1959

THE SIEGE OF PARIS

The Café Voisin's most famous chef, Choron, is remembered today for the tomatoed bearnaise sauce which bears his name. The restaurant was frequented by Zola, the Goncourt brothers and Alphonse Daudet, among other literary celebrities. The contents of its once famous cellars were sold at auction in 1932.

By Christmas 1870, the ninety-ninth day of the Siege of Paris, there was little to eat in the capital; the zoos were being emptied out to furnish meat. The choice of wines and the order of their service represents a formula which evolved during the nineteenth century and persisted until the Second World War: Sherry or Madeira with the soup, Sauternes with a noble fish in sauce (the paucity of salmon and turbot during the siege would account for the fried goujons, which were netted in the Seine), red Bordeaux, followed by red Burgundy, and Champagne with a sweet preparation. Today the words *entremets* and *desserts* are used interchangeably and one thinks of cheese and Port, served after the pudding, as a specifically British tradition. In the last century, an entremets could be either sweet or savory, depending on its placement in a menu, and a dessert simply indicated the last service, usually composed of fruits, pastries, and cheeses, hence Brillat-Savarin's aphorism, "A dessert without cheese is a belle who is missing an eye" [Un dessert sans fromage est une belle à qui il manque un oeil]. It is not easy to bring into focus, in one's imagination, the Mouton-Rothschild, the wolf's leg and the cat flanked with rats, but the Romanée-Conti would certainly have been very much at home with a truffled antelope terrine and with the *cèpes à la Bordelaise*.

§

Le Siège de Paris

Café Voisin, Paris, 25 Décembre 1870

99me JOUR DU SIÈGE

Hors-d'OEuvre:

Beurre, Radis, Tête d'Ane Farcie, Sardines

Potages :

Purée de Haricots rouges aux Croûtons

Consommé d' Éléphant

Entrées :

Goujons frits, Le Chameau rôti à l'anglaise

Le Civet de Kangourou

Côtes d'Ours róties sauce Poivrade

Rots :

Cuissot de Loup, sauce Chevreuil

Le Chat flanqué de Rats

Salade de Cresson

La Terrine d'Antilope aux truffes
Cèpes à la Bordelaise
Petits-Pois au Beurre

Entremets :
Gâteau de riz aux Confitures

Dessert :
Fromage de Gruyère

VINS

1er Service	2me Service
Xérès	Mouton Rothschild 1846
Latour Blanche 1861	Romanée Conti 1858
	Bellenger frappé
Ch. Palmer 1864	Grand Porto 1827

Café & Liqueurs

Café Voisin. — G. Braquessac, 261, rue Saint-Honoré

CHRISTMAS CHEZ GARIN

Georges Garin, formerly restaurateur in Nuit-Saint-Georges and caterer for the banquets at the Château du Clos de Vougeot, organized by the Confrérie des Chevaliers du Tastevin, opened "Chez-Garin," 9 rue Lagrange, in Paris in 1961. It rapidly became one of the most sought-out restaurants of the capital and, to many of his clients, Garin was France's greatest chef. He closed and retired to the South of France in 1973 and died in 1979.

This meal was prepared at the Garins' flat. The wines came from the restaurant cellar. The pheasant was stuffed with quartered truffles mixed with grated pork-back fat and roasted for not quite half an hour in a hot oven; after twenty minutes the bard and trussing strings were removed and the legs were opened out from the body to hasten their cooking. The wild rice was soaked, drained, and cooked in three times its volume of salted water for an hour or so, until dry, then tossed with butter. The intermingling of the pheasant's and the truffles' juices with the wild rice was a new and memorable experience for all of us and a great gift to the wine. La Tâche 1954, I have tried to describe earlier in this chapter. The Richebourg 1952, which was Henri Leroy's favorite bottle in his last years, is to this day dense, deep-colored though brick-hued, chewy, powerful, and opulent.

§

Paris, Christmas Day 1968

Apéritif: Roederer Cristal 1961; Caviar

Homard à la Nage, Beurre Blanc
Musigny Blanc (de Vogüé) 1959

§

Poule Faisane aux Truffes; Riz Sauvage
La Tâche 1954

§

Fromages
Richebourg (DRC) 1952

Homage to Dumaine

The meal was at the restaurant, Chez Garin. Alexandre Dumaine, the great chef at the Hôtel de la Côte d'Or, in Saulieu, had retired and this meal was conceived in his honor. All of Garin's terrines drew their silken texture and an element of mysterious flavor from the foie gras puréed into the basic mixture; chopped truffles and pistachios were always present. The woodcock terrine's savors were heightened by the incorporation of the birds' entrails, a fumet drawn from the carcasses and several days' ripening after cooking. Its placement on the menu imposed a white wine but, served after the liver, it would have performed wonders with the Tâche "Les Godichots."

A braised calf's liver, firm but moist and pink throughout, thinly sliced, is a marvel of delicacy, perfectly suited to a fine red Burgundy. In a home kitchen, it may be more easily roasted (about 10 minutes per pound in an oven declining from hot to medium-low, with a 10- or 15- minutes rest in a warm place). The liver need not be whole but the section should weigh at least a couple of pounds to cook correctly: the outside membrane should be first removed and it is a good idea to wrap the liver in caul before roasting. Another good garnish is a white purée of potatoes, onions, garlic, celeriac, and turnips.

Hommage à Dumaine

Chez Garin, Paris, February 1970

Apéritif: Laurent-Perrier "Cuvée Grand Siècle"

	Terrine de Bécasses au Foie Gras
Bâtard-Montrachet (Leflaive) 1961	§
	Turban de Saumon à la Mousseline de Homard aux Truffles, Sce. Homard, Subrics d'Epinards
	§
Musigny (de Vogüé) 1937	Foie de Veau Entier Braisé, Sauce Echalote à la Moëlle, Purée de Champignons, Galettes de Maïs
	§
La Tâche "Les Godichots" 1929	Plateau de Fromages
	§
	Poires Dijonnaises
	§
Rhum Blanc 1878	Café

A Truffle Lunch

Elizabeth David was a phenomenon. Among food writers in Britain, everyone agrees: first, there is Elizabeth David, then come the others. With her dedication to all that is pure, simple, and fresh in the kitchen and with the vitality and often wicked wit of her writing, she dominated the field for forty years. Alice Waters is also very special. Something over twenty years ago, in Berkeley, California, inspired by Elizabeth David's culinary ideals, Alice opened the restaurant Chez Panisse, so-named because of her love for Marcel Pagnol's "Marius" film trilogy and for everything Provençal. Since then, five hugely successful Chez Panisse cookbooks have appeared, the most recent of which is for children. Today, Chez Panisse is an American gastronomic mecca, Alice is idolized and clients must book tables far in advance for the single-menu dinners, changed daily and announced in advance, which are famous across the country.

The aim of this lunch was to introduce my two friends, pioneers and crusaders with a common passion for Burgundy, for truffles, and for austerely simple food with exquisite flavors. Scrambled eggs, cooked in a double boiler to a thick but pourable cream, and poached sausages, served hot with their court bouillon, are both perfect vehicles for truffles and perfect companions to either white or red Burgundy. The Montrachet was no more than a pleasant mouth-rinse but I was very pleased with it, for I had bought it at auction at a price closer to that of a Mâcon Blanc than to that of a Montrachet. The Volnay was a marvel of playful delicacy. The Domaine's Grands Echézeaux 1953 is famous and was, at that time, breathtaking. I have not tasted it since.

Alice arrived from Italy a couple of hours before lunch, her handbag heavy with tender parmesan and fresh white truffles—really pearl gray with scattered faint veins of lilac and rose; we decided to replace my cheese platter with parmesan and white truffles. We chipped away at parmesan and white truffles and sipped away at Grands Echézeaux until nightfall. It was heaven.

A Truffle Lunch for Elizabeth David and Alice Waters
London, a Sunday, November 1979

Apéritif: Bollinger 1973

Brouillade aux Truffes
Montrachet (Prieur) 1975

§

Cervelas Pistaché aux Truffes, Pommes Vapeur
Volnay Champans (de Montille) 1974

§

Parmesan Frais, Truffes de Piémont
Grands Echézeaux (DRC) 1953

A TASTING CHEZ TAILLEVENT

Bipin Desai is a remarkable person. He arrived in the United States from India at the age of nineteen to continue his studies, received his doctorate in nuclear physics from the University of California, Berkeley, in 1961, and is at present professor of elementary particle physics at the University of California, Riverdale. Bipin was a vegetarian and teetotaler until well into his career. He first tasted wine in 1970, but the passion for wine developed later as a result of meeting European wine-connoisseur colleagues at the Center for Nuclear Research (CERN) in Geneva. His cellar contains about four thousand bottles of "anything that is great." He regularly organizes tastings of rare wines and publishes articles in various wine journals. Jean-Claude Vrinat, proprietor of Le Taillevent, is a special kind of genius. His staff is trained to finely honed perfection; his wines are treated with great respect, always served at an ideal temperature; and glasses remain filled to a precisely correct level throughout the meal.

Thanks to Jean-Claude Vrinat's collaboration, the menu, a heroic concept, was a great success. Bipin's guests rose from table light in body and spirit. The choice of Champagne and an *escabèche* to bridge the passage from Yquem to Montrachet, although surprising, succeeded in returning palates to a perfect receptivity after Yquem's enveloping penetration. The Romanée Saint-Vivant and the Grands Echézeaux were poured side by side, a back-and-forth comparative tasting of '71s, sharing first the sweetbreads, then the *côte de boeuf*; henceforth, we drank one monument after another, each with its chosen course. The uncomplicated flavors and the simplicity of the preparations chosen to accompany the red wines succeeded perfectly in throwing the wines into relief. The sweetbreads were braised, the côte de boeuf grilled, the pigeon squabs roasted, kept slightly pink at the leg joint ("*en bécasse*" refers simply to the pigeon's presentation, split and arranged on a plate in the manner associated with a woodcock), and the truffles were served in a demiglace. The cheeses were carefully chosen to respect the wine.

Dégustation Chez Taillevent
Organized by Bipin Desai
Restaurant Taillevent, Paris, 18 March 1987

CHÂTEAU D'YQUEM 1948	Foie Gras d'Oie et de Canard au Natural
CHAMPAGNE DOM RUINART 1979	Rougets de Roche en Escabèche
MONTRACHET 1967 (DRC)	Coquilles Saint-Jacques aux Moules
ROMANÉE SAINT-VIVANT 1971 (DRC)	Noix de Ris de Veau aux Primeurs
GRANDS ECHÉZEAUX 1971 (DRC)	Côte de Boeuf à la Moëlle
RICHEBOURG 1966 (DRC)	Pigeonneau de Bresse en Bécasse
ROMANÉE-CONTI 1959	Truffe du Quercy en Cocotte
LA TÂCHE 1949	Fromages de nos Provinces
CHÂTEAU D'YQUEM 1959	Glace au Lait d'Amandes et au Coulis de Groseille

A Summer Dinner in Provence

The bottle of Romanée-Conti 1926 was offered to me by the Domaine for my sixtieth birthday (the vintage of my conception rather than my birth, since no 1927 remains in the Domaine's vinothèque). I cellared it for something over a year until my brothers and sisters were gathered in Solliès. In summer, one lives out of doors. Special bottles are reserved for evening meals because of the lunchtime heat. The grapevines which cover the terrace and the garlands of multicolored lights which illuminate it create a very special atmosphere. The juxtaposition of a young, vigorous Echézeaux and an extraordinarily relaxed Romanée-Conti was beautiful. The Echézeaux was an explosion of joy. The Romanée-Conti was a slightly dusty, light red without the tile edge of color normal to a wine of that age. It was all nuance and nostalgia with, nonetheless, a surprisingly fresh, floral scent, mingled with a suspicion of feathered game, an odor which I associate with gutting fresh partridge—a wine full of memories.

The onglet (hanger steak, butcher's cut, hanging tender, bloody skirt) was grilled whole over fruitwood embers, then sliced thinly on the bias. The potatoes were spaghetti-shredded, rinsed, dried in towels, and sautéed for a few seconds in butter to coat them. A first batch was layered, salted, in a gratin dish with peeled whole garlic cloves tucked in here and there. A layer of sliced truffles was spread over this, and a second batch of sautéed potatoes was pressed atop. The dish was baked for 35–40 minutes, until the surface was golden.

§§§

Solliès-Toucas, 23 June 1988

Apéritif: Krug 1979

§

Filets de Sardines Crues en Marinade

Hermitage Blanc (Chave) 1981

§

Onglet Grillé; Gratin de Pommes de Terre aux Truffes

Echézeaux (DRC) 1978

§

Fromages
Romanée-Conti 1926

§

Château Ricaud (Loupiac) 1929

Lunch at Solliès-Toucas

I was anxious to taste a bottle of Romanée-Conti 1935 which had been lying in my cellar for a couple of years, waiting for its moment to come; I asked my friends Kermit Lynch (wine merchant and importer in Berkeley, California, who lives half the year in the South of France near Bandol), and Lucien and Lulu Peyraud (proprietors of Domaine Tempier, Bandol), the Peyrauds' sons François and Jean-Marie, and Catherine, Jean-Marie's wife, to join me for lunch. They proposed that each of them should furnish an element on the menu. Kermit had discovered a splendid *jambon persillé* in Nuits-Saint-Georges which he had shipped to him for the occasion and he brought along the Echézeaux 1979 and the Tâche 1954 to complete the suite of wines. Because I had only one bottle of Montrachet, I preceded it with a couple of bottles of Chevalier-Montrachet, an opulent, golden, old-fashioned wine which could only have been followed by the Domaine's Montrachet. It is always intimidating to uncork a bottle of rare old wine, lest one find it dead, or dying, in the bottle. It was our good fortune to find all of the wines in perfect condition. La Tâche '54, in fact, had shed years of age, was much deeper in color and much fuller-bodied than it had seemed five years earlier in its ethereal phase. A note for the Romanée-Conti, assembled from my guests' notes, is included in Chapter 8.

The jambon persillé was very good, finely seasoned and not at all vinegary; after a bit of hesitation, however, everyone agreed that it would be much more at home with a Bourgogne Aligoté than with this Chevalier-Montrachet. The olives, on the other hand (picked very ripe, tossed regularly in salt for several days, first in a terrine, the last few days in a wicker basket to drain them well, then tossed with fresh twigs of thyme, bay leaves, freshly ground pepper, and olive oil), threw the wine beautifully into relief. Lulu's ragout of snails (previously cooked for two or three hours in a fennel-flavored white wine court bouillon) was remarkable. It consisted of three heads (forty or fifty cloves) of garlic, peeled and simmered with chopped parsley in part water, part snails' court bouillon until nearly dry, simmered then with thick cream and puréed; mushrooms cooked in butter until nearly dry, then simmered with a little of the court bouillon; chopped, butter-stewed shallots; snails, garlic, cream, mushrooms and shallots assembled and simmered together. A mysterious new taste was born in which the presence of garlic was imperceptible (Jean-Marie complained that he could not taste the garlic) and the marriage with the Montrachet was exquisite. The Montrachet was of course very young, a bit green and very steely, but nonetheless fantastically impressive. Kermit apparently found it to be distinctly masculine, for he wrote, "Challenging aristocracy. Asks nothing of the taster. It stands by itself. You give yourself to him. Extraordinary quality of oak. Still young but easy to taste, enjoy. Like a fountain 'en bouche' and the aftertaste exudes. France still has its Kings." The Echézeaux was direct, clean, uncomplicated, with nonetheless great finesse, an immediate scent of fresh, feathered game and a lovely sharp fruit on the palate; the Romanée Saint-Vivant, more veiled, more complex, velvety and mysterious. They were drunk side by side, both perfect with the just-done pheasants and the salad. The traditional terror of placing a vinaigrette in the presence of a wine should not be taken too seriously. The vinegar should be the very best, neither sharp nor aggressive, but rather sweet, gentle, aromatic, and used with discretion; the olive oil should be virgin, from the first pressing, and fruity. *Coustelline* is a perennial wild salad green which grows on Provençal hillsides from a tough, black, chicory-like root. The plant dies back to the root during the hot, dry summers, and, after autumn rains, tender, sharply dentellated gray-green leaves begin to grow. Its flowers resemble those of a dandelion, but the leaves are finer flavored, more subtle and less bitter. In Provence, a garlicky salad of coustelline is an obligatory accompaniment to brochettes of little birds turned before the flames. Coustelline needs garlic, but to respect the wines we used it discreetly. The following notes are compiled from my guests' notes. Echézeaux: "Color shows some age. Nose no sign of age, yet no longer youthful, smoky, small game [animal de venerie], cabinetmaker's oak [chêne d'ébénisterie], reseda; palate still tannic [en bouche encore du tanin], cedar, cypress, ripe fruits, full, round [plein, gras], racé. What finesse!" Romanée Saint-Vivant:

"Color more somber and dense than the Echézeaux. Nose more closed, palate more complex, full, meaty [charnue] . . . thicker nose and palate with no loss of finesse. Aromas and flavor which seem to go beyond other Burgundies. Echézeaux very direct, Romanée Saint-Vivant full of mystery." La Tâche: "Extraordinary nose, wild things, fur, pastureland; palate round and full; finishes clean, light—perfection—round but no sign of alcohol." The Tâche and the Romanée-Conti were drunk separately. Everyone agreed that the Tâche was perfect with the cheeses; Jean-Marie wrote, "Extraordinary nose which goes like a glove with the cheeses, especially the pelardon and the coulommiers".

I think that no one ate cheese with the Romanée-Conti. Lucien wrote, "It's a crime to drink that while eating—it has to be analyzed with joy in all its fullness." Compliments were showered on the Krug and the Yquem, as well. Briefly, Lulu wrote, "Krug, finesse and majesty; Yquem, discretion and grandeur . . . these are the joys which can be shared only among friends, warmth, fruits, unforgettable aromas."

Only Voltaire (who, thanking a benefactor for a gift of Corton, wrote, "I serve quite good Beaujolais to my guests . . . but I drink your Corton in hiding") could have disagreed with Lulu.

Lunch, Solliès-Toucas, 17 November 1990

Apértif: Krug 1973

§

Jambon Persillé, Olives Noires

Chevalier-Montrachet (Michel Niellon) 1981

§

Ragoût d'Escargots Lulu

Montrachet (DRC) 1985

§

Poules Faisanes Rôties; Salade de Coustelline
Echézeaux (DRC) 1979
Romanée Saint-Vivant (DRC) 1979

§Fromages
La Tâche 1954
Romanée-Conti 1935

§
Yquem 1980

VINTAGES

VIII

A VOYAGE IN TIME

TWENTY-EIGHT MARCH 1991: a voyage never taken before and one which can never be repeated. We were six who immersed ourselves in the mystery and the myth of La Romanée-Conti, glimpsed the infinite variations on the theme of a terroir, recovered a past—*un temps retrouvé*—which we had never experienced but which was hauntingly familiar, Romanée-Conti's memories fusing with ours and with those of Burgundy and history, the centuries-old tradition of *provignage,* the prince de Conti's suppers at the Palais du Temple, and the priors of Saint-Vivant. The leap from the ethereal filigree wines of the early 1950s, the first vintages to issue from the reconstituted vineyard, to the wines from the old provined vines inspired the same kind of sensation as that of a recurrent dream in which, after taking a deep breath of air, one discovers that one is weightless and able to fly; we soared into a world in which time no longer existed.

Forty-five vintages of Romanée-Conti, several of which represented the last remaining bottle in the vinothèque and many of which Lalou Bize-Leroy and Aubert de Villaine had never tasted—bottles which had lain tranquilly in the Domaine's cellars since their *mise en bouteilles,* which had never experienced the traumas of travel or radical temperature variations—were served throughout the day in decade relays:

1980s, eight vintages; 1970s, seven vintages; 1960s, six vintages; 1950s, seven vintages; 1940s, two vintages; 1930s, four vintages; 1920s, eight vintages; 1910s, three vintages. The youngest wine, 1989, had recently been fined and was ready to be bottled; the oldest, 1915, a famous vintage in its time and the only bottle in the vinothèque, had unfortunately taken a wrong turn and is therefore not included in the following notes. At midday, a buffet was laid—hams, sausages, terrines and pâtés, quiches and other savory tarts, cheeses, and fruits.

Present, in addition to Lalou Bize, Aubert de Villaine, and myself, were Serena Sutcliffe M.W., director of the wine department at Sotheby's, London and New York, and author of a number of books on wine, including *Serena Sutcliffe's Guide to the Wines of Burgundy;* Michel Bettane, editorial adviser to *La Revue du vin de France,* the wine periodical founded in 1927 by Raymond Baudouin; and Michel Dovaz, also a member of the staff of *La Revue du Vin de France* and author of a number of wine books. Of the following notes, all those signed "S.S." (Serena Sutcliffe), "M.B." (Michel Bettane), and "M.D." (Michel Dovaz) are from the 28 March 1991 tasting. Michael Broadbent M.W., director of the wine department at Christie's, London, author of *The Great Vintage Wine Book,* among others, kindly shared his prepublication notes for *The Great Vintage Wine Book II,* published in 1991. The notes by Robert Parker, American author and publisher of the monthly review *The Wine Advocate,* are taken from his book *Burgundy* (1990). Other notes are from Geoffrey Troy, East Coast associate editor of *Wine Journal,* a monthly review published in Los Angeles, and *Dégustation Sélection,* a commercial wine-tasting agency in Beaune. The date following each entry is that of the first day of picking at the Domaine, not necessarily the day on which Romanée-Conti was picked. The figures following the name Romanée-Conti represent the production in hectoliters per hectare (hl/ha, multiply by 65.3 for gallons per acre). The available figures (some, from the late thirties to the mid-forties, have disappeared because the records were kept in the de Villaine home in Moulins, which was requisitioned by the Germans during the war) are especially interesting for the pre-phylloxera vines, for they represent the same level of production—an average of 11 to 12 hectoliters per hectare—as that of La Romanée at the time of the prince de Conti, some three or four hectoliters per hectare fewer than the production level in the mid-nineteenth century.

1990 22 September

(32 hl/ha): "A 'cathedral' wine, no doubt the only vintage, along with 1988, able to support the comparison with the greatest and most sublime of the prewar vintages of Romanée-Conti. Such aromatic refinement in a wine as concentrated as this is difficult to believe!" (M.B.)

1989 20 September

(30 hl/ha): "Très belle couleur, blue/crimson. Wonderful rich blackberry nose—heady, opulent, rich in alcohol. A touch smoky. Smells like very expensive leather! Maraschino cherries au nez. Taste: Great glycerol, alcohol, tannic—incredible power. Excellent acidity, so will last beautifully. Le paradis." (S.S.) "Dense purple robe, no shading at rim, no blue-violet reflections. Perfect marriage of new wood (vanilla and spices) and secondary aromas of violets plus delicate smoky nuances of admirable grace. Astonishing stability in presence of air. A rich and fleshy wine, powerfully built, supported by a natural acidity far superior to the average in this vintage. Assertive wood tannins. Wine in its infancy with great promise." (M.B.) "Intense robe, one of the strongest. Dense, fruity nose, tightly woven, new wood already integrated! Lively attack, the acidity maintains the wine at the top of the palate—no somber notes." (M.D.)

1988 28 September

(32 hl/ha): "Deep colour, crimson, has lost blue notes. Glorious nose of black cherries; heather and all of the maquis on the nose—imposing. Taste: Very vif, V.G. balance fruit, tannin, acidity. Tannins less envelopés qu'en '89—plus visibles—wonderful raspberries en bouche. Chewy. Vin de garde." (S.S.) "Purple robe, slightly pink rim. Complex and refined scents of roses with nuances of mint, crème de moka and spices. A lean wine with a particularly tight texture and a rare tannic power for a modern pinot noir. Closed and rigid, typical of the vintage. Throughout the tasting, this 1988, held aside, demonstrated a fullness and a richness comparable with the greatest vintages of the past." (M.B.) "A bit less robe—very young. Nose: vanilla coats the fruit—smoky. Palate: acute concentration—still no somber notes." (M.D.) "Staggeringly concentrated with a bouquet that almost defies articulation. There is no doubting what it is or who made it." (Robert Parker, last tasted fall 1989) "A powerhouse of a wine with a great future." (Michael Broadbent, last tasted January 1991)

1987 5 October

(11.5 hl/ha): "Colour much lighter and more evolved, bricky notes. Rich évolué, even liqueur nose. Wet earth. Taste: no red fruits, wet earth, acidity quite marked. Strong centre to it—kernel [noyau] of flavour. Long finish. Lacks the fat [gras] of '88 & '89 but concentration." (S.S.) "Surprisingly exotic nuances of macerated orange zest. With aeration, the wood dominates. Very lean and serious wine with less flesh than the 1988. The breed is evident in a finish of supreme elegance. Tight, serious wine, still austere, from a minuscule harvest. It will age admirably." (M.B.) "Transparent fruit. Superficial wine, held together by its acidity." (M.D.)

1986 1 October

(26.5 hl/ha): "Quite a bit more brown—warm earth and roasting chestnuts on the nose. Also warm peach skins—rare for a red wine! Taste: Surprisingly strawberryish in flavour. Delicious now, long flavour, but not big." (S.S.) "Loss of color (a bit too much for a five-year-old wine). The nose is in its musky phase with nuances of leather and earth. The terroir is well defined but with less rigor than 1987. A bit more fluidity in the middle mouth but, in a way, greater harmony, especially on the finish when nuances of violets and earth develop freely." (M.B.) "Normal robe. Fuller nose. Extremely homogeneous. First vintage which begins to melt in the mouth but to the detriment of the extract." (M.D.)

1985 5 October

(24 hl/ha): "The bouquet is deep and complex, like cherry kernels. The taste followed through with immense cherry concentration . . . marries opulence to tannin in such a way that one almost drowns the other—at the moment, it is the swamping, glycerine-rich opulence that wins, but the backbone is all there." (Serena Sutcliffe, *Decanter,* February 1988) "Utterly mind-blowing . . . Red burgundy and red wine do not get any better than this." (Robert Parker, last tasted fall 1989)

1984 8 October

(13.5 hl/ha): "Deep colour. Slightly vegetal nose, nonetheless great finesse. Very supple and very full-bodied for this vintage. Superb '84." (*Dégustation Sélection,* 1990)

1983 3 October

(16.5 hl/ha): "Couleur *très* profonde—tuilée but toffee-dark. Warm funghi—nose of *roses*. No dry notes—cannelle, mais 'différent.' Nose does not get better en verre. Taste: Dry en bouche, lack of fruit—but rich. Aftertaste of pruneaux." (S.S.) "Color very deep with brown nuances. Two dominant aspects to the nose: surmaturity (nuances of fig) and, alas, the bitterness of hail damage, which is accentuated in contact with air. Monumental constitution. Finishes on a bitter note. Perhaps very long aging (25–30 years) will bring suavity and harmonize the bitter finish." (M.B.) "Fabulous—the most intense. The first to achieve warm and somber notes—richness and pleasure on the nose . . . density, balance—the dominant acid structure of the preceding vintages is smothered—great length—fine grain." (M.D.)

1982 27 September

(40 hl/ha): "Very brown colour—quite clear. Rich, warm, toasty nose—violets—nez de plus en plus séducteur—A temptress of a wine. Cèpes!! Taste: *Délicieux*. En Pleine beauté. Soft. Chocolate on finish—lovely and 'creamy.'" (S.S.) "Very evolved robe, almost bronze. Ravishing voluptuous nose of grapes with nuances of muscat. Same voluptuousness of texture, but with aeration, alcohol dominates and interferes with the aromatic purity of the nose. Finishes on a slightly sweet note . . . this fault will be less apparent at table than in a clinical tasting." (M.B.) "Evolved robe. Powerful—long and full. Balance in facility. Can be drunk now." (M.D.)

1981 5 October

(16.5 hl/ha): "Deep brown—like a Barolo! Nose rather dead and flat in comparison to others—but compact and concentrated; will open out—cabbage and truffles—*later:* has opened out—Now superb and élancé—spicy—Marché de Caire! Taste: lovely rich taste, especially middle—seulement un peu sec en bouche (à la fin) like a walnut liqueur." (S.S.) "Mahogany robe. Much more discreet but more elegant nose than 1982. Very distinguished violet nuances. Admirably clear, rigorous expression. La Romanée in all its divine elegance, thanks to a finish without excessive alcohol. Superb success for this vintage." (M.B.) "Very pure—crystal. Aristocratic palate, a bit disdainful of facility—best of the series [1980s]. Great class." (M.D.)

1980 18 October

(18 hl/ha): "Couleur marron mais un peu plus vif—plus clair, quand-même. Nose of tabac et café—first like this in range so far—seize it now. Taste: lovely coffee taste—ready—soft—tails away a bit at end but lovely coffee flavour that lingers." (S.S.) "Robe more bronze than mahogany. Lots of esters with already very complex notes of leather and fine musk. More enveloping palate than 1981, a bit more sensation of alcohol. Rich wine, more suave and better structured but less ideally pure. One can begin to drink it now." (M.B.) "Period robe. Nose melting, discreet. Very soft, ready to drink, medium complexity." (M.D.)

1979 11 October

(14 hl/ha): "Brown at edges. Nez de vanille—cannelle—touch of cloves . . . Taste: Bouteille très fermée. Saveurs masquées." (S.S.) "Bronzing robe. Full nose, very 'muscat'. Limp attack, accentuated softness not altogether franc. Opulent and decadent but will not please purists." (M.B.) "Normal robe. Charcoal? Slight reduction—which disappears if one waits. Nose grenadine. Balanced palate with good grain, nice finish. Good without being astounding—too short." (M.D.)

1978 16 October

(27 hl/ha): "Much deeper colour than '79—that is as expected—*Glorious* raw black truffles/damp earth smell—adore this—Attack— woodsmoke—sauvage!! Palais: Incredible taste—rich and yet young. Divin! All the wildness of a grand vin in a great year—untamed—pas domestiqué!" (S.S.) "Mahogany robe. Very affirmative and powerful nose mingling with great style musk, spices, caramel and which becomes increasingly complex with aeration. Beautifully balanced palate. Richness (but with no sensation of sweetness), very good acidity and a long and brilliant finish. The expectations of a great year fulfilled. Wait at least five years before drinking!" (M.B.) "Beautiful. Full alcohol? Quite rich, slightly smoky. Classic, long but stays on the surface (at first), fills out in glass—leans toward truffles—could be longer." (M.D.)

1977 19 October

(39 hl/ha): "Rather a yellow brown, like a yellowy winter sky!! Soft, surprisingly clean nose of roses . . . Palais: Soft, un peu "torchon humide"! Mais aussi easy, accessible, some fruit, lingers quite prettily." (S.S.) "Bronzing robe. Extremely delicate nose

(very musky) of a light-bodied, fading wine. Full of charm if drunk during the first twenty minutes. Thins out with long aeration." (M.B.) "Old and light. Transparent from every point of view and abnormally evolved." (M.D.)

1976 24 September

(38 hl/ha): "Deep molasses brown—roasted prunes. Surmaturité—dried currants. Taste: liqueur texture—alcohol—Quite something, superb on gibier—Coats mouth—Glycerol—Impressive. Rich." (S.S.) "Coffee robe. Pronounced character of the vintage (aromas of humus, nutmeg, far away from grapes). Beautiful constitution, develops lots of nuances with aeration, rigorously constructed palate. Very far from its peak." (M.B.) "Deep and bronzed. Nose smooth, rich. Lots of fruit, a wine for pleasure. No doubt not a model of balance—medium length." (M.D.) "Heavenly fragrance, 'ethereal beetroot'—the inimitable, almost theatrical D.R.C. pinot scent. On the palate, sweet, mouthfilling flavour, still hard. Anticipate full blossoming after 1996." (Michael Broadbent, last tasted September 1990)

1975 11 October

(26 hl/ha): "Jaune . . . Difficult to get anything from nose other than caramel . . . Soft but far too vegetal." (S.S.) "Bronze robe. Aroma of celery betrays damaged raw material. But it does not lack its own kind of charm. A curiosity to be uncorked just before the service." (M.B.) "Very light. Classic nose but not full. Light palate—light in poverty. A bit short. (M.D.)

1974 7 October

(30 hl/ha): No recent notes.

1973 6 October

(40 hl/ha): No recent notes.

1972 18 October

(40 hl/ha): "Très dark de couleur—Evolué, mais profond—Nez sauvage et concentré, typiquement '72 en Côte de Nuits, rich, heathery—les roses de Bulgarie—opulent, almost meaty—like all 1972s, really spicy. Taste: V. powerful—still basic acidity—tannin. Lots of

very frank fruit—long—sauvage." (S.S.) "Color of old tiles. Powerful nose of leather. Few noble nuances on the nose and the palate. The leathery notes are accentuated. Alcohol out of balance and short. All the same, it is far from fading and can be drunk for a long time still. It may yet find its balance." (M.B.) "Concentrated color. Serious nose, tertiary or autumnal, leaning toward meaty and finishing on truffles and mushrooms. Taut wine, a bit stiff—a military wine—long." (M.D.)

1971 27 September

(22 hl/ha): "Colour similar to '72—hail nose—more noticeable than '83, but perhaps because older—Palais: Oh dear! Begins well, all the richness and opulence that the wines had des le départ en fût, mais the finish is so touched by grêle—completely dries up taste." (S.S.) "Mahogany robe. An aromatic festival (spices, violets, earth, fine leather, a bitter note of hail). Great fullness and pith. Very voluptuous notes of muscat. Bitter hail taste less present than in 1983. Menthol finish. Should please a great many wine drinkers even though it is in no way a classic Romanée." (M.B) "Still deeper color. Lacks superficial charm, smoky, resin, pine forest. Surmaturity, something of crystallized fruits. Long. I defend this wine." (M.D.) "Sweet, full, richly flavoured. A vast, complete wine, packed with fruit, with great length and flowery aftertaste . . . magnificent now and will keep." (Michael Broadbent, last tasted May 1983)

1970 9 October

(40 hl/ha): No recent notes.

1969 13 October

(30 hl/ha): "Advanced nose and colour—light ruby—Dominance of alcohol—wine somewhat out of balance which, in our opinion, is not representative of the vintage or the growth." (*Dégustation Sélection,* 1990) "Make no mistake about it, this wine is magnificent: an almost inimitably glorious bouquet; great power and length. No words of mine can do justice to it." (Michael Broadbent, tasted September 1986)

1968 14 October

No red wines bottled at the Domaine.

1967 6 OCTOBER

(30 hl/ha): "Yellow at rim—orangey smell—tawny—a touch of tar. Palais: Madérisé en bouche—middle flavour is good, fruity and earthy. Finish has a glimpse of oxidation." (S.S.) "Tile robe. Reduction at first but, with aeration, becomes cleaner. Not much flesh, a lean wine, almost monotonic, but which is holding well and presents all the breed of its terroir. It improves greatly after half an hour. But don't expect voluptuousness." (M.B.) "Medium intensity. Supple, spindly palate." (M.D.)

1966 5 OCTOBER

(35 hl/ha): "Deep colour—Mature, but healthily so. Nez enivrant—wonderful champignon nez, *but* healthy mushrooms—comme chanterelles avec quelques truffes aussi. Grande classe—grande richesse et opulence. Wet, spicy earth. Taste: Enormous freshness. Rich, macerated fruit—great fruit. Incredibly rich—opulence—glycerol—alcohol. Melts in the mouth. Backbone of tannins. Perfect structure—Grand vin. The star, the Classic [of the 1960s]." (S.S.) "Marvelous, explosive nose (violets, spices) of extraordinary charm. Perfect maturity on palate—all of the 'feminine' qualities of La Romanée—finesse, suavity, intense perfume, aerial form, impressive length. Prestigious balance. It is difficult to leave one's glass." (M.B.) "Beautiful robe. Harmonious, distinguished, voluptuous, rich. Length and balance. Supple and civilized. Very GOOD." (M.D.)

1965 23 OCTOBER

(24 hl/ha): "Very deep colour. Old, dried champignons nose . . . Taste: Good middle fruit—'torchons' à la fin. Some richness—but not clean." (S.S.) "Mahogany robe. Festival of mushroom nuances on the nose (oyster mushrooms, meadow mushrooms), due no doubt to a certain proportion of rotted grapes. Surprising mellowness. Astonishing uncommon complexity. Much more class than 1975 or 1963. Wine outside of the norm but very exciting." (M.B.) "Fading (a bit of mushroom). Short." (M.D.)

1964 4 OCTOBER

(38 hl/ha): "Deep colour, but not as deep as '65! Amazing smell of cooking beef—muscular. Scent—touch of violets. Palais: Sévère—Plus sec que le 66. V.G. acidity." (S.S.) "Mahogany robe. Absolute opposite of 1966. Much less expressive but much

more serious and profound nose (blond tobacco, earth, liquorice) which, for Lalou Bize expresses rigorously its terroir. Solid structure, demands a long aeration to open out. Fat and muscular tannins. Built to age for a couple of decades more, at least. It is not, at present, in an amiable mood." (M.B.) "Very evolved. RICH nose. Balanced palate, chewy fruit—but not elegant enough." (M.D.)

1963 15 October

(35 hl/ha): "Dark and brown but not yellow as the '67! Nez pur de Porto! Palais: Un Porto en Bourgogne! Rich. Je le préfère au '65 . . . Plus net." (S.S.) "Solid robe. Slightly volatile nose. Lots of spices. Astonishing freshness of conservation. The initial faults have faded and melted. But a bit less personality than 1965." (M.B.) "Feeble. Short and cross." (M.D.)

1962 15 October

(35 hl/ha): "Last tasted, in jeroboam, almost exactly a quarter of a century after the grapes had been picked. Not deep now but medium deep, richly coloured, looking mature. When first poured, the nose was low-keyed, rather twiggy. It took twenty minutes to get its act together in the glass, developing richly and after half an hour was rich and toasty. Medium dry, full bodied, a powerful assertive wine, with hints of liquorice, holly, walnuts. Great length. Mouthfilling. Best beyond 2000." (Michael Broadbent, September 1987)

1961 7 October

(25 hl/ha): "Deep to rim!! And thick to rim. Quelle *intensité*—unbelievably rich *fruit*. Heady. Reached all corners of nose. Spice bazaar . . . Taste: Rich, liqueur, sweet, soft, moins "nerveux" que le '64." (S.S.) "Brilliant expression of La Romanée. Mahogany robe. Great, dazzling nose of spices and musk, tremendous fullness on palate with a comfortable softness which will seduce lovers of opulent Burgundies. Great radiance but displays a tendency to oxidize with prolonged aeration." (M.B.) "Superb robe. Impression of concentration. *Very elegant nose. Homogeneous*—something spicy. Long on palate. Great style." (M.D.)

1960 4 October

(30 hl/ha): Only Romanée-Conti and La Tâche bottled at the Domaine. No recent notes.

1959 26 September

(40 hl/ha): "Deep colour—mature at edges—Rich, café nose, rich sous-bois, violettes aussi. Vegetal undertones—cocoa avec oxydation. Cocoa and alcohol en bouche. Manque un peu de vivacité—Aging." (S.S.) "Mahogany robe. Less explosive nose than 1961. Nuances of dried beef which evolve in refinement with long aeration. Very full-bodied, no doubt still too young to reach the complexity of 1953 and 1952. But it is hard to imagine how it could be more elegant!" (M.B.) "Deep mahogany. Highly civilized nose, completely harmonious. *Very* long, great class . . . a great noble." (M.D.)

1958 9 October

(28 hl/ha): No notes.

1957 10 October

(27 hl/ha): "Quite an angry orange brown. Un peu 'musty' and 'mousy'—then that goes and it is very *roasted.* Roasted raisins. Palais: très rôti en bouche—sec, but extremely concentrated. Lacks 'allure,' but is very 'serious' wine." (S.S.) "Tile robe. Subtle nuanced nose (with a flair of muscat which seems decidedly to be the signature of the Domaine's wines). Opens out (without the perfection of the aromas of the 1953)—fragile in contact with air. Should be uncorked at the moment of service." (M.B.) "Old wood on the nose. Subtle, deep and disguised acidity. Surface beauty. Half long." (M.D.)

1956 18 October

(25 hl/ha): "Very dark. Café . . . Cannelle, comme le café à Vienne (Vienna!!) where one puts cinnamon in the coffee. Smells almost of rum later—then oxidizes. Good fruit in middle, but dishcloths at end." (S.S.) "Tile robe. Strong scent of muscat, purer and fruitier than 1959 or 1957. Ravishing contours, no heavy notes, bouquet of infused aromatic herbs. Marvelous illustration of this terroir's capacity to succeed in small years." (M.B.) "Lots of class in the range of somewhat isolated tertiary, autumnal aromas—with aeration evolves toward muscat. On the palate, immediate finesse—powerful singleness of expression—round fruit later." (M.D.)

1955 14 OCTOBER

(30 hl/ha): "Same colour. *Richly* aromatic nose. Like toffee made of clover—*intense*—deeply concentrated—like roasting coffee beans. Nose stays constant in a remarkable way. Palais: Extremely powerful—Great centre of concentration and alcohol—Kernel of character. Imposing—strong." (S.S.) "Bronze robe. Extremely nuanced nose (spices, fine moka), ideally suave texture; superb bottle but fragile with aeration. After twenty minutes in the glass, nuances of iodine appear and the inevitable decline proves that a wine from eight-year-old vines is not immortal." (M.B.) "Mahogany. Tertiary fruit—smoky coffee. Long palate, very long—indisputably fading, a profile but a beautiful profile." (M.D.)

1954 16 OCTOBER

(30 hl/ha): "Deep colour . . . coffee beans—smoky. Taste: Rather bitter. Some fruit—like coffee beans that are roasted too long." (S.S.) "Mahogany robe. At first, the nose has none of the finesse of the 1955 but it is much more resistant to air. Lovely softness on palate, very elegant nuances of fine leather, but no great length. Altogether astonishing for the vintage." (M.B.) "Lots of (period) robe. Rich. Complex, spicy nose . . . a certain rigidity. (M.D.)

1953 4 OCTOBER

(29 hl/ha): "Very *golden* brown—like the glints in a Cognac—coloured topaz—Extravagant, meaty nose, cigar box—an old one that has had the best Havanas, like smoked meat. A siren of a wine au nez cedary. Palais: Soft, charming tabac en bouche, melts in the mouth, en dentelle." (S.S.) "Bronze robe. Really sublime bouquet with subtle nuances of jasmin, smoky China tea and spices. Fabulous delicacy, perfect harmony. An aerial wine, miracle of young vines in an ideal year of aromatic purity for pinot noir." (M.B.) "Very evolved. Very complex nose—muscat, smoky. Very concentrated palate—astringence of age but, all the same round and fruity." (M.D.)

1952 29 SEPTEMBER

(24 hl/ha): "Very dark and far less yellow. Wonderfully scented. Violetty—musky—smoked sous-bois. Grand vin de la Côte de Nuits—signé! Vanilla pod, La race même. Palais: GRAND grand vin, toujours avec son côté sauvage. Pour la première fois aujourd'hui un vin qui a le goût du gibier—surtout de la grouse faisandée.

Glorious explosion of 'fauves' tastes—like La Tâche '52 mais peut-être plus jeune." (S.S.) "First vintage of reconstituted vines. Much more earthy nose than 1953 with, nonetheless, the same exotic nuances of jasmine. Astonishing body for a wine from young vines, suave texture, extremely complex bouquet (spices, humus), still holding admirably. Belongs to the family of 'serious' vintages like 1964 and 1959." (M.B.) "Very dense robe. Anthology of fruit, traces of mushroom. Classic and long . . . Cleansed." (M.D.)

The vines of Romanée-Conti were torn up after the 1945 harvest. The following vintages issue from the old vines which were propagated by *provignage* and cultivated *en foule:*

1945 2 October

(2.5 hl/ha): "(From a bottle in perfect condition) . . . This bottle was absolutely magnificent! Deep, dark colour, with a wonderful nose of Oriental spice mixed with plums and exotic berry fruit. In the mouth, there are layers of rich fruit and tremendous length. This wine goes on and on in the mouth, finishing with spice in perfect harmony. Perhaps one of the greatest Burgundies ever made." (Geoffrey Troy, 1990)

1944 6 October

"Medium colour with some browning at the rim . . . wonderful nose of oriental spice, with amazing concentration of fruit. In the mouth, the wine has perfect balance, lovely Pinot noir fruit with soft tannins that go on and on. An incredible tasting experience." (Geoffrey Troy, 1990)

1943 8 October

"Good colour, although brown/yellow. Nez of wet linen—immensely smoky. Taste: Un peu rôti—liqueur. Un peu amer maintenant, raisiny, très fort et concentré." (S.S.) "Brick-red holding better than 1952 and 1953. Slightly volatile nose. The wine shines better on the palate with its astonishing texture and its firm, stable tannins. Earthy bouquet like 1952. Wine outside of the norm to which one must adjust." (M.B.) "Old and deep. Somber mushrooms. Very, very long—lemony concentration." (M.D.)

1942 8 October

"A *touch* darker. Caramel nose—Heady—Incredible chocolate/coffee nose—unctuous nose. Légèrement fumé—réglisse. Palais: Réglisse en bouche aussi. (Superbe avec le Reblochon!) Le '42 a des paramètres classiques." (S.S.) "A masterpiece: Wine with fantastically straightforward texture and aromas, of unbelievable concentration, more clearly defined than 1943, with tighter grain, born of raw material of a totally different nature than that of the wines of the '50s. All of the tasters were struck by its intensity." (M.B.) "Must have been VERY dark, still is with age. Extremely tightly woven. Incredible density. Concentration of the essence of wine." (M.D.)

1941 12 October.

No notes.

1940 7 October.

No recent notes.

1939 October.

No notes.

1938 October

"Très jaune, couleur profonde. Nez de café et réglisse—Smoky—Aromatique—chocolat—lead pencil—Palais: Figues sèches en bouche—termine en café froid." (S.S.) "Blond tobacco nose. Fabulous aromatic expression: voluptuous essence, fullness and length, immeasurably deeper than modern norms. With aeration evolves toward nuances of figs, recalling 1983." (M.B.) "Deep robe. Great noblesse. Round, full palate, great rigueur." (M.D.)

1937 October

"*Golden* brown—nez de caramel—Taste: Unfortunately, too caramel for me—oxidation. Mais un côté rôti que j'aime. Hot, dry year, the wine is the same." (S.S.) "Last bottle in the Domaine's cellar. Poor example which gives no idea of the vintage." (M.B.) "Long, concentrated, but too old." (M.D.) "Magnificent. Four good notes, most recently, in magnum, medium deep, lovely warm, broad autumnal colour with fine gradation to mature, mahogany-hued rim; ripe, rich, classic 'beetroot' pinot, gentle, fragrant, sustained bouquet; very sweet, fairly full-bodied, fleshy, lovely flavour. Seemed to grow richer in the glass. Perfect tannin and acidity." (Michael Broadbent, last tasted September 1988)

1936 October

"La couleur d'un Malaga. Couleur profonde, extrême oxydation. Palais: Completely 'gone' even if you like old Malaga! Like a raisiny Oloroso! Rich, though." (S.S.) "Moka color. Spectacular nose of Malaga which evolves with aeration. Very rich, soft and round, but time has taken its toll . . . Difficult to judge." (M.B.) "Perfect robe for the period. Great richness. Sweet palate, decadent, sublimity slipping—probably low acidity." (M.D.)

1935 15 October

"Couleur très jeune pour un vin de cet âge—nez of mothballs! Des fruits exotiques. Some more 'pure' scents appear later. Taste: like an old lacy lady. Elegant." (S.S.) "More transparent, youthful robe. No brown nuance. Needs aeration to get rid of unpleasant meaty nuances. After half an hour, presents a ravishing nose of violets, quintessence of the terroir of La Romanée. Aerial, caressing wine, the soul of elegance." (M.B.) "Light-colored wine. Meaty—barnyard . . . comes together—good balance on palate—gets better in glass." (M.D.) "Nose of Russia leather, tobacco, stubble mulch, clayish earth. On the palate, a fresh acidity which gives the impression of youth. Very solid. Marvelous!" (from menu of 17 November 1990 assembled from guests' notes; see chapter 7)

1934 6 October

No recent notes.

1933 7 October

(6 hl/ha): No recent notes.

1932 15 October

No recent notes.

1931 10 OCTOBER

No recent notes.

1930 11 OCTOBER

No recent notes.

1929 1 OCTOBER

(30 hl/ha): "Très bonne couleur pour son age. *Wonderful* scented, bready nose. A racehorse. Enivrant—un peu de vanille, une touche de Guerlain, spice box, sweetness cedary. Traces of coffee. Taste: Dentelle—Glorious breed. Ultra-racé. Totalement franc—What grace—what delicacy. Une merveille!" (S.S.) "Really divine bouquet, impossible to describe, in which the finesse and delicacy of exquisitely musky nuances excludes all traces of time . . . the essence of fruit on the palate: incredible depth—unbelievable savor and persistence. Textbook wine." (M.B.) "Mahogany. Heady nose holds in glass. Great elegance, fluidity—medium length—a Matisse." (M.D.)

1928 10 OCTOBER

(7.5 hl/ha): "Bonne couleur comme '29—nez *très* aromatique—moins en dentelle que le '29, plus fort, plus prononcé, *plus* aromatique—spiced coffee. Taste: What an *incredible* taste—Full, rich, extremely puissant, beaucoup de mâche—Extraordinary power and richness. On est dans l'époque spirituelle—the '28 and '29 are incredible." (S.S.) "Extra-ordinary concentration. Less voluptuous nose than 1929, but the form is much more carved and sculptural, a monument of intensity and solidity. It is built of bronze. These old vines planted "en foule" are irreplaceable. What a pair of vintages!" (M.B.) "Deep mahogany. Serious, dense, rigid? Balance, power, density. Long—full. A Braque." (M.D.)

1927 4 OCTOBER

(11.5 hl/ha): No recent notes.

1926 4 OCTOBER

(6 hl/ha): "Couleur un peu caramel sur les bords—profonde quand-même—nez sauvage—un peu de madérisation—Wet dog fur!—gets better—spices. Taste: un peu amer—Café fort. Lots of central fruit—plums and prunes—Acidity at end." (S.S.) "Older robe. Some volatility, nuances of walnuts and leather, mushrooms and earth,

wilder than 1929 and 1928. Somewhat more worn also but what force of expression and what intensity!" (M.B.) "Deep mahogany. Concentrated suint—fruity. Very concentrated. Some astringency but not fading. Long but not very long." (M.D.)

1925 22 September

(19 hl/ha): No recent notes.

1924 25 September

(9 hl/ha): "Perhaps palest of série [1920s]. Scented and musky—oxidé—turning to Madeira—smoky—gets more pronounced with oxidation—Taste: Very Madeira/Malaga en bouche. Great pruneaux d'Agen taste . . . prune liqueur." (S.S.) "Orangy robe. Macerated fruits and cinnamon on nose, quinine, beginning to fade but without madeirizing. A very moving relic." (M.B.) "Less color, old mahogany. Sapid concentration. Warm and long but imperturbably monochord." (M.D.)

1923 13 October

(3 hl/ha): "Yellow-brown but same depth. Smelling a bit Porty now—element of pruneaux, walnut liqueur again. Taste: beginning to separate but was very good—alcohol on one side, acidity on other." (S.S.) "One of the tiniest harvests in history (3 hl/ha!). Monumental concentration, incredible fat and tannic force but without the aromatic distinction of 1928/1929. Staggering stability in contact with air and fantastically rigorous structure for this 68-year-old bottle!" (M.B.) "Firm mahogany. discreet—sapid wine. Concentrated—short." (M.D.)

1922 7 October

(7.5 hl/ha): "Deep golden-brown-Nose un peu banana caramel—scented sous-bois underneath the caramel. Taste: Rôti et sec en bouche." (S.S.) "Firm color. Ample nose of quince, angelica with no trace of oxidation. Astonishing subtlety of nuances which show no sign of fading after a half-hour of aeration!" (M.B.) "Firmer robe than 1924. Stretched leather, evolved tertiary scents. A bit short, lengthens somewhat." (M.D.)

1921 24 September

"Same colour as '22. Great heady concentration—Epices envoûtantes. Smells of the bazaar au Caire où on vend les essences de parfum—Taste: *Extraordinary*—opulence but on a solid base. Unequalled! Le '21 fait partie des mythes et des légendes." (S.S.) "Unbelievable transparence of robe. Ravishing aroma, undoubtedly the most extraordinary bouquet of pinot noir that I have ever known, its nuances of fading roses indefinitely prolonged. Aerial wine, fluidity which literally coats the mouth . . . leaves the mouth fresh. The very essence of La Romanée. A sublime bottle, absolutely unforgettable." (M.B.) "Normal robe, that is to say that it must have been very dark at first. Very deep nose, slightly meaty—smoky/smoked tea/immense harmony-balance. Fluid palate, perfect balance. The greatest, the most perfectly balanced, the most sublime." (M.D.)

1920 5 October

(12 hl/ha): "Same colour as '22 and '21—Nose of walnut liqueur—Also wet earth and raw roots—nez fumé, aussi très fruité, même avec l'oxydation. Taste: tarry taste . . . Acidity on one side—has gone 'spiky,' but was very impressive." (S.S.) "What a decade! Admirable transparency of robe, spicier nose than 1921, slightly denser texture, tannins more in evidence. Perfectly preserved bottle of a purity which holds perfectly with aeration. Fabulously complex tannins. A dream wine." (M.B.) "Very deep robe for its age. No trace of age on the nose. Straight, rigorous. Very concentrated, beautiful continuity on the palate. Solid acid support." (M.D.)

1919 2 October

(23 hl/ha): "Same colour as '18—*Very* good depth. Lovely scent—truffley—raisins murs—Taste: So delicate. Lovely fruit en équilibre, toujours avec l'acidité—un peu de thé." (S.S.) "Opens with a divine bouquet (fading roses, smoked tea, lichen and moss), palate nearly as fluid as 1921 but a bit less perfection of balance. Fragile in contact with air, began to fade after a quarter of an hour, but what a quarter of an hour!" (M.B.) "Beautiful. Aging nose. Fruity palate. Medium length. Elegant." (M.D.)

1918 1 October

"A *touch* darker? Plus aromatique, heathery. Taste: Wonderfully *sweet.* Glorious. Fatal attraction . . . reste *très* constant dans le verre—Quel équilibre!" (S.S.) "Firmer color than 1919. Superb constitution, bouquet of extraordinary complexity without quite the grace of 1929 and 1921 or the purity of the 1920. But what texture! What a history lesson on the evolution of style of the great Burgundies!" (M.B.) "Deep color. Violets . . . very long, fine grain. Concentrated—hard." (M.D.)

1917 23 September

No recent notes.

1916 10 October

No recent notes.

1915 20 September

No recent notes.

1914 10 October

No recent notes.

1913 4 October

No recent notes.

1912 5 October

(11 hl/ha): No recent notes.

1911 21 September

(7.5 hl/ha): No recent notes.

The Rarest Wine in the World has no Price

IX

THE WINE OF la Romanée has always fetched a price higher than the others . . .
EXPERTISE OF ROMANÉE-CONTI, 1794

All of the Domaine's red growths, with the exception of Romanée-Conti, are available in case lots. Romanée-Conti, which represents about one-fifteenth of the Domaine's production of red wine, is available only in assorted cases of twelve bottles, each containing one bottle of Romanée-Conti. The changing composition of these assortments from year to year reflects the variable production from one growth to another. The 1988 assorted case consisted of one Romanée-Conti, three La Tâche, two Richebourg, three Romanée Saint-Vivant, one Grands Echézeaux, and two Echézeaux. The price of the assorted case, announced in July 1990 for release in January 1991, was: Fr 10,200 (for ten cases or more); Fr 11,875 (five or more cases); Fr 13,880 (fewer than five cases). Within France, the government imposes an additional 18.6 percent "value added tax" (TVA). The composition of the assorted cases may shift from year to year to sustain the balance. When stocks fall out of balance, so do the assortments; in 1981, for instance, the 1966—and again, in 1987, the 1978—was composed of two Romanée-Conti and ten Romanée Saint-Vivant.

The augmentation of prices in a ten-year period is illustrated by those announced for 1978 (in March 1981) and for 1985 (in July 1987), vintages of great reputation, for assortments comparable to that of 1988, in fewer than five-case lots: 1978 (one Romanée-Conti, three La Tâche, two of each of the other growths), Fr 5,440; 1985 (one Romanée-Conti, three La Tâche, one Richebourg, two Romanée Saint-Vivant, two Grands Echézeaux, and three Echézeaux), Fr 8,085.

In principle, only the mixed cases of red growths or cases of a single growth, with the exception of Romanée-Conti, are offered to private individuals. The Domaine's agents may buy one bottle of Romanée-Conti to every fifteen bottles of other red wines of the same vintage. Montrachet, whose production is half that of Romanée-Conti, is not offered to private individuals; it is sold to négociants on the basis of one case of Montrachet to from thirty to fifty cases of other growths of the Domaine in the same vintage, depending on the year.

The Domaine has often been criticized for this system of rationing, the purpose of which is to maintain a balance in the reserves of all the growths and, above all, to ensure the continuing availability of Romanée-Conti for as long as a given vintage remains in stock; if Romanée-Conti were not rationed, its entire production would disappear into the cellars of a handful of wealthy collectors, never to be seen in the marketplace, unless it be for purposes of speculation in the auction rooms. The proprietors are the first to admit that the formula is imperfect, for they have no control over what happens to the wines once they leave the Domaine's cellars. A sort of economic alchemy takes possession, thrusting into motion a mysterious shifting of values which varies in different parts of the world. The price of Romanée-Conti, above all, assumes a life of its own, soaring to startling heights, thanks to its rarity and to its immensurable power as a status symbol.

Although the single bottle of Romanée-Conti in each mixed case bears no price tag, it is easy enough to affix a presumed value to it, since the other growths are priced.

For ten or more cases of 1988, the prices per bottle in 1991 were: La Tâche, Fr 1,000, Richebourg, Fr 900, Romanée Saint-Vivant, Fr 800, Grands Echézeaux, Fr 700, Echézeaux, Fr 500. These figures place the bottle of Romanée-Conti at Fr 1,300, the same price as the bottle of Montrachet, fractionally more expensive than La Tâche, and about two and a half times the price of Echézeaux. By the time these wines reach the marketplace and the auction rooms, Romanée-Conti will command about three times the price of La Tâche, four to five times that of Richebourg, five to six that of Romanée Saint-Vivant and Grands Echézeaux, and eight times that of Echézeaux. In France, Romanée-Conti can often carry a price five times that of La Tâche and twelve times that of Echézeaux: in October 1990, La Cave à Millésimes, Paris, listed Romanée-Conti 1981 at Fr 3,200 per bottle (plus TVA) and Echézeaux 1981 at Fr 300; Millésimes in Fontvieille listed Romanée-Conti 1987 at Fr 3,200 (plus TVA) and, in the same vintage, La Tâche at Fr 600; Richebourg, Fr 550; Romanée Saint-Vivant, Fr 450; Grands Echézeaux, Fr 390; and Echézeaux, Fr 260! Prices in the chic shops at Place de la Madeleine are considerably higher.

Auction rooms provide the best barometer of prices. The 1989 edition of *Christie's Price Index of Vintage Wine* lists the following prices, fetched in Christie's London rooms in 1987 and 1988, for twelve-bottle cases of the 1978 vintage: Romanée-Conti, £3,300; Montrachet, £2,500; La Tâche, £1,300; Richebourg, £720; Romanée Saint-Vivant, £660; Grands Echézeaux, £620; Echézeaux, £480. In September 1990 a case of Romanée-Conti 1969, estimated at £3,000 to £4,000, went for £7,200. Bottles of Romanée-Conti from the pre-1945, ungrafted vines are rare on the market. Christie's lists seven vintages, mostly single bottles, which have appeared in their London auction rooms since 1984. In December 1988, five bottles of 1875, from the cellars of Café Voisin, acquired in 1932 by the Paris wine firm Nicolas, went for a low of £980 and a high of £1,200 per bottle. A bottle of 1899 was sold in 1987 for £1,550. In December 1992, *La Revue du vin de France*, whose figures are based on transactions from the preceding two months, estimated Romanée-Conti 1971 and 1978 at Fr 7,500 per bottle, 1953, 1959, 1961, 1964, 1966, and 1985 at Fr 7,000 or more; the lowest estimate is 1977 at Fr 3,000.

Restaurants in Europe who buy directly from the Domaine tend to base their prices on the Domaine's original tariffs rather than on those created by the international markets; because some restaurants alter their prices very little, or not at all, after the initial markup, it is not uncommon to find a Romanée-Conti on a restaurant wine list at a price considerably lower than that commanded for the same vintage in a retail shop, whereas the Domaine's other growths are usually at least as expensive on the restaurant lists. Because of the Domaine's formula for marketing their Montrachet, it is extremely rare to find a Domaine de la Romanée-Conti Montrachet in a restaurant cellar (Roger Vergé lists both a 1982 and a 1985).

FRAUDS

The reputation of the Domaine and the prices of its wines act as a magnet to fraudulent activity.

The most frustrating variety of fraud is that in which the truants attempt to remain within the limits of the law by creating denominations or labels which resemble, without perfectly imitating, those of the original. In the early 1960s a German distributor, in collaboration with a French firm, specialized in the export of wines from cooperative cellars in the South of France, marketed vins rosés under the registered trademarks "Remané" and "Remany"; they were constrained to remove them from the market after the INAO presented the case before the Civil Tribunal in Düsseldorf. In 1969 an ordinary table wine (*vin sans appellation*) appeared on the French market labeled ROMAIN CONTE. The defense claimed that, because it was a cheap wine, its clientele was totally different from that of Romanée-Conti. The court judged, nonetheless, that not only was a prestigious reputation thus tarnished but that the confusion with the name Romanée-Conti permitted the wine to be sold at a higher price than that of other wines of a similar quality.

In Texas in the early 1980s, Lalou and Aubert were served a bottle of wine labeled "Romanée-Conti 1947." There was no Romanée-Conti between 1945 and 1952. The wine, however, was an authentic Domaine wine and the cork was original: it was branded "Domaine de la Romanée-Conti, Echézeaux 1964." The bottle's origin was traced to New Orleans, but the artist's identity was never uncovered. A bottle of the same wine, from a New Orleans collection, was listed in a Christie's catalog for an auction in Chicago, 15 September 1990. The Domaine was notified; the bottle was withdrawn from the sale and destroyed. In September 1990 a Japanese wine merchant bought five sealed cases of wine marked "Domaine de la Romanée-Conti, Montrachet 1986" from a Beverly Hills wine merchant. One of his clients discovered the otherwise perfectly imitated labels to bear the legend "Appellation Romanée-Conti Contrôlée," instead of "Appellation Montrachet Contrôlée," beneath the large letters MONTRACHET. The Japanese clients contacted the Domaine, as well as their U.S. agents, whose falsified colleret was affixed to the bottles. Lalou, on a business trip to Japan, profited to buy a bottle of "Montrachet, Appellation Romanée-Conti Contrôlée," which is now being held under bailiff's seal in France. The Japanese wine merchant is said to have paid $5,000 per case, he is said to have been reimbursed by the California wine merchant, and the remaining wine is said to have been destroyed. The affair is under investigation by the U.S. Bureau of Alcohol, Tobacco, and Firearms.

The surprising aspect of both the Romanée-Conti and the Montrachet falsifications is the extraordinary innocence of the counterfeiters: the first was unaware that Romanée-Conti 1947 did not exist, that the basic design which served as a model for the false label did not exist before 1951, that numbered bottles, the total number of bottles produced, and Henri de Villaine's signature appeared on the labels for the first time in 1953—and he failed to note that the corners of the Domaine's labels are always rounded instead of square; the Montrachet falsifier apparently had no idea of the meaning of the words *appellation contrôlée,* but assumed that two famous names on a label would be twice as good as one.

Genealogical Tree of the Second House of Conti

The House of Conti took its name from the town of Conti-sur-Selles, near Amiens, in Picardy. The marquisate of Conti was acquired by Louis de Bourbon, first prince de Condé and uncle of Henry IV, in 1551, through his marriage to Eléonore de Roye. Their third son, François, bore the title of marquis de Conti until the marquisate was elevated to a principality at the end of the sixteenth century. The first House of Conti disappeared in 1614 with the death of François, first prince de Conti, who left no legitimate heirs.

At the birth in 1629 of Armand, second son of Henry II, prince de Condé, Louis XIII resurrected the House of Conti in the child's favor.

Henri II de Bourbon
prince de Condé
(1588-1646)

Charlotte Marguerite de Montmorency
(d. 1650)

Louis de Bourbon, duc d'Enghein
prince de Condé after 1646
(1621-1686)

Armand de Bourbon
prince de Conti
(1629-1666)

Louise Marie Martinozzi
(1637-1672)

Louis Armand de Bourbon
comte de Pézenas
prince de Conti in 1666
(1661-1685)

Marie Anne de Bourbon
(1666-1739)

François Louis de Bourbon
comte de La Marche
prince de La Roche-sur-Yon
prince de Conti in 1685
(1664-1709)

Marie Thérèse de Bourbon-Condé
(1666-1732)

Louis Armand de Bourbon
comte de La Marche
prince de Conti in 1709
(1695-1727)

Louise Elisabeth de Bourbon-Condé
(1693-1775)

Louis François de Bourbon
comte de La Marche
prince de Conti in 1727
(1717-1776)

Louise Diane d'Orléans
(1716-1736)

Louis François Joseph de Bourbon
comte de La Marche
prince de Conti in 1776
(1734-1814)

Fortunée Marie d'Est
(1731-1803)

Genealogical Tree of the Croonembourg Family

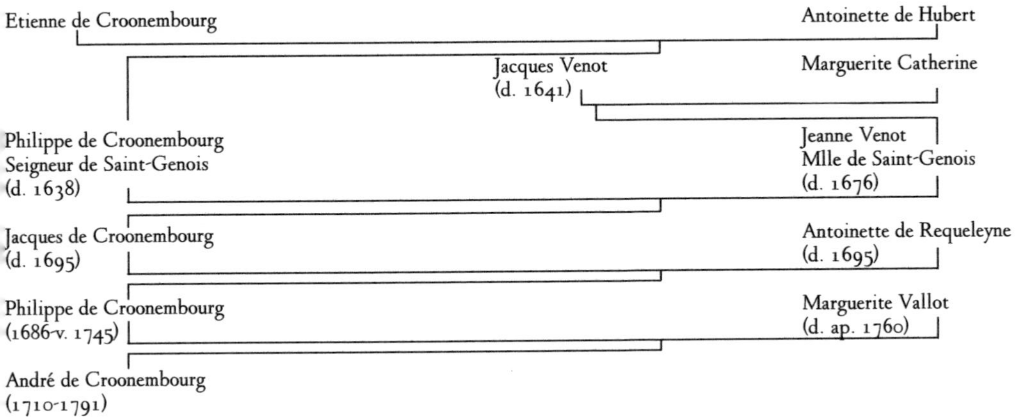

Proprietors and Directors of the Domaine de la Romanée-Conti since 1869

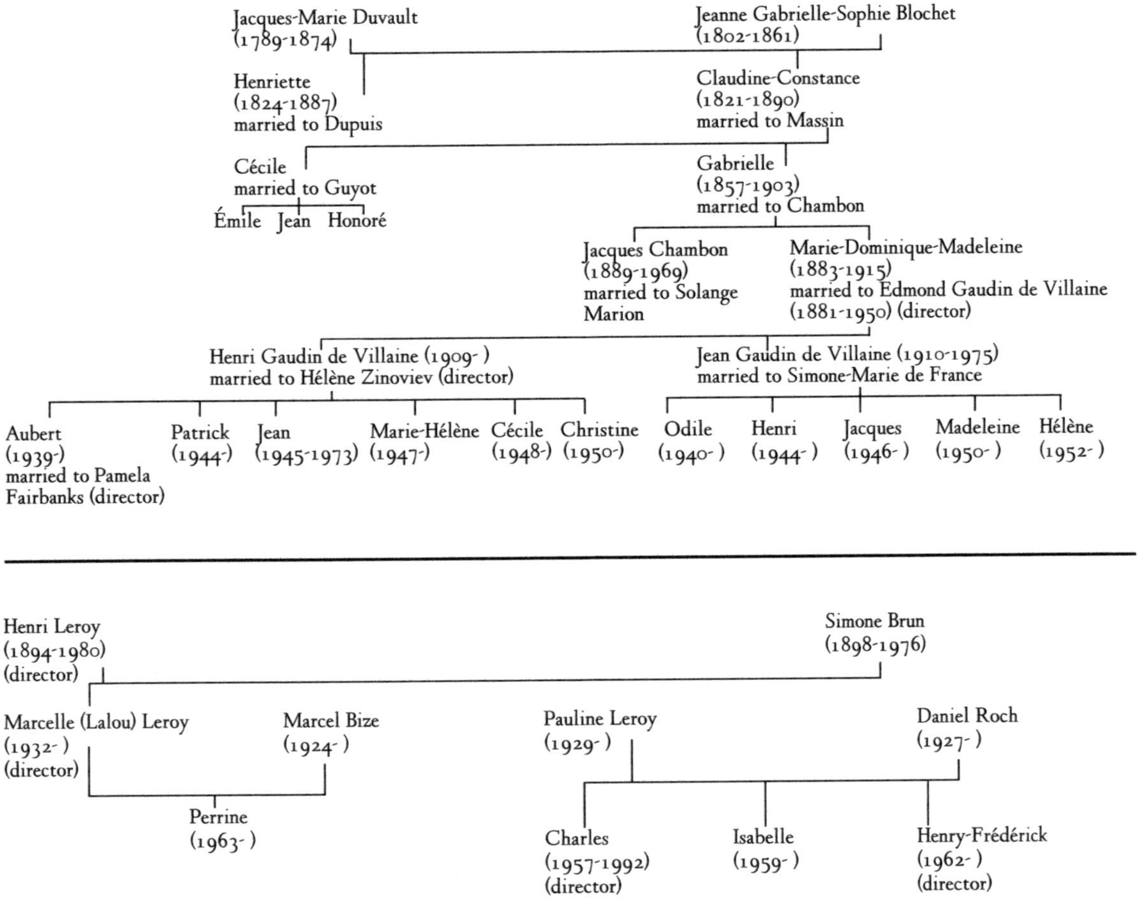

HISTORICAL CHART

	BURGUNDY AND FRANCE		ROMANÉE-CONTI
	Dukes of Burgundy		
880	Richard le Justicier, First Duke of Burgundy (d. 921)	ca. 900	Foundation of the Priory of Saint-Vivant by Manassès, Sire of Vergy (d. 918)
1032–1361	House of Capet	1131	13 November—Hugues II, Duke of Burgundy, cedes all woods and uncultivated lands that he possesses in Flagey and Vosne, including those to become Romanée-Conti, to the prior of Saint-Vivant
1364–1477	House of Valois : Death of Charles le Téméraire, 5 January 1477; Annexation of Burgundy by Louis XI, King of France		
	Kings of France	1241 1276 1285	Acquisitions of vines by the priors of Saint-Vivant, among which are the future Romanée-Conti
1328–1498	House of Valois (. . . Louis XI, Charles VIII)		
1498–1515	House of Valois-Orléans (Louis XII)	1512	First declaration and description of "Les Cloux de Saint-Vivant"

1515–1589 House of Valois-Angoulême (François I, Henri II, François II, Charles IX, Henri III)

1589 House of Bourbon : Henri IV (d. 1610)

1610 Louis XIII (d. 1643)

1643 Louis XIV (d. 1715)

1715 Louis XV (d. 1774)

1584 19 February—sale (perpetual lease) by the prior of Saint-Vivant of the Cros des Cloux to Claude Cousin

1603 Germain Danon, Claude Cousin's nephew, inherits the Cros des Cloux

1621 Jacques Venot acquires the Cros des Cloux from Germain Danon

1631 28 August—Jacques Venot transfers his properties to his son-in-law, Philippe de Croonembourg, and his daughter, Jeanne Venot

1651 First mention of "La Romanée"

1760 18 July—contract of sale of La Romanée to Jean-François Joly de Fleury "for himself or his friend of election"; transfer of property "au profit de Son Altesse Sérénissime Monseigneur Louis-François de Bourbon Prince de Conty Prince du Sang"

1762–1763 The prince de Conti buys two adjoining parcels of vines, lieu dit "au meix Gaillot" (aux Goillotte) to be used for the construction of vinification and storage cellars for La Romanée and lodging for the prince's vigneron and régisseur

1774	Louis XVI (d. 1793)		
		1776	2 August—Death of Louis-François de Bourbon; Louis-François-Joseph de Bourbon becomes prince de Conti
	The Revolution and the Modern Age		
1789	14 July—taking of the Bastille		
1792–1804	First Republic:		
		1793	April—the prince de Conti is arrested and imprisoned at Fort Saint-Jean, Marseilles
	21 January 1793—execution of Louis XVI; 16 October—execution of Marie-Antoinette		
		1794	13 February—first expertise of la Romanée-Conti; 6 July—second expertise; 24 December—La Romanée sold to highest bidder, Nicolas Defer de la Nouèrre
	27–28 July, 1794–fall and execution of Robespierre		
	4 September 1799—coup d'etat		
		1797	5 September—the law of 19 Fructidor exiles all members of the House of Bourbon; the prince de Conti takes refuge in Barcelona (d. 1814)
1799–1815	Bonaparte: 1799—coup d'etat; 1802—Consul for Life; 1804—proclamation of the First Empire; 1814—abdication (first restoration of the monarchy, Louis XVIII, King of France); 1815—Hundred Days ends with second abdication of Napoleon		
1814–1848	Bourbon Restoration:		
	1815—Return of Louis XVIII		
		1819	22 September—Julien-Jules Ouvrard acquires Romanée-Conti at auction
	16 September 1824—death of Louis XVIII		

	29 May 1825—Coronation of Charles X	1828	19 May—Ouvrard moves to Château de Gilly to manage his vineyards and fashion a public life
	2 August 1830—abdication of Charles X; 9 August—Louis-Philippe, duc d'Orléans, accepts the crown		1837—Ouvrard mayor of Gilly; 1840—councillor general of the Côte d'Or; 1852—Deputy of the Côte d'Or
1848–1852	Second Republic:		
	24 February 1848—abdication and flight of Louis-Philippe; 26 February—proclamation of the Second Republic; 10 December—Louis-Napoléon Bonaparte, president of the Republic		
	2 December 1851—coup d'état of Louis-Napoléon Bonaparte (Napoleon III)		
1852	2 December—proclamation of the Second Empire	1861	22 June—death of Ouvrard; de Rochechouart nieces and nephews inherit Romanée-Conti
		1869	7 August—sale of Romanée-Conti to Paul Guillemot; 25 November—Jacques-Marie Duvault-Blochet, already proprietor in Les Gaudichots, Richebourg, Grands Echézeaux, and Echézeaux, buys Romanée-Conti
1870–1871	Franco-Prussian War: 19 July 1870—France declares war on Prussia; 4 September—collapse of Second Empire; establishment of Third Republic; 19 September—Siege of Paris; 28 January 1871—Franco-Prussian armistice		
		1874	23 February—death of Duvault-Blochet

		1876	Duvault-Blochet properties divided between his two daughters, Claudine-Constance Massin and Henriette Dupuis; subsequently, through successive inheritances, Romanée-Conti is divided among cousins
		1911	Edmond Gaudin de Villaine, husband of Marie-Dominique-Madeleine Chambon and manager of the Domaine, hires Louis Clin as régisseur
1914–1918	First World War	1912	M.-D.-M. Gaudin de Villaine and Jacques Chambon purchase Guyot cousins' shares of Romanée-Conti
1939–1945	Second World War:	1933	Acquisition by Domaine de la Romanée-Conti of La Tâche Joly de Bevy
	3 September 1939—France declares war on Germany		
	10 July 1940—Defeat by Germany and end of Third Republic; Occupation;	1940	July—André Noblet hired by Louis Clin
	6 September, 1944—provisional constitution of new republic	1942	31 July—Société Civile du Domaine de la Romanée-Conti formed; Henri Leroy buys Jacques Chambon's shares in Domaine
1946–1958	Fourth Republic		
1958–present	Fifth Republic	1950	24 November—death of Edmond Gaudin de Villaine; Henri de Villaine becomes co-director with Henri Leroy

1963–1980	Acquisition by the Domaine of vines in Montrachet
1966	Romanée Saint-Vivant Marey-Monge farmed out to the Domaine de la Romanée-Conti
1974	New bylaws of Domaine: Lalou Bize-Leroy and Aubert de Villaine are named co-directors; Henri de Villaine and Henri Leroy are named Board of Supervisors
1979	Domaine acquires La Goillotte
1980	21 February—death of Henri Leroy; Pauline Roch, his eldest daughter, replaces him on the Board of Supervisors
1984	André Noblet retires; Bernard Noblet, chef de cave; Gérard Marlot, chef de culture
1986	30 May—death of André Noblet
1988	September—purchase of Romanée Saint-Vivant Marey-Monge by the associates of the Domaine de la Romanée-Conti
1992	January—Lalou Bize-Leroy cedes co-directorship of the Domaine de la Romanée-Conti to her nephew, Charles Roch; 10 March—death of Charles Roch; 28 April—Henry-Frédéric Roch named co-director

NOTES

1. Official declarations of wine production today are expressed in hectoliters (hundred-liter units). Among vignerons, volumes are designated in terms of the *pièce*, the *feuillette*, and the *quartaut*. A pièce (also called a *muid*, a *tonneau*, or a *poinçon*) is the traditional cask of the Côte d'Or filled with its measure of wine (when the cask is empty, it is called a *fût*). The queue, or double barrel, is a measure used in the past for pricing wine; double barrels have never been in common use for raising or storing wine in the Côte d'Or. Following are some equivalents:

1 queue	= 2 pièces	= 456 liters	≈ 608 bottles
1 pièce		= 228 liters	≈ 304 bottles
1 feuillette	= 1/2 pièce	= 114 liters	≈ 152 bottles
1 quartaut	= 1/2 feuillette	= 57 liters	≈ 76 bottles

2. This definition of *climat* is not applicable to the Clos de Vougeot, which is today officially classified as a single climat, or cru, but which in fact is composed of a number of different climats. Climat and lieudit (place-name) often coincide, as in Romanée-Conti, but a climat may also encompass several lieudits or contain only a portion of a lieudit; the climat of Les Echézeaux, for instance, contains, in part or in their entirety, eleven different lieudits. A finage embodies all of the climats, or lieudits, contained within a community's boundaries. Thus, a climat is to a finage as an individual is to a family. The climats of Romanée-Conti, La Tâche, Richebourg, and Romanée Saint-Vivant are situated in the finage of Vosne; the climats of Echézeaux and Grands Echézeaux are in the finage of Flagey.

3. In August 1988, thanks to a persistent and incomprehensible confusion between the Domaine de la Romanée-Conti and its distributor the Société Leroy, the international press announced, in some instances flatly, in others by inference, that the Japanese were buying into the Domaine de la Romanée-Conti. There was an immediate uproar concerning the violation of national heritage (*le patrimoine*). The retractions were numerous, but they were given less space than the original false information, and in any case the damage was already done. The following formal repudiation appeared, 26 July 1990, on the front page of *La Journée vinicole*, beneath the headline "*Nationale Heritage*: No Japanese in La Romanée-Conti":

> The Société Civile du Domaine de la Romanée-Conti would like to put a stop, once and for all, to the rumors, inexactitudes, and false interpretations concerning a foreign investment in its capital. The capital of the Société du Domaine de la Romanée-Conti belongs entirely and in equal parts to two family groups: de Villaine and Leroy.
>
> S.A. Leroy possesses no part of the capital of the Société Civile du Domaine de la Romanée-Conti and has no connection with the Domaine apart from the same kind of contract which binds the Domaine to its other agents.
>
> The minority participation by the Takashimaya Company in the capital of S.A. Leroy is, therefore, the affair of the Société Leroy S.A. and of it, alone.

4. Nineteenth-century classifications are parsimonious in their attributions of superior status. André Jullien (1816) listed eight growths as "superior wines of the first class": "la Romanée-

Conti, le Chambertin, le Richebourg, le Clos-Vougeot, la Romanée-de-Saint-Vivant, la Tâche, le clos de Saint-Georges, and le Corton." The English writer Cyrus Redding, in his classification of wines of the world (1833), listed the same eight growths, in the same order, at the head of "Wines of the First Class," described as "the first and most delicate red wines in the world." Dr. Lavalle (1855), in his "Tête de Cuvée n° 1" category, separates out Romanée-Conti, Clos de Vougeot, Chambertin and (Chambertin) Clos de Bèze, designated as "*vins hors ligne*," followed by those listed above and a couple of others. Among the whites, only Montrachet receives superior status from these writers.

In today's official classification of the wines of the Côte d'Or, the ultimate category is that of Grand Cru, its Appellation d'Origine Contrôlée (AOC) being the specific name of the climat, or cru, to the exclusion of any more generalized information—for example, Appellation Romanée-Conti Contrôlée. The Institut National des Appellations d'Origine (INAO), created in 1935, grants, with democratic largesse for the Côte d'Or, Grand Cru status to twenty-five red growths (of which twenty-four are in the Côte de Nuits) and nine white growths (of which eight are in the Côte de Beaune), with no distinctions made within the category (among the Grand Cru appellations in the finage of Gevrey-Chambertin, Clos de Bèze is part of the Chambertin appellation, just as Mazoyères is part of the Charmes appellation: Chambertin-Clos de Bèze, however, because of its reputation, never relinquishes its name; on the other hand, much of Mazoyères-Chambertin, which is a less well known name than Charmes-Chambertin, is commercialized under the Charmes-Chambertin label). The AOC Grands Crus of the Côte d'Or, reading from north to south, are as follows:

Côte de Nuits

Finage	Growth
Gevrey-Chambertin	Chambertin-Clos de Bèze
	Chambertin
	Chapelle-Chambertin
	Charmes-Chambertin
	Griotte-Chambertin
	Latricières-Chambertin
	Mazis-Chambertin
	Mazoyères-Chambertin (or Charmes-Ch.)
	Ruchottes-Chambertin
Morey-Saint-Denis	Clos Saint-Denis
	Clos de la Roche
	Clos des Lambreys
	Clos de Tart
	Bonnes Mares
Chambolle-Musigny	Bonnes Mares
	Musigny (red and white)
Vougeot	Clos de Vougeot

Flagey-Echézeaux	Echézeaux Grands Echézeaux
Vosne-Romanée	Romanée-Conti Romanée Saint-Vivant Richebourg La Tâche La Romanée La Grande Rue

Côte de Beaune

Finage	Growth
Ladoix-Serrigny	Corton (red and white) Corton-Charlemagne (white)
Aloxe-Corton	Corton Corton-Charlemagne (white) Charlemagne (white)
Pernand-Vergelesses	Corton Corton-Charlemagne (white) Charlemagne (white)
Puligny-Montrachet (all white)	Chevalier-Montrachet Bienvenues-Bâtard-Montrachet Bâtard-Montrachet Montrachet
Chassagne-Montrachet (all white)	Montrachet Bâtard-Montrachet Criots-Bâtard-Montrachet

The next-best appellation is that of Premier Cru. A Grand Cru owes allegiance to no appellation other than that of its own climat, whereas a Premier Cru is a superior village appellation, as differentiated from an AOC *communale*. The label of an AOC Premier Cru usually includes—in addition to the village name and the designation Premier Cru—the name of the climat, in letters which must not measure more in height than those of the village name (AOC communales may also include the name of the climat on the label, if the wine is of a single origin, but the letters must be no more than one-half the height of those of the village name). The designation Premier Cru on a label is not obligatory; if its omission is justified by the fame of a climat, it is sometimes absent.

5. During the eighteenth century, outside of the royal family, the only extant branches of the House of Bourbon, from which issued the princes of the blood, were those of Orléans, Condé, and Conti. In rank, the princes of the blood came immediately after the king of France and his family; only they were entitled to the ritual address Son Altesse Sérénissime (SAS), which derived from divine right. A striking illustration of the importance attached to this form of

address was furnished by Louis-François, prince de Conti, when he refused to sign as a witness to the reading of the will of the duchesse d'Orléans until "Son Altesse Sérénissime" had been crossed out before the names of all the witnesses, because one among them, the duc de Penthièvre (son of the comte de Toulouse, a natural, "legitimized" son of Louis XIV), was not of the blood.

6. The earliest use of the name Romanée in relation to Les Clos de Saint-Vivant, occurs in a 1765 lease to Barthélemy Fistet, farmer of the Clos de Saint-Vivant and tax and tithe collector for the prior of Saint-Vivant, of "approximately eighteen *journaux* of vines in a single *pièce*, as they are without guarantee of measure, called la Romanée de Saint-Vivant, situated in Vosne, adjoining the aforesaid buildings and house [of the prior] and extending to la Romanée of His Serene Highness, Monseigneur le prince de Conty."

7. "I, Alix, duchess of Burgundy, hereby make known to whomever it may concern that the prior and the monastery of Saint-Vivant de Vergy have given and conceded to Aimon d'Aiserey, provost of Saint-Jean, a parcel of vines situated in Vosne, in the terrain of Maizières, that he may possess it in peace for as long as he may live. But when he is taken from our midst, the aforesaid parcel of vines, with all improvements and additions, if there be any, will be returned freely and without protest to the Priory of Vergy. In witness of which, I have confirmed these present letters by our seal. Done in the year of grace 1232."

8. Quoted by Comte Liger-Belair, *Vosne*, 1981.

9. Fagon also attributed to Louis XIV's use of champagne his "frequent fevers, hot flushes, itchings and anxieties" and observed that the wine of Champagne "sours easily because it contains more tartar and less spirit than that of Burgundy and, consequently, reinforces and augments the sourness of the melancholic humor and its effects."

10. Throughout its history, Romanée-Conti has been described as containing either forty ouvrées or five journaux. *Ouvrée* and *journal* both mean "a day's work." An ouvrée is the measure of vineyard surface that a vigneron could work in a day's time using only hand tools; a journal is the measure of land that could be covered by a man, a horse, and a plow in a day's time. Both terms are still in common usage.

The hillside, planted to noble grape varieties, where the vines were crowded and disordered from centuries of reproduction by *provignage* (see chapter 5), could only be worked by hand; on the plain, the gamay vines were cultivated in rows, and the soil was tilled with horse and plow. For this reason, Danguy and Aubertin observed that "vignerons evaluated surfaces planted to quality varietals [pinot or chardonnay] in terms of ouvrées . . . whereas those planted to gamay are ordinarily measured by the journal." In practice *ouvrée* is mostly used for vineyard parcels measuring less than a journal; parcels measuring less than an ouvrée were, in the past, measured in terms of perches. Following are some equivalents:

1 perche = 102.5 sq. ft. = 9.523 m^2
1 ouvrée = 45 perches = 4,612 sq. ft. (.11 acres) = 428.5 m^2 (.0429 ha)
1 journal = 8 ouvrées = 36,900 sq. ft. (.85 acres) = 3,428 m^2 (.3428 ha)

11. Courtépée wrote, of the fortress of Vergy, "This château was very old; some attributed its foundation to Vercingentorix [sic] . . . ; others to Virginius, a Roman captain. However that

may be, it existed at the time of St. Léger [seventh century]." The canon Jean Marilier wrote that the château "dated from no later than the 7th century."

12. Some authors have placed the foundation of the priory of Saint-Vivant in the year 890, others in 894. Jean Marilier (*Le Monastère de Saint-Vivant de Vergy*, 1977) wrote, "I believe it impossible to determine precisely the year of the foundation of Saint-Vivant; it was between 894 and 918." All information concerning the early history of Saint-Vivant is taken from this publication.

13. The deed reads as follows: "Dom Bouchard, prior of Vergy, with the consent of all his chapter, has given freely, without having been asked, to Dom Guillaume, abbot of Val-Sainte-Marie, to the other brothers in charge, and to their successors, all of the land that he had in the village of Créault . . . For this, Hugues, duc de Bourgogne, with the approbation of his spouse, Mahaut, and of his sons, Eudes, Hugues, Robert, Henri, Raymond, and Gauthier, has given, in compensation, to the monks of Vergy, all the uncultivated lands, woods and fields [that he owned] in Flagey and in Vosne . . . Finally, he forbids any and all seigneurs de Vergy to encroach upon what he has given and decrees that the church to which he has made this gift freely shall possess it inviolably . . . Enacted in the presence of S. Abbot [Dom Bouchard] and of the duke . . . [Witnesses] Simon, sire de Vergy, Gales, chapelain de Gilly, Maître Raoul, Gales Motet [chevalier de Vergy], Doon de Vergy, Lécelin Motet, Constantin familier, Othe de Fangey, Simon de Gilly, Robert Maire, Boniot forestier, Hugues d'Izier."

14. With the passage of centuries, the rights, both of the priory of Saint-Vivant and of the Cistercians, had to be reconfirmed from time to time. Dr. Lavalle is the first modern writer to cite a treaty, probably from the end of the twelfth century, that begins, "Let it be known to all sons of the Church that Etienne, prior of Vergy, and his Chapter have permitted and conceded to the monks of Citeaux all that these monks had and were able to acquire [within defined limits, which included the Clos de Vougeot] . . . for an annual tithe of four sols on each and every ten journaux." Two and a half centuries later, the tithe had increased thirtyfold: Frère Marcel Lebeau (*Essai sur les vignes de Citeaux des origines à 1789*, 1986) cites a deed from 1452 in which Cistercians recognize that they owe to Saint-Vivant an annual tithe of one hundred livres on the vines and dependencies of the Clos de Vougeot.

15. *Cloux* is the antique form of *clos*, meaning an enclosure or enclosures; the singular and the plural spellings are the same for both cloux and clos. In Burgundy, a clos usually defines a vineyard—often the totality of a climat—that is, or has been in the past, enclosed partly or entirely within walls. Romanée-Conti is enclosed to the south and to the east today, as it was in the sixteenth century.

16. The Clos des Cinq Journaux and the adjoining three ouvrées of vines which together make up Romanée-Conti today, were thus described: "Another parcel of vines in the aforesaid cloux called Les Cinq Journaux of the said cloux, containing five journaux or thereabout, facing on the southwind side a communal road leading from Vosne to Vergy and on the northwind side a communal footpath which leads to aforesaid Vergy, and beneath facing a street called rue de la Barre, and above [the properties] belonging to Monsieur de Fangey because of his wife, to Jehan Breton and to several others; another parcel of vines containing three

ouvrées, being next to the above five journaux, bordering on the footpath which leads from Vosne to Vergy toward the southwind and, to the side of the northwind, Messires the venerable Cistercians, and at the lower end bordering the rue du Noyer Saint-Martin which leads to the coomb of Vosne."

17. Of this scourge, Abbé Bavard (*Histoire de Volnay*, 1887) wrote, "Everything leads us to believe that we are here in the presence of an early invasion of phylloxera. Local tradition reports that our ancestors, no doubt in memory of the infamous black death of 1349 . . . gave the name of *maladie noire* to the vineyard scourge . . . To replant the vineyards, one was obliged to bring in plants from the Crimea." However implausible the notion of phylloxera's paying but a passing visit and the Crimea's furnishing pinot noir to repopulate the Côte d'Or, Camille Rodier (*Le Clos de Vougeot*, 1949) repeated these words; speaking of the Clos de Vougeot, he added, "Dom Menrique relates in the annals of Citeaux that he read in the convent library that the disease consisted of legions of tiny insects which attached themselves to the roots like clusters of lice. The leaves first turned yellow, the vinestock dried out and, finally, the vine died. The monks had to leave the domaine fallow for some time . . . It took more than a century to replant the vineyards of Burgundy."

18. The Chambre des Comptes of Dijon was a royal record office, or archives, housing all kinds of official contracts, titles, deeds, and royal charters. It was charged with population census, auditing accounts and incomes for taxation, overseeing Crown lands and revenues, and with surveying and reclaiming lands belonging to the Crown. Founded under the Capetian dukes, the Chambre des Comptes was considered by the dukes of Burgundy and, later, by the kings of France to be of such great importance that, among other privileges, its officers were exempted of all taxes and other payments normally exacted by the state.

19. A purchased seigneurie was a *seigneurie engagée* (as opposed to a *seigneurie patrimoniale*, whereby the lands and the seigneurial rights were nobly inherited). In this case, the seigneur engagé, Jacques Venot, purchased not the land itself, which remained technically the possession of the Crown, but the seigneurial rights of dispensing justice (superior, intermediate, and inferior) and collecting tithes and other dues. The title of seigneur de Vougeot was of minor importance, for the seigneurie did not embrace jurisdiction over the possessions of the Cistercians monks, the Clos de Vougeot and its cellars and dependencies; out of 200 journaux of vines within the community boundaries, nearly 150—and all of the best—were contained within the walls of the Clos de Vougeot.

On 13 September 1631, two weeks after the date of the contract by which Jacques Venot ceded his properties to Jeanne Venot and Philippe de Croonembourg, Henri de Bourbon, prince de Condé, father of Armand, prince de Conti, by an exchange of properties with his cousin Louis XIII, became proprietor of the Châtellenie d'Argilly, "with the option to reabsorb parts and portions of the seigneuries that had been sold and engaged, upon reimbursing the buyers with the price of their acquisitions."

Although the Croonembourgs had always claimed to be seigneurs de Vougeot, in fact the seigneurie, under pressure from the Cistercian monks, was reclaimed by the prince de Condé and ceded to the Cistercians, proprietors of the Clos de Vougeot. The seigneurie remained in the possession of the Cistercians from 1631 until 1709, during which time the Châtellenie d'Argilly passed by inheritance into the hands of the prince de Conti.

In 1709, as a result of Philippe de Croonembourg's discovery of a decree declaring the Seigneurie de Vougeot to be reunited to the domain of the Crown, the prince de Conti instituted court proceedings and, by a court decision, 10 February 1722, was able to reintegrate the Seigneurie de Vougeot into the Châtellenie d'Argilly.

Three days later, the prince de Conti leased the Seigneurie de Vougeot to Philippe de Croonembourg. The terms were 1,000 livres for right of entry, 300 livres in annual rent, and the stipulation that the Cistercians be reimbursed for their loss. Five years later, Philippe de Croonembourg managed to have this contract broken and replaced by a contract, dated 18 April 1727, by which he received the seigneurie outright for 1,000 livres, payable over a nine-year period with an interest of 5 percent. The price was ridiculously low, the conditions incomprehensibly generous; the Cistercians were outraged.

Only the first year's rent of 300 livres in the original contract was paid. Neither the 1,000 livres of the original contract nor the 1,000 livres of its replacement was paid; whether or not the Cistercians were reimbursed is not recorded. Sixteen days after the second contract was signed, ten-year-old Louis-François de Bourbon, at his father's death, became the prince de Conti.

20. The contract begins: "So be it, by contract received by Me. Pierre Coquille Vinant Royal notary in Flagey, the twenty-eighth day of the month of August one thousand, six hundred thirty-one, Noble Jacques Venot, Conseiller du Roy, Me. ordinaire de la Chambre des Comptes à Dijon, Sieur du Vougeot—and by consent of damlle. Marguêrite Catherine, his wife, having sold, left, handed over, and transferred to the nobleman Philippe de Croonembourg, Sr. de St. Genois, their son-in-law, and to damlle. Jeanne Venot, their daughter, wife of the said Sr. de Croonembourg, the land and Seignerie of Vougeot together with all the domain and its appurtenances situated in said Vougeot, as well as the finages and territories of Gilly, Flagey, Vosne, and Chambolle, consisting of houses, shareholders' income, mills, fields, food stocks, vineyards, wines, and money rents, in return for the price and sum of thirty thousand livres, to be paid, be it known, twelve thousand livres liquid by the said Sieur de Croonembourg and thirteen thousand livres for which the said Sieur Venot and Damlle. Catherine, his wife, shall be quitted of the dowry (which to this effect will be entirely paid) promised by them to the said Jeanne Venot, their daughter."

21. Until the Revolution, the official unit of tender was the livre. It was a "unit of account" or "currency unit", an abstract unit of value which, in itself, did not exist as a unit of exchange. The livre tournois was royal money stamped in Tours. The livre was broken down into twenty sols and the sol into twelve deniers.

In May 1726, under Louis XV, the livre was stabilized. Until then, the coins in circulation, the écu d'argent, the louis d'or, and their derivatives (which were not stamped with a given value in currency units) had fluctuated in value constantly (in the two years preceding the stabilization, the louis varied from fourteen to twenty-four livres). With the stabilization, the livre was defined as 4.45 grams of 90 percent pure silver, the louis d'or was worth twenty-four livres, and the écu d'argent was worth six livres. The principal coins in circulation were: in gold, the double louis, the louis, and the demi-louis; in silver, the écu, the petit écu (three livres), and the pièces de 24, 12, and 6 sols; in copper, the double sol, the sol, the demi-sol and the liard (3 deniers or 1/4 sol).

The law of 18 Germinal, Year III (7 April 1795) states, "The currency unit will take the name of franc to replace that of livre, in use until today." The livre and its subsequent alias, the franc, remained stable, by the above definition, from 1726 until the First World War. Paper money was not trusted; the only sure values were land and precious metals.

The fact of a stable currency should not tempt one to believe that any dependable equivalents or comparisons may be drawn between moneys of different historical periods, for even though a unit of money may have been legally frozen to represent a specific weight in precious metal, the value of everything else was constantly changing and the worth of gold and silver was variable.

22. During the first six months of 1760, at the same time that the terms of the sale of La Romanée were being arranged, Claude Marey, wine négociant and mayor of Nuits, bought nine separate parcels of vines, all in climats that are today either Echézeaux or Grands Echézeaux, totaling twenty-four ouvrées, for 4,223 livres in all, or an average of 176 livres per ouvrée.

23. An *intendant* was an administrator of a province, acting in the name of the king, a role that coexisted with that of the *gouverneur*, who was more noble figurehead than active administrator. The Joly de Fleury family were well-known magistrates; Jean-François's father was Crown Attorney and his brother was a president of the Parlement of Paris. Jean-François Joly de Fleury was intendant de Bourgogne from 1749 to 1761; from 1781 to 1783, he was Louis XVI's minister of finance.

24. The comtesse de Boufflers (née Marie-Charlotte-Hippolyte de Campet de Saujon, separated from the comte de Boufflers-Rouverel) should not be confused with the marquise de Boufflers, mistress of Stanislas Leszczyński, the king's father-in-law, or with the duchesse de Boufflers, who later became the maréchale-duchesse de Luxembourg and was a close friend of the prince de Conti and the comtesse de Boufflers.

25. Saint-Simon noted, "Mme la princesse de Conti gave birth to M. le prince de Conti today, whilst monsieur her husband was at L'Isle-Adam." The marriage of Louis-Armand, prince de Conti, and his cousin, Louise-Elizabeth de Bourbon-Condé, which neither wanted, had been imposed by Louis XIV, at the same time as that of Louis-Armand's sister and Louise-Elizabeth's brother, the prince de Condé. Louis-Armand and his princesse were both unfaithful (the prince de Condé nicknamed his brother-in-law "the prince de Montaran" because he was keeping a lady named Mlle Haran). Their quarrels were famous. Saint-Simon wrote, "Mme la princesse de Conti, who hardly ever restrained herself, told him [the prince] in public that he needn't bother trying to order her around because he should know that he couldn't make a prince of the blood without her whereas she could make one without him." Some scholars believe that Louise-Elizabeth did not solicit Louis-Armand's collaboration in the making of Louis-François.

26. To be a member of the society at court and to partake of its honors one had, in principle, to prove, to the satisfaction of the royal genealogist, an impeccable noble lineage reaching back to 1400 before being presented to the royal family by a member of the inner circle. The marquise de Pompadour was a special case, as was, much later, the comtesse du Barry.

27. Louis XV practiced a secret diplomacy which was at odds with the official diplomacy of his ministers. Twenty-five years after the prince de Conti's withdrawal from the court of Versailles, the comte de Broglie wrote, "The late M. le prince de Conty passed on to me, the day of my nomination to the embassy of Poland, orders from the king to correspond secretly with His Majesty and to prefer H.M.'s orders, passed on to me by this prince, to those which I would receive through normal channels from the King's Counsel. I was, I admit, terrified by such conflicting orders; I envisaged making dangerous enemies. I begged M. le prince de Conty to urge His Majesty to choose another ambassador. The following day, I received a second order from the king. I obeyed and, since them, nothing has shaken my loyalty or my zeal. In 1757, when M. le prince de Conty retired from these occupations, His Majesty deigned to confide in me his secret correspondence, for which I was responsible until his death."

It was in his unofficial role as chief of the king's bureau of secret affairs that the prince de Conti launched his tempestuous young friend the chevalier d'Eon, on a bizarre and scandal-ridden counterespionage career. For his first mission, to Russia, Eon disguised himself as Mlle Lia de Beaumont, accompanied by her Scots guardian, Sir Douglas Mackenzie. After a brief and brave career as captain in the Dragoons (he was honored with the Croix de Saint-Louis), Eon was recalled by the king, who sent him on a second mission to Russia, this time in masculine habit (as the brother of Lia), and subsequently to England, where he passed a number of tumultuous years in Louis XV's secret service. At the time of the king's death, the chevalier d'Eon held secret papers which Louis XVI and his minister of foreign affairs, Vergennes, were anxious to obtain. With Beaumarchais, who was acting as an agent for Louis XVI, Eon used the papers as a bargaining tool for the continuation of the pension granted him by Louis XV, for the payments of his debts and for his reentry in France. Their agreement, signed 5 October 1775, specified that "Mlle d'Eon" would henceforth quit wearing masculine attire, but that she would be allowed to keep the Croix de Saint-Louis. Beaumarchais proposed marriage to the *chevalière* d'Eon but was rejected on the grounds that his having a venereal disease was an insult to a virtuous girl and proof of the playwright's infidelity.

28. Shortly after the prince de Conti's return from the army, 16 January 1747, there was an incident, quite foolish, but one which must have deeply offended a proud prince: the marquise de Pompadour had organized a theater troupe, the Théatre des Petits Cabinets, composed of members of the court, of which she was the star performer. The stage was large, the sets and costumes sumptuous, and the seating capacity limited. At the first performance (Molière's *Tartuffe*), the prince de Conti was refused entry; and it was not even a full house. Luynes wrote, "There were very few spectators: the King, Mme d'Estrades, Mme du Roure and M. le maréchal de Saxe, and, I think, M. de Tournehem, M. de Vandières, Champcenetz and his son, a few other of the King's domestics; in all, there were only fourteen people."

29. The Enclos du Temple was, in the twelfth and thirteenth centuries, the priory of the religious-military Order of the Chevaliers de la Milice du Temple, which was suppressed in 1312. It then became the property of the Order of the Hospitaliers de Saint-Jean de Jérusalem, who were given the island of Malta in 1530, when they came to be known as the Chevaliers de Malte. The Palais du Grand Prieur was rebuilt in 1667 by the architect Jules Hardouin-Mansart; it was demolished in 1853 on orders from Baron Haussmann.

30. The Hôtel de Conti, built in 1663 by François Mansart and André Lenôtre for Guénégaud, secretary of state under Louis XIV, was acquired in 1670 by Louis-François's great-grandmother, the widow of Armand de Bourbon. It was sold to the king in 1750 for 1.6 million livres. The final choice for the Place Louis XV was today's Place de la Concorde (the equestrian statue of the king was inaugurated in 1763 and destroyed twenty-nine years later, when the Place Louis XV became the Place de la Révolution). The Hôtel de Conti was demolished in 1768, and the present Hôtel des Monnaies, on the Quai de Conti, was erected in its place between 1771 and 1777.

31. A few months earlier, after thirteen years, the prince had separated from Mme Marie-Louise d'Arty, daughter of the financier Samuel Bernard and Mme de Fontaine. In 1770 the prince took another mistress, Mme Dailly, who bore him two sons, François-Claude-Faust and Marie-François-Félix. They received the titles of marquis de Rémoville and chevalier d'Hattonville, from the names of the lands given them by their father, who also recognized them in his will as his natural sons and left each a pension. Both received letters from their legitimate brother, the prince de Conti, from his exile in Barcelona, confirming their paternity, and on the basis of these letters Louis XVIII granted them the right, in 1815, to assume the name Bourbon-Conty. Both the marquis François-Claude de Bourbon-Conty and the chevalier Marie-François de Bourbon-Conty died childless.

A lady, known as the comtesse de Montcairzain (anagram of Conti-Mazarin) published a book during the Revolution in which she claimed to be the natural daughter of the prince de Conti and the duchesse de Mazarin. Capon and Yves-Plessis investigated her rights to the claim without coming to any conclusion. The same authors presented brief biographical sketches of some forty mistresses of short duration; they lamented the fact that the prince's sentimental adventures were so numerous that they were forced to renounce establishing a complete list.

32. The prince had organized Rousseau's flight from France in June 1762, when his book *Emile* was condemned and orders for his arrest issued. A fugitive ever since, he was back in Paris in December 1765 *incognito* (wearing a fur-trimmed, long Armenian gown and matching fur-lined bonnet, a costume by which he was identified everywhere, since he had realized "all the advantages of a long dress"), in preparation for a new flight to asylum in England, when the prince whisked him away to temporary asylum within the Enclos du Temple. He was established in luxury there, in his own private little palace, the Hôtel de Saint-Simon, where the prince sent around his musicians each morning to soothe his guest at the waking hour. Of that sojourn, Rousseau wrote, plaintively, "I have the honor, whilst awaiting [the flight to England] to be M. le prince de Conty's guest. He has insisted that I be housed and served with a magnificence which he well knows is not to my taste: but I can understand that, under the circumstances, he wanted this to be a visible testimony of the esteem with which he honors me."

After the English debacle, the prince persuaded Rousseau to assume the pseudonym Jean-Joseph Renou and settle into the Château de Trye (June 1767–June 1768), a Conti domain halfway between Paris and Rouen. Rousseau pleaded repeatedly with the prince to permit him to turn himself in, to face his accusers; the prince, who had spent his life defying authority, would have none of it.

33. The duc de Chartres, later duc d'Orléans, known during the Revolution as Philippe Egalité, voted for the death of Louis XVI and was shortly thereafter beheaded himself. His son Louis-Philippe was king of France from 1830 to 1848.

34. The sale was a disaster. Louis-François's biographers, Capon and Yves-Plessis, estimate conservatively that the prince had spent 2,725,000 livres on his collection; it brought 1,091,345 livres at auction. The 1,085 paintings, alone, included works by Titian, Veronese, Correggio, Raphaël, Rubens, Velázquez, Rembrandt, Poussin, Brueghel, le Lorrain, Watteau, Chardin, le Nain, Guido Reni, Boucher, Greuze, Van Dyck, Murillo, Philippe de Champaigne, Salvator Rosa, Fragonard, all of the seventeenth-century Dutch and Flemish masters, and so forth.

35. Mougel, *La Fortune des Princes de Bourbon-Conti*: In 1790 the prince de Conti's income was 3,743,000 livres, his expenses, 3,290,000 livres; in 1791, his income was 4,394,000 livres, his expenses, 4,004,000 livres.

36. The contract read,

> The vigneron assigned to cultivate the vines of la Romanée will be held responsible to stake the vines at his own expense, to work the soil with pickaxe and hoe three times a year, to prune the vines correctly, to practice each year twelve or thirteen *provins* [see chapter 5] per ouvrée, and as many more as may be judged necessary. He will also keep the vines clean and free of weeds and will maintain them in good condition, in his own interest and at his own cost.
>
> As for substantial repairs in the vineyard, he will be obliged to work with the hired workers without exacting any retribution for his personal time.
>
> He will, moreover, pay all workers whom he employs to cultivate the vines.
>
> In addition, he will be responsible for the expenses of the harvest. He will feed the pickers, of whom he will be required to hire up to forty, and if it is judged necessary to hire more, he will be responsible only for feeding the surplus, whose wages will be paid by the proprietor.
>
> He will pay half the price of the casks furnished each year for the harvest.
>
> On the other hand, the vigneron will be lodged free of cost in the house of Vosne belonging to the proprietor and the adjoining garden will be his to cultivate.
>
> For each queue of wine making up half of the harvest of La Romanée, he will be paid the highest official price for the wines of Vosne, and twenty livres in addition.
>
> Plus the sum of fifteen livres every year for the tilling, staking and culture of each journal of vineyard.
>
> Plus six livres on condition that he will plant in the vines neither bean fodder [*feverolles*], nor any other legumes.
>
> Substantial repairs in the vineyard of La Romanée will be entirely at the charge of the proprietor.
>
> Each year the vigneron will receive an advance of three hundred livres, payable quarterly, which sum will be deducted from the half of the wine concerning him when the official prices [of the wines of Vosne] are announced.
>
> I, the undersigned, Etienne Magnien, vigneron domiciled in Nuits, accept to transport my domicile to Vosne and to cultivate the vineyard of La Romanée in accor-

dance with the above outlined conditions. Enacted in Nuits 17 February 1782. [signed] *Etienne Magnien*.

37. Except for the figures, the text of the accounting is identical each year. It begins, "On St. Martin's Day 1783, the harvest of La Romanée consisted of one queue, one quartaut and twenty-four bottles of wine. The price of the wines of Vosne was fixed by the municipal officials of Nuits, for 1783, at 270 livres per queue, which makes 290 livres for the account of the vigneron of La Romanée, it being understood that he is paid twenty livres per queue above the price of Vosne.

38. Fistet died before 1774, the year of the last declaration of Les Clos de Saint-Vivant, which is signed "widow Fistet." The priory of Saint-Vivant had fallen upon difficult times; the Fistets seem to have been given an extraordinary liberty in their role as farmers and collectors and no doubt lined their pockets along the way. In 1786, two years before the monastery was closed down, the widow Fistet was trying to extort a portion of the harvest of la Romanée from the last prince de Conti instead of the sum of money that had been settled upon for the tithe. In a letter dated that year, addressed to Ligeret, Margue, the prince's steward, observes, "Between you and me, the new proposition to pay the tithe in kind [wine] to the farmer [of Saint-Vivant] is not to the taste of Monseigneur—he pretends that he is being taken advantage of which puts him in an ill humor."

39. After twenty-seven months in the Marseilles prison, the prince de Conti's health had declined alarmingly. The Committees of National Urgency and of National Security decreed, 28 Thermidor, Year III (15 August 1795): "(1) That Louis-François-Joseph Bourbon Conty be immediately liberated; (2) That he move to Autun to remain provisionally under the surveillance of the municipailty and to re-establish his health by the use of mineral waters and other curative means."

The prince and Jacquelin moved to Autun, one of the more active revolutionary and anti-aristocratic centers in France; it was another kind of prison.

On 18 Thermidor, year IV (5 August 1796), about a year after the prince's arrival in Autun, the minister of police, Cochon, wrote the municipal authorities of Autun, "The citizen Bourbon-Conty has obtained from the Executive Directory, the 6th of this month [24 July], permission to move to Melun, department of Seine et Marne, to remain under the surveillance of the authorities . . . [the local administration should] place no obstacle in the way of this citizen's departure or in that of anyone in his service."

The prince de Conti remained in Melun until the coup d'état of 18 Fructidor (4 September 1797). The law of 19 Fructidor banished all members of the Bourbon family from French territory. Louis-François-Joseph de Bourbon, prince de Conti, died in exile in Barcelona, 10 March 1814; buried with him was his most prized possession, the gold-handled sword that his father had carried to battle seventy years earlier.

Fortunée-Marie d'Est, princesse de Conti, with whom Louis-François-Joseph had never shared a hearth, died alone, 21 September 1803, in Venice, in the Convent of the Visitation.

40. The Republican calendar places the first day of the first year of the Republic on 22 September 1792, the day following the first session of the National Convention, the proclamation of the Republic and the abolition of royalty. The calendar was, however, not conceived until the following year.

There were twelve thirty-day months, each broken into three ten-day weeks, or *décades*:

Autumn	*Winter*	*Spring*	*Summer*
Vendémiaire	Nivose	Germinal	Messidor
Brumaire	Pluviose	Floréal	Thermidor
Frimaire	Ventose	Prairial	Fructidor

The days of the week were primidi, duodi, tridi, quartidi, quintidi, sextidi, septidi, octidi, nonidi, and décadi. The five days—six every fourth year—between the last day of Fructidor and the first day of Vendémiaire, named Les Sans-culottides in glorification of the defenders of the Republic, were devoted to celebrating the different qualities of the Republic, each fête-day taking a different name: de la Vertu, du Génie, du Travail, de l'Opinion, and des Récompenses. In leap year, the sixth day was "La Sans-Culottide par excellence," on which national games were celebrated. The Republican calendar was officially abandoned during the first year of the Empire, 10 Nivose, Year XIV (31 December 1805).

41. The first assignats, 400 million livres' worth issued at the end of December 1789, were bonds, whose security was in undefined national land holdings, earning 5 percent interest, non-negotiable except as payment for national land holdings. The following year, all ecclesiastical property was seized and declared as security for new assignats, which were no longer bonds earning interest but negotiable paper money: 800 million were printed in September 1790, 900 million the following year, then a billion, then more. By 1796, 45 billion had been printed. Pierre Gaxotte (*La Révolution Française*), from whom these figures are borrowed, wrote, "In 1796, a 100-livre assignat, which was worth six sous (one-third of one percent of its face value) was accepted, in government offices, in payment for 100 livres worth of good land." The worthless assignats were replaced by a new paper money called *mandats*, claiming the same security, with transactions in real coin punishable by prison sentences; a year later, both assignats and mandats were "demonitized," but could be officially exchanged for coupons representing 1 percent of their face value, admissible only for payment of national land holdings.

42. For twenty years, Louis Tourton had been a close friend of the flamboyant, intrepid, profligate speculator and financial visionary Gabriel-Julien Ouvrard, protector of Joséphine de Beauharnais, father of several children by the famous beauty Mme Tallien, and inventor of a financial system based on credit, confidence, and depreciation (the same which makes the world run today). Ouvrard made and lost uncountable fortunes, was, by turns, Napoleon's banker, creditor, arms supplier, scapegoat, and prisoner (in debtors prison), despite which, he again accepted to finance the government and to furnish the army during the Hundred Days. His financial theories, which had been rejected by preceding governments, who wanted his money but not his ideas, permitted the duc de Richelieu to reduce the national debt and render Louis XVIII's government solvent, in gratitude for which Richelieu arranged the marriage of Ouvrard's daughter Elizabeth to his friend and cousin comte Louis-Victor-Léon de Rochechouart, master of the house of one of the oldest noble families in France; at the same time, Richelieu recognized a state debt to Ouvrard that previous ministers had refused to pay, from which was abstracted one million francs for his daughter's dowry (confirmed by the comte de Rochechouart, who wrote, in his *Souvenirs*, "I invested the million which my wife had brought in her dowry . . . I insist on this point because it was said at the time and has

perhaps been written in memoires, 'Rochechouart got the woman but Ouvrard kept the dowry.' I formally deny this signal calumny."

G.-J. Ouvrard was also a master of the slight-of-hand methods accountable for the disappearance of money coveted by avid creditors, and its reappearance in a laundered form in other hands. So it was that, on April 1818, Louis Tourton, specially appointed guardian (*curateur ad hoc*) to Julien-Jules Ouvrard, Gabriel's son, who was not yet of age, appeared with the boy before the Justice of the Peace of the First Arrondissement in Paris to have him legally emancipated, a condition essential to being an independent property owner. Two days later, for the sum of Fr 540,830, Victor Ouvrard, Gabriel's nephew, purchased, from Tourton and Ravel, the Château de Gilly and appurtenances including the 125-acre (50 ha) vineyard of the Clos de Vougeot, and, the same day, by a transferral-of-property declaration, registered them in the name of Julien-Jules Ouvrard.

43. The Clos de Vougeot found no takers at the opening price. After several indecisive beginnings, it was finally sold, in 1889, in parcels, to a real estate agent and five Burgundian négociants, for a total of Fr 600,000; the agent sold his part in more parcels. In 1891, there were fifteen proprietors; today, there are more than eighty.

44. The ledgers from these years contain day-by-day notes on the work and the weather. Each vigneron family was under contract to cultivate a specified surface of vineyard, "according to local custom" at variable annual rates per ouvrée, depending on whether the vines required "man and woman behind the plow," "woman behind the plow," or cultivation with pickaxe.

The vignerons' names—Soucelyer, Lécrivain, Niquet, Tisserandot, Mongeard, Esmonin—often reflect the history of Romanée-Conti: Michel Soucelyer was witness to the perpetual lease of the Cros des Cloux in 1584; in 1631, Jehan and Symon Lescrivain were proprietors of one of the parcels of vineyard lying above the Cros des Cloux; François Niquet, vigneron of La Romanée, paid dues to Saint-Vivant, in the name of Mlle de Saint-Genois, 1685–93; Nicolas Tisserandot was vigneron of La Romanée until 1735, Denis Mongeard from 1735 until 1782; J. Esmonin, municipal officer of Vosne, was one of the signers of the 1794 expertise of La Romanée.

Beginning 3 December 1910, the notes record rain, torrential rains, continuous rain, rain storms . . . 15 December, men floated through cellars in balonges—open wooden tuns, used for transporting grapes—to rescue submerged kegs of wine and eau-de-vie; the rain continued. The note for 17 December reads, "Brought up all the wine and eau-de-vie from the cellars, completely submerged."

45. Dr. Lavalle, whose authority is generally accepted, misread the expertise and failed to check the sale record. He wrote, "Before the Revolution (La Tâche) belonged to the Chapitre de Nuits and was acquired by M. Marey Cadet for 900 francs per ouvrée."

46. In order to make La Tâche "monopole," Edmond Gaudin de Villaine purchased also, from the Maison Reigner, a small parcel of La Tâche-Gaudichots, which had formerly been commercialized as "La Tâche-Romanée."

47. The oldest bottle in the Domaine's cellars is a Richebourg 1911, souvenir of Edmond Gaudin de Villaine's first year as *gérant*. From 1911 until 1959, all of the remaining stock in

the cellars is contained in the vinothèque, the inviolate personal reserve of the Domaine. From between 1911 and 1945, when the pre-phylloxera vines of Romanée-Conti were torn up, nine vintages of Romanée-Conti are now contained in the vinothèque, rare treasures sometimes limited to a single bottle (five unique bottles were sacrificed for the March 1991 tasting). Until 1929, with the exception of the bottle of Richebourg 1911 and five bottles of Richebourg 1923, the other growths are not represented in the vinothèque. From 1952 onward, most growths are well represented. In 1978 a formula was established of retaining, each year, fifty bottles of each growth for the vinothèque. The vintages 1959-79 have been refurbished to the fifty-bottle mark when stocks permitted.

BIBLIOGRAPHY

UNPUBLISHED SOURCES

Archives Départmentales de la Côte d'Or, Dijon.

Prieuré de Saint-Vivant: H 21

Hugues II, gift of lands (1131), Alix de Vergy letters

(1232 and 1240) and Saint-Vivant acquisitions

(1241, 1276, 1285, 1520) H21 700

Declaration of property holdings (1512) H21 1800

Declarations, receipts for dues, etc., 1603–1774 . . . . H21 1848

Dowry-marriage deed, Jeanne Venot and Philippe de Croonembourg (1631) . . . . E 635

Revolution, Sales of Confiscated Properties: . . . . .Q

Correspondence between Parisian officials and officials
of the Côte d'Or concerning Romanée Conti . . . . .Q 914

Expertises and sales of Romanée Conti and La Tâche . . . . Q 248

Estimation, Romanée de Saint-Vivant . . . . Q 191

Archives Nationales, Paris:

The Bourbon-Conti file, R3 75, contains the perpetual lease of the Cros des Cloux, 1584, by the Prior of Saint-Vivant to Claude Cousin, documents concerning the Châtellenie d'Argilly, collated notaries' deeds concerning la Romanée, 1584–1720, notaries' deeds concerning the sale of la Romanée by André de Croonembourg to the prince de Conti, the surveyor's map of the la Romanée, the architect's plans for la Goillotte and all documents pertinent to la Romanée during the princes de Conti's proprietorship.

Private Archives of the Domaine de la Romanée Conti and the Domaine Marey-Monge.

"Recherche de la Noblesse," 1666, manuscript n° 926, Bibliothèque Municipale de Dijon, contains useful information concerning the Venot and the Croonembourg families.

PUBLISHED SOURCES:

Actes du congrès de vignerons français, 4e session tenue à Dijon en anoût 1845, Dijon, 1845.
Andrieux, P., *Petite Histoire de la Bourgogne et de son vignoble*, 1955.
Arbaumont, J. d' (see also Beaune), *Armorial de la Chambre des comptes de Dijon*, Dijon, 1881.
Arnoux, *Dissertation sur la situation de Bourgogne*, London, 1728.
Aubertin, Ch. and Danguy, R., *Les Grands Vins de Bourgogne*, Dijon, 1892.
Bavard, Abbot, *Histoire de Volnay*, 1887.
Bazin, J.-F., *Le Clos de Vougeot*, Paris, 1987 ; *Montrachet*, Paris, 1988.
Beaumarchais, P.-A. Caron de, *Mémoires* (complete works), Paris, 1826 ; *Œuvres* (Pleiad), Paris, 1988.
Beaune, H. and Arbaumont, J.d', *La Noblesse aux états de Bourgogne de 1350 à 1789*, Dijon, 1864.
Béguillet, E., *Œnologie ou discours sur la meilleure méthode de faire le vin et de cultiver la vigne*, Dijon, 1770.
Bluche, F., *Louis XIV*, Paris, 1986 ; *La Vie quotidienne de la noblesse française au XVIIIe siècle*, Paris, 1973.
Bréjoux, P., *Les Vins de Bourgogne*, 1967.
Broadbent, M., *The Great Vintage Wine Book*, London, 1980 ; *Christie's Price Index of Vintage Wine*, 1989.
Calmette, J., *Les Grands Ducs de Bourgogne*, Paris, 1949.
Capon, G. (see Yves-Plessis).
Carlieu, *Guy-Crescent Fagon*, 1901.
Cavoleau, J.-A., *Œnologie française ou statistique de tous les vignobles de France*, 1827.
Cazalis, dr F., *Traité pratique de l'art de faire le vin*, 1890.
Chalmandrier, J.-E., *Histoire du village de Gilly-les-Vougeot*, Dijon, 1894.
Chaptal, J.-A., *Traité théorique et pratique sur la culture de la vigne*, Paris, 1801 ; *L'Art de faire le vin*, 1819.
Choiseul, Duke of, *Mémoires*, Paris, 1982.
Columella, *De re rustica*, vol. I, book III, London, 1941.
Courtépée, Abbot C. (begun with Béguillet), *Description générale et particulière du duché de Bourgogne et Description historique et topographique du duché de Bourgogne*, 1774-1788 ; also *Description générale et particulière...*, edition of 1847, ed. P. Gras et J. Richard.
Chrétien, J. (see Mériaux).
Danguy, R. (see Aubertin).
Dion, R., *Histoire de la vigne et du vin en France des origines au XIXe siècle*, 1959.
Drouot, H., *La Côte d'Or*, Paris, 1925.
Duby, G., *Histoire de la France*, 1970.
Duchesne, A., *L'Histoire de la maison de Vergy*, Paris, 1625.
Dumaine, A., *Ma cuisine*, 1972.
Dumay, G., *Géographie historique du département de la Côte d'Or*, 1902.
Durand, C.-H., *Détails particuliers sur la journée du 10 août 1792*, 1822.
Durand, E. (see also Guicherd, J.), *Manuel de viticulture pratique*, 1900.
Dutens, M., *Mémoires d'un voyageur qui se repose*, Paris, 1806.
Duvault-Blochet, J.-M., *De la vendange*, Dijon, 1869.

Engel, C.E., "Un individualiste du XVIIIe siècle : Louis François de Bourbon, prince de Conti" (*Versailles*, 2nd trim. 1965).
Engel, R., *Vosne-Romanée*, 1980.
Escoffier, A., *Le Livre des menus*, 1912.
Fabre, J., "Jean-Jacques Rousseau et le prince de Conti" (*Annales de la société J.-J. Rousseau* ; t. XXXVI, 1963-1965, p. 7-48).
Fagon, G.-C., *Journal de la santé du Roi Louis XIV de l'Année 1647 à l'Année 1711 par Vallot, d'Aquin et Fagon* (introduction by J.-A. Leroi), Paris, 1862.
Ferré, L., *Cours pratique d'œnologie*, Beaune, 1933 ; *Traité d'œnologie bourguignonne*, Paris, 1958.
Forgeot, P. (see also Poupon), *Guide de l'amateur de Bourgogne, Paris*, 1967 ; *Pèlerinage aux sources de Bourgogne*, 1971.
Frère, H., *Notes sur Fagon, premier médecin de Louis XIV*, Rouen, 1903.
Gadille, R., *Le Vignoble de la côte bourguignonne*, Paris, 1967.
Galet, P., *Cépages et vignobles de France* t. II, Montpellier, 1958.
Gandilhon, R., *Naissance du Champagne*, Paris, 1968.
Gaxotte, P., *Le Siècle de Louis XV*, Paris, 1974 ; *Louis XV*, Paris, 1980 ; *La Révolution française*, Paris, 1988.
Genlis, Mme de, *Mémoires inédits*, 1857.
Girault, C.-X., *Détails historiques et statistiques du département de la Côte-d'Or*, 1818.
Glotz, M. and Maire, M., *Salons du XVIIIe siècle*, Paris, 1949.
Goubert, P., *The Course of French History*, New York, 1988.
La Grande Encyclopédie, Paris (without date–end of XIX century).
Guicherd, J. and Durand, E., *Culture de la vigne en Côte d'Or*, Beaune, 1896.
Guyot, J., *Étude des vignobles de France ; région du centre-nord*, 1876.
Huglin, P., *Biologie et écologie de la vigne*, Lausanne, 1986.
Joigneaux, M.-P. (under the direction of), *Livre de la ferme et des maisons de campagne*, 1864.
Jullien, A., *Topographie de tous les vignobles connus*, 4th ed., Paris, 1866.
La Chenaye-Desbois, de, and Badier, *Dictionnaire de la noblesse*, 1868.
Ladrey, C., *Traité de viticulture et d'œnologie*, Paris, 1872-1879.
La Force, Duke of, *Le Grand Conty*, 1923.
Landrieu-Lussigny, M.-H., *Le Vignoble bourguignon, ses lieux-dits*, 1983.
Larousse, *Grand Dictionnaire universel du XIXe siècle*, 1869.
Laurent, R., *Les Vignerons de la Côte-d'Or au XIXe siècle*, 1958.
Laussere, J.-J., *Lettre à mon cousin*, Paris, 1832 ; *Les Grands Vins de table*, 1855.
Lavalle, Dr. J., *Histoire et statistique de la vigne et des grands vins de la Côte d'Or*, 1855.
Lebeau, Brother Marcel, *Essai sur les vignes de Cîteaux des origines à 1789*, 1986.
Léglise, M., *Principes de vinification*, Beaune, 1979 ; *Élevage et conservation du vin en cave*, 1979 ; *Une initiation à la dégustation des grands vins*, 1984.
Leneuf, N. (see Mériaux).
Levron, J., *Madame de Pompadour*, 1961.
Liger-Belair, Count Henry, *Vosne, ses origines et ses seigneurs*, 1981.
Ligne, Prince of, *Mémoires*, 1923.
Luchet, A., *La Côte d'Or à vol d'oiseau*, 1858 ; *Le Clos de Vougeot et la Romanée Conti*, 1859.
Luynes, Duke of, *Mémoires sur la cour de Louis XV*, Paris, 1860-1865.
Lynch, K., *Adventures on the Wine Route, New York*, 1988 ; *Mes aventures dans le vignoble de France*, Paris, 1990.

Maire, M. (see Glotz).
Marilier, Canon Jean, *Le Monastère de Saint-Vivant de Vergy*, Dijon, 1977.
Mériaux, S., Chrétien, J., Vermi, P. and Leneuf, N., "La Côte viticole, ses sols et ses crus" (*Bull. Sci. Bourg.* 1981, t. XXXIV, p. 17-40).
Morelot, Dr., *Statistique de la vigne dans le département de la Côte-d'Or*, Dijon-Paris, 1831.
Mougel, F.-C., "La fortune des princes de Bourbon-Conty, 1655-1791" (*Revue d'histoire moderne*, t. XVIII, 1971).
Odart, Count, *Ampélographie universelle ou traité des cépages les plus estimés*, 6th ed., Paris-Tours, 1874.
Ombiaux, M. des, *Nouveau Manuel de l'amateur de Bourgogne*, 1921.
Ouvrard, G.-J., *Mémoires de G.-J. Ouvrard sur sa vie, etc.*, Paris, 1826.
Pacottet, P., *Viticulture*, Paris, 1905.
Parker, R., *Burgundy*, 1990.
Payard, M., *Le Financier Ouvrard*, 1770-1846, Paris, 1958.
Peynaud, E. (see also Ribéreau-Gayon), *Connaissance et travail du vin*, 1971.
Pinsseau, P., *L'Étrange Destinée du chevalier d'Eon*, Orléans, 1945.
Pitiot, S. and Poupon, P., *Atlas des grands vignobles de Bourgogne*, Paris, 1985.
P.L.M. (Paris–Lyon–Marseille railway), *Instructions pour le traitement des vignes par le sulfure de carbone*, Paris, 1878.
Pomerol, Ch. (under the direction of), *Terroirs et vins de France*, 1984.
Poupon, P. (see also Pitiot) and Forgeot, P., *Les Vins de Bourgogne*, 1952.
Ramain, P., *Les Grands Vins de France*, 1931.
Redding, C., *A History and Description of Modern Wines*, London, 1833.
Rendu, V., *Ampélographie française*, 1857.
Ribéreau-Gayon, J. and Peynaud, E., *Traité d'œnologie*, Paris, 1964.
Richard, J., *Les Ducs de Bourgogne et la formation du duché du XIe au XIVe siècle*, Paris, 1954 ; *Histoire de la Bourgogne*, Paris, 1957.
Rodier, C., *Le Vin de Bourgogne*, Dijon, 1948 ; *Le Clos de Vougeot*, 1949.
Roupnel, G., *Histoire de la campagne française*, 1932 ; *La Bourgogne*, 1936.
Rousseau, J.-J., *Les Confessions* (Pleiad), Paris, 1959.
Saint-Simon, *Mémoires* (Pleiad), Paris, 1983-1988.
Siegrist, J., *Les Tanins et les anthocyanes du cépage Pinot* (Commission of research and progress, viticulture and enology, March 1985, Beaune).
Sutcliffe, S., *Serena Sutcliffe's Pocket Guide to the Wines of Burgundy*, 1986 ; *Guide des vins de Bourgogne*, 1987.
Theuriet, C.-D., *Histoire de Vergy*, 1885 ; *Histoire de Nuits-sous-Beaune*, 1886 ; *Alix de Vergy, duchesse de Bourgogne*, 1897.
Thiers, *Histoire du Consulat et de l'Empire*, vol. V, VI, 1845.
Tulard, J., *Les Révolutions*, Paris, 1985.
Vergnette-Lamotte, A. de, *Le Vin*, 1868.
Vermi, P. (see Mériaux).
Vie privée et politique de Louis François-Joseph de Conti, prince du sang, et sa correspondance avec ses complices fugitifs. . . par J.P. (anonymous), Turin, 1790.
Vienne, H., *Essai historique sur la ville de Nuits*, Dijon, 1845 ; *Notices historiques, topographiques et statistiques sur les sept communes de la Côte dijonnaise dépendantes du canton de Gevrey*, 1845.
Yves-Plessis, R.-C. and Capon, G., *Vie privée du prince de Conty*, Paris, 1907.

ACKNOWLEDGMENTS

My thanks, above all, are due to Lalou Bize-Leroy, Pauline Roch, Aubert de Villaine, and Henri de Villaine, for the patience and the equable good nature with which they have met my barrage of interrogations over the past few years; to the office staff at the Domaine, Mmes Madeleine Jayer-Haegelen, Chantal Noblet-Jovin and Françoise Juillet; to Gérard Marlot, chef de culture, and Bernard Noblet, chef de cave; to the vigneronnes, vignerons, and cellar staff of the Domaine, Mmes Annick Basar, Charlotte Basar, M.-Andrée Chevaux, Danielle Genet, Michelle Marlot, Gino Morey, Séraphine Persico, Cécile Raillard, Lisiane Sanchez, Louby Secic, and MM. Bernard Chevaux, Emmanuel Chevaux, Pascal Chevaux, Khémis Haouamed, Bernard Legou, Gaston Mignon, Roger Morey, Patrick Pépin, Domenico Persico, José Sanchez, and Daniel Surier; to Mlle Geneviève Clin and Mme Madeleine Noblet, retired members of the Domaine de la Romanée-Conti family.

I owe a very special note of gratitude to the late Chanoine Jean Marilier, medieval ecclesiastical scholar, who uncovered precious documents from the twelfth and thirteenth centuries, among others, and willingly translated them from medieval Latin into modern French.

And to Mlle Françoise Vignier, director of the Archives de la Côte d'Or, Dijon; M. Bernard de Montgolfier, director of the Musée Carnavalet, Paris; Mlle Claudie Barral, curator of prints, Musée des Beaux Arts, Dijon; Mlle H. Joanelle, librarian, and M. Gilles Eboli, chief librarian, at the Bibliothèque Municipale de Dijon; Mlle Darbois, researcher.

To Mmes Serena Sutcliffe and Rebecca Wasserman and to MM. the marquis Jacques d'Angerville, Jean-François Bazin, Michel Bettane, Michael Broadbent, François Chambon, Clive Coates, Bipin Desai, Michel Dovaz, René Fleurot, Russel Hone, Albert Hotchkin, Louis Latour, Michel Lemonnier, Professor Noël Leneuf, Kermit Lynch, the marquis Humbert de Montlaur, Lucien Peyraud, Peter Thustrup, John Tilson, Geoffrey Troy, and Kyril Zinovieff.

To my sisters, Margaret Olney McBride and Elizabeth Stecher, to my brothers, Byron, James, and John Olney, and to my nephew John Olney, for repeatedly reading and criticizing my text in the course of its evolution.

To my editor, Ghislaine Bavoillot, whose genius for coordination and whose belief in me has permitted this book to evolve in its own time.

INDEX